Learning Assistance and Developmental Education

Martha E. Casazza
Sharon L. Silverman

· ·

Learning Assistance and Developmental Education

A Guide for Effective Practice

Jossey-Bass Publishers
San Francisco

Substantial discounts on bulk quantities of Jossey-Bass books are available to corporations, professional associations, and other organizations. For details and discount information, contact the special sales department at Jossey-Bass Inc., Publishers (415) 433–1740; Fax (800) 605–2665.

For sales outside the United States, please contact your local Simon & Schuster International Office.

Selected excerpts from *Higher Education in Transition*, 3rd. ed. by John S. Brubacher and Willis Rudy. Copyright © 1958, 1968, 1976 by Harper & Row, Publishers, Inc. Reprinted by permission of HarperCollins Publishers, Inc.

Manufactured in the United States of America on Lyons Falls Pathfinder Tradebook. This paper is acid-free and 100 percent totally chlorine-free.

Library of Congress Cataloging-in-Publication Data

Casazza, Martha E., date.
    Learning assistance and developmental education : a guide for effective practice /
Martha E. Casazza, Sharon L. Silverman. — 1st ed.
      p. cm. —(The Jossey-Bass higher and adult education series)
    Includes bibliographical references and index.
    ISBN 0-7879-0211-X
    1. Developmental studies programs—United States. I. Silverman, Sharon L.,
date. II. Title. III. Series.
LB2331.2.C37   1996
374'.012—dc20
                                               95-45303

FIRST EDITION
HB Printing 10 9 8 7 6 5 4 3 2 1

The Jossey-Bass
Higher and Adult Education Series

Contents

Part Three: Shaping the Future

Preface

When we started writing this book, we had a focus and a definite purpose in mind. We wanted to provide an up-to-date handbook for both novices and experienced practitioners in the field of developmental education and learning assistance. Our primary goal was to integrate our own experiences with theory and research in order to construct a new model of practice.

We hope we have accomplished what we set out to do. However, in the process, we have also discovered the excitement that accompanies seeing things from a new perspective. We have found different ways of looking at the field through our readings and conversations with colleagues. We have reorganized many of our informal ideas about theory and practice through critical reflection and through synthesizing the work of others. The act of writing has forced us to articulate clearly ideas that had blurred over time.

We will feel successful if the reader goes through even a portion of the process that we have experienced: reflection, reorganization of ideas, and a clear articulation of a philosophy for maximizing student potential.

Philosophy and Language

We felt strongly that the book should integrate theory with practice and encourage the active participation of the reader. To that end, case studies and practical checklists have been embedded in the text to facilitate immediate, individualized application.

Our diverse backgrounds reflect the interdisciplinary nature of the field in general and contribute to the philosophy that has guided our writing. Our formal education includes training in the fields of educational psychology, learning disabilities, reading instruction, curriculum and instruction, and counseling. Our practical experience includes learning center management, counseling and advising, direct instruction, and program design.

Our philosophy reflects a positive, inclusive approach to learning assistance. Rather than focusing solely on students who need help with basic skills—a focus that has traditionally fought a negative connotation—this approach seeks to provide assistance to all learners, from the underprepared to graduate students. The goal in all cases is to maximize the individual's potential so that his or her goals can be met. The philosophy assumes that the learner and the practitioner bring equal commitment to their tasks and share the responsibility for producing successful outcomes. It also assumes that the learning process takes place in a meaningful context and is sensitive to the cognitive, emotional, and social needs of the learner.

We have chosen this inclusive philosophical stance in order to promote a positive belief system. Rather than highlighting differences in terminology and practice, we have decided to examine the field through a lens that magnifies the overall goal of maximizing student potential. Whether practitioners are considered developmental educators or learning assistance professionals is of little consequence; they have much in common. To underscore the shared foundation, we have used the two terms interchangeably throughout the book.

In a glossary of developmental education terms compiled by a group of professionals in the field (Rubin, 1987), *learning assistance* and *developmental education* were defined in different words, but the same underlying concept was expressed: improving student performance. Developmental education was described as a process, a subdiscipline, and a field of research, teaching, and practice. Learning assistance was described more in terms of its activities and programs.

Frequently, professionals who operate within a learning center where services do not include coursework refer to their practice as learning assistance, whereas those who deliver formal courses, often through a department, call themselves developmental educators. This latter term may be used because coursework is housed in academic departments, and the practitioners may want to emphasize that they are operating within a discipline. It is also the case that practitioners who work within academic affairs units are more often called developmental educators, whereas those who are housed within student affairs units tend to be referred to as learning assistance professionals.

Whatever practitioners call themselves, they frequently exist on the margins of academia. It is in their best interests and those of their students to strengthen their professional field of study through collaborative research and documentation of their very effective practices. All practitioners need to become more visible and articulate about what they do. In large part, it is their responsibility to provide a model for all educators that emphasizes the enhancement of academic standards and realistic access to continuing education for all populations. We believe the foundation has been laid; practitioners now need to hold to their important mission and share their expertise with others.

Audience

The primary audience for this book is the community of practitioners, both novices and the more experienced. Novices will gain insight into the comprehensive nature of the field of developmental education and learning assistance and become acquainted with its history and theoretical foundations. If they are engaged in setting up a learning center or developing curriculum, this book may offer practical suggestions on how to get started.

For more experienced practitioners, this book may offer what it did to us—an opportunity to look again at ideas that may have fallen dormant. It may also inspire the practitioner to conduct research and to share it with others in the field. We hope the book will confirm much current practice and help us all to define ourselves more professionally.

In addition to the practitioner, we hope that this book will be useful to our colleagues in related fields. Professionals in student affairs, administrators and faculty across the curriculum of formal education, community-based leaders involved in teaching adults, and those involved in workplace training will all find practical suggestions for managing learning programs, providing instruction, and understanding students.

Overview

The book is divided into three sections. Part One, "Examining the Foundations," consists of two chapters designed to provide an overall framework for practice. The first chapter reviews the history and evolving philosophies of learning assistance and developmental education at the college level. The second chapter overviews learning theories representing five different approaches. Through a sample case study, we offer suggestions for constructing an integrated approach to providing assistance.

Part Two, "Creating an Integrative Approach for Practice," leads the reader through various components of the field and culminates in a comprehensive model for practice. In Chapter Three, we discuss the fundamental principles and practices involved in developing successful programs. Chapter Four takes a look at student assessment. Assessment is discussed as a process, and the reader is given an opportunity to apply an overall plan to a case study. Chapter Five focuses specifically on the tutor training component of a comprehensive program and how to implement it effectively.

Chapter Six describes four successful programs that represent different types of institutions and organizational frameworks. In Chapter Seven, we construct an innovative model for practice. This model, TRPP, emphasizes interconnections among the four variables of theory, research, principles, and practice, all of which have as their focus the maximizing of student potential. Critical reflection is an overriding variable that reinforces the interdependence of the other variables .

In the final section, "Shaping the Future," we challenge readers to confirm their practice by conducting research and affirming their professionalism as they prepare to meet the challenges of the twenty-first century. Chapter Eight presents a practical model for research that takes readers through the scientific thought process necessary for using research to strengthen practice. Chapter Nine looks at the professionalism of the field and the philosophical foundation that has emerged from decades of practice. Chapter Ten considers some of the challenges that will face practitioners as student needs and government mandates increase, as resources dwindle, and as learning technology proliferates.

Acknowledgments

As with any project that takes over two years to complete, there are many individuals who have helped along the way. Special thanks go to our colleagues who allowed us to disrupt their learning centers by conducting interviews, observing, and collecting materials. Juele Blankenberg, Barb Eichler, Lisa Kerr, and Karen Quinn were particularly understanding and provided valuable feedback as they critically reviewed Chapter Six.

A great deal of appreciation is also due to those who spent time reading our initial drafts and offering their feedback: Angela Durante, Jiazhen Hu, Martha Maxwell, and Pat Fiene. Cheryl Sporlein tirelessly converted our disks to the correct format, and Esperanza Esparza wrote out countless bibliographic note cards.

We particularly want to acknowledge the constant stimulation provided by our graduate students. Their challenging questions cause us to continually rethink our ideas and refine them.

Our institutions, Loyola University Chicago and National-Louis University, provided support through flexible scheduling, staff assistance, and in one case, a sabbatical leave. Without colleagues like Carol Eckermann, a long-time mentor, and Ed Risinger, an avid supporter of developmental education, this project would not have been completed.

Special thanks also to Daniel Barnes, who was the administrator responsible for supporting learning assistance at Loyola University Chicago and who gave us the opportunity to develop many of the ideas in this book.

To our families, we can finally say, "It's over!" We won't ask you to pronounce "TRPP" any more or to stop asking how many pages we have written on a particular day. So, Larry, Josh, Dan, Christopher, and Justin, "It's over!"

Chicago   Martha Casazza
January 1996   Sharon Silverman

aron Silverman directs the learning assistance center and is act-
g dean of student services at Loyola University Chicago. She
ches in the school of education at Loyola and in the develop-
ntal studies graduate program at National-Louis University. She
lso a member of the governing board of St. Augustine College
Chicago. Silverman received her undergraduate degree (B.S.)
m Indiana University in elementary education, her M.A. degree
m DePaul University in learning disabilities, and her Ed.D.
gree from Loyola University Chicago in educational psychology.
verman designed and developed the award-winning Learning
richment for Academic Progress (LEAP) program at Loyola. In
89, LEAP was recognized by the Noel Levitz Center for Student
tention for excellence in retention programming and in 1993 by
American Association of University Administrators for exem-
ry practice in achieving campus diversity. Silverman's research
d writing activities have focused on students on academic pro-
ion, programming for underrepresented student populations in
her education, and tutor training. She consults regularly in these
as and runs faculty development workshops on learning styles
d study strategies. She actively participates in the Midwest Col-
e Learning Center Association and the National Association for
velopmental Education.

Tl

Martha Casazza directs the developmental stud
gram in the adult education department at Nat
versity (NLU), Chicago. She received her docto
from Loyola University Chicago in the area o
instruction. Her master's degree is in reading. U
coordinated the undergraduate reading program
focus for her has been the area of curriculum o
designed the curriculum for both the developme
uate program and the undergraduate reading prog
dent assessment and program evaluation are two
areas, and she has implemented a portfolio asse
the undergraduate level. As chair of the devel
department, she initiated a process of self-ass
resulted in new program development and a set
for the department. Casazza regularly consults in
ing and writing strategies and program evaluat
active in establishing standards and evaluat
through her committee involvement with the l
tion for Developmental Education. She has
regionally as president of the Midwest College
Association and as founding chair of the Midwe
opmental Education Symposium.

Learning Assistance and Developmental Education

Part I

. . . .

Examining the Foundations

In this opening part, we describe the historical, philosophical, and theoretical foundations of our practice. Professionals in our field have diverse backgrounds, ranging from education to psychology to teaching English as a second language. Although this cross-disciplinary training has enabled us to construct an integrated practice, it also has contributed to the perception that we lack a formal, cohesive body of knowledge and a shared history and philosophy.

Chapter One provides the building blocks for a shared history and philosophy by describing how our practice has been a part of the educational system from the beginning. The history of American higher education is divided into three time periods so that we can examine the role that learning assistance and developmental education have played in each. Readers will discover that the challenges we face today are similar to those that have confronted education through the ages.

Once our historical and philosophical roots have been outlined, we move into another significant building block for our practice, a more theoretical one. Chapter Two provides an overview of various learning theories that contribute to the integrated approach that makes our practice so effective. As noted earlier, an important aspect of our field is the range of perspectives represented by its practitioners. Chapter Two describes five different learning theories and how they connect to provide the best possible approach to student learning. To facilitate a direct application to practice, two case studies are included. The first case models how the theories can be integrated, and the second allows readers themselves the opportunity to apply the principles that have been presented.

Evolution of Learning Assistance and Developmental Education in Higher Education

It may surprise the reader to discover that some of today's familiar questions about higher education have been asked for centuries—for example, What is the purpose of postsecondary education? Who should attend college? What should the curriculum look like? The responses to such questions have provided the fuel for academic debate as long as colleges have existed. The current educational arena is not totally new; only the names and faces have changed as institutions of higher education have tried to redefine themselves and remain viable, both academically and financially.

Developmental education and learning assistance have a very definite historical foundation within American higher education. This chapter provides a historical framework for the current state of learning assistance by examining how institutions have dealt with the issues surrounding the diversity of students' academic preparation over the past several decades.

A major thread running through the chapter is the tension that has always existed in higher education between traditionalists and reformists. Frequently, traditionalists come from within the educational system; they argue that student enrollment must be selective so that high academic standards can be maintained. They also defend the merits of prescribed curricula and often disparage institutions that tailor their offerings to the particular needs of students. Typically, traditionalists would charge individuals rather than institutions with the full responsibility for succeeding or failing in an educational endeavor.

By contrast, reformists have frequently, though not always, come from outside the system of higher education. Often, it is the federal government, through its funding policies or legislation, that promotes the reformist ideal of granting more access to colleges and universities. Potential employers also have advocated for greater access because of the changing demands of the workplace. Such advocates argue that in a democracy, education is the right of every citizen and certainly a means for advancement. They further point out that curricula must be relevant and must prepare individuals for their roles in society. And they also urge colleges and universities to facilitate student success by providing the necessary support mechanisms.

It is the tension between these two philosophies that has led to gradual changes in the educational system. The reader is invited to notice how this tension recurs throughout the history described here. In each historical period, specific issues emerge that divide traditionalists and reformists.

The act of reviewing this history and showing that a wide range of institutions has provided academic assistance for underprepared students acknowledges a tradition in American higher education. It is this tradition that helps make postsecondary education in a democratic society unique. Furthermore, the tradition helps those of us in the field to define our professional roles. By increasing our own historical awareness, we can help our administrators and colleagues across the institution understand that we have been a part of American higher education from the very beginning. This acknowledgment alone lends credibility and validity to our field.

It is also important for us as professionals to view learning assistance from a perspective that illuminates the ways in which our field has been affected by the history of higher education in general. If we look at our work through this broader lens, we are better able to serve our students. By examining data and research from higher education and integrating it with our own, we can promote a more symbiotic relationship with faculty and administrators from other disciplines. We can decrease the tensions that have often created a barrier between our programs and others within our institutions.

This chapter divides the history into three periods, each organized around a general theme. The first period (1700–1862) is characterized by the tension associated with founding colleges in a new democracy with only the classical institutions of Europe available as reference points. The second period (1862–1960) demonstrates the impact of the federal government on the opening of higher education to diverse populations. The last period (1960–2000) covers changes that had to be made by institutions to facilitate success for the new students.

For each time period, the three questions stated earlier are asked: What is the purpose of postsecondary education? Who should attend college? What should the curriculum look like? The answers help to define the periods, highlighting both their differences and their similarities.

Integrating a Classical Tradition with Democratic Ideals, 1700–1862

With only the classical institutions of Europe as reference points, there was predictable confusion as higher education was established in the new American democracy.

What Is the Purpose of Postsecondary Education?

Ezra Cornell, founder of Cornell University, approached the professor responsible for admissions decisions and asked why so many applicants were not passing the entrance exam. The professor replied that they didn't know enough. Cornell then asked why the university could not teach the students what they didn't know. The professor replied that the faculty was not prepared to teach the alphabet. "Can they read?" asked Cornell. The professor's response was that if Cornell wanted the faculty to teach spelling, he should have founded a primary school and not a university (Brier, 1984, p. 3). This anecdote is from the 1830s, when Cornell University stated in writing that it would admit only qualified, prepared students. As a result of Ezra Cornell's conversation with the faculty admissions representative, the rejected students were allowed to retake the entrance exam. In addition, according to faculty minutes from 1864, there was a committee at Cornell on "doubtful cases," whose responsibility it was to make decisions regarding marginal student applicants. It is evident that the definition of "prepared" was not clear-cut at Cornell.

The tension between democratic ideals and classroom reality so evident in the Cornell story has been present in American higher education from the beginning. The primary mission of early colleges such as Harvard and Yale was to train clergy and to preserve and maintain the cultural norms that were brought from Europe. The goal was to create an educated elite that could lead the new society. This was supported by statements such as this one from a seventeenth-century Harvard commencement address, in which the speaker expressed appreciation of the fact that the college had been founded by the first Puritan settlers; otherwise, "the ruling class would have been subjected to mechanics, cobblers, and tailors, the gentry would have been overwhelmed by lewd fellows of the baser sort, the sewage of Rome, the dregs of an illiterate plebs which judgeth much from emotion, little from truth" (Brubacher and Rudy, 1976, p. 10).

Although the goal of preserving traditional norms was widely accepted as the primary mission of the early colleges, it was not without its challenges. In the seventeenth century at Harvard, for example, 10 percent of the student body came from families of artisans, seamen, and servants, and the university continued to reserve places for poorer students whose tuition was paid either through work or assessments on the wealthier students (Brubacher and Rudy, 1976). In 1654, an Indian College was founded at Harvard to fulfill part of the university's charter to reach out to the local Native

American population. One entire room was to be devoted to this endeavor! However, it failed because the president complained that the facility was being underused and also because of the "unspoken assumption that the Indians should aspire to the same social and cultural ends as the whites" (Cremin, 1970, p. 222). It is apparent that the colleges of the time, though attempting to reach out to more diverse populations, were not willing to modify their curricula to meet individual needs.

An attempt was made by Thomas Jefferson in 1779 at the College of William and Mary to reform this uncompromising attitude toward minority populations. He recommended that instead of trying to christianize the Indians through schooling, the college should try to understand the Indian culture by studying its laws, languages, religions, and so on, and then constructing grammars and vocabularies that would become areas for further study (Butts and Cremin, 1953, p. 85). This recommendation was rejected, but it demonstrates again the tension between the traditional purposes of education and the reformist ideas that were continually being proposed.

Another reform suggested by both Jefferson and Benjamin Franklin in the eighteenth century was that the mission of colleges be broadened, to prepare students for "leadership in public service, in the professions, in science and technology and in the arts in place of preparation for the ministry, classical scholarship and inculcation of the tenets of an established religion" (Butts and Cremin, 1953, p. 83). Somewhat later, Francis Wayland, president of Brown University, proposed one of the most democratic missions for a college of the time. He described the college as the "center of intelligence for all classes" and developed a university extension division that included classes taught by the faculty of Brown. His program lasted until 1854, when "unmistakable evidence began to accumulate that the quality of the student body was deteriorating." There was also a widespread perception that he had lowered the standards of the bachelor's degree with his innovative "partial" coursework that did not lead to a degree (Brubacher and Rudy, 1976, p. 107).

Other schools tried to provide alternatives for students who had not received sufficient college preparatory training by offering different degrees. The bachelor of philosophy and bachelor of science degrees were designed as alternatives to the traditional liberal arts degree, but again the feeling was widespread that they led to a lowering of standards (Brubacher and Rudy, 1976).

Even though these attempts at reform were put on hold, they reflected the constant struggle to "Americanize" higher education, and they seemed to mirror the changing needs of those attending college. In the seventeenth century, 70 percent of college graduates went into the ministry; in the eighteenth century, that percentage dropped to 20, and by 1840, it was less than 10 (Butts and Cremin, 1953).

Who Should Attend College?

"Qualified" students during this time were narrowly defined as males with the proper family background. Preparation for higher education consisted mainly of private tutoring, with each individual tutor deciding when the student was ready for the more formal study offered at the colleges. In 1700, the requirement for college entrance was a demonstrated knowledge of Greek and Latin along with evidence of good moral character. Yale added an arithmetic exam to its entrance requirements in 1745.

Qualified students were not numerous during this early period. Harvard had only 465 graduates during the entire seventeenth century; in 1710, there were only 36 students at Yale and 123 at Harvard. This small pool of appropriate students, coupled with the lack of secondary schools and standardized preparation, forced the colleges to admit and then accommodate students with minimal training. It was during this period that the president of Vassar College declared that "the range of student achievement extends to a point lower than any scale could measure" (Brier, 1984, p. 2).

In order to extend educational opportunity to a broader population, colleges like Amherst and Williams were founded to accommodate those who could not afford the education offered by Harvard and Yale. These schools helped to open the doors to education, but they also had the effect of segregating those students who, because of their lesser means, were most likely less prepared. The students at Williams were described as "rough, brown featured, schoolmaster-looking, half-bumpkin, half-scholar, in black, ill-cut broadcloth" (Brubacher and Rudy, 1976, p. 40).

Although standardized preparation for college was unknown during this period, it was assumed that all students, once accepted, would proceed at the same pace and with the same instructional delivery techniques. Students were assigned a tutor, who was charged with reading their lessons to them and then listening to their recitations to verify that they had memorized the text. A professor at Harvard published a pamphlet in 1825 criticizing this practice. The pamphlet stated: "The attempt to force together sixty or eighty young men, many of whom have nothing . . . in common . . . and to compel them to advance . . . (at the same pace) . . . giving to the most industrious and intelligent no more and no other lessons, than to the most dull and idle is a thing that is unknown to the practical arrangements for education in other countries" (Butts and Cremin, 1953, p. 226). Though his emphasis was on how the lack of individualization failed to stimulate the most intelligent students, it could be added here that nothing was being done to assist the slower students. Unfortunately, records were not kept during this period to inform us of the rates of persistence or the reasons for dropping out of school. We are left to imagine the effects on many students of trying to learn by a single method and at the same pace as everyone else.

Nineteenth-Century Reflection

Harvard's approach to stirring the student to self-exertion was not so much to push the average student to raise his minimum achievement as it was to excite the superior one to his maximum attainment. The average cannot expect to achieve more than mediocrity, but it is a major misfortune to thrust mediocrity on the talented. It was feared, and with some reason, that gifted American students would not elect in sufficient numbers a special honors course if offered, but they might rise to the bait of achieving honors in an examination which would test their resourcefulness in exploring and organizing a whole area. To provide individual assistance Harvard instituted a tutorial system. Harvard tutors, however, unlike preceptors at Princeton, were drawn from all ranks of the faculty and did not form a subordinate rank of the teaching staff [Brubacher and Rudy, 1976, p. 268].

While the learning needs of students were not considered individually, colleges did recognize that to cover expenses, they needed to accept students who were not ready for college study. To this end, preparatory departments were formed. Designed to provide the academic preparation that students had not received earlier, these departments proliferated on college campuses; indeed, "at many institutions preparatory enrollments matched or exceeded the 'regular' college enrollments" (Brubacher and Rudy, 1976, p. 156). This can be explained in part by the lack of secondary schools at the time; students came to college lacking the basic skills of spelling, writing, geography, and mathematics (Brier, 1984). Viewed as secondary schools within colleges, the preparatory programs delivered training that often led to a six-year program for underprepared students. One of the most enduring preparatory departments was developed at the University of Wisconsin. It was designed in 1849 to "bridge the gap" and lasted until 1880 despite being continuously under fire from faculty.

Those colleges without preparatory departments often offered precollege courses and/or tutoring to students who needed assistance. Students admitted on a "conditional" basis were required to fulfill certain criteria such as taking extra or special classes or receiving individual tutoring (Brier, 1984). In addition to the resources offered by the colleges themselves, there were proprietary tutoring schools. These private enterprises delivered tutoring in college and college preparatory coursework as well as prepared students for college entrance examinations (Brier, 1984).

What Should the Curriculum Look Like?

College in the first half of the nineteenth century was not directly tied to professional aspirations, but was designed simply to provide the elements necessary for the life of a gentleman. The curriculum provided for this training was borrowed from the classical tradition and mainly offered coursework in Greek, Latin, and mathematics. The education was expected to discipline the mind by providing it with difficult material and forcing recitation to prove effectiveness. The *Yale Report of 1828* reinforced this notion with its implication that the difficulty of the ancient languages led to a strengthening of character and a mental power that would serve students well in whatever they chose to pursue after college (Brubacher and Rudy, 1976). The *Yale Report*, recognizing that these intellectual exercises were not for everyone, also called for an end to the admission of students with "defective preparation."

Even though the notion of a classical curriculum and training for an elitist group of gentlemen was supported by the majority of the American population, there was ongoing tension. Educators and statesmen led the debate over both the relevance of the curriculum and the students it was serving. A complaint from the Massachusetts legislature in the mid nineteenth century stated, "A college should be open to boys who seek specific learning for a specific purpose. It should give the people the practical instruction that they want, and not a classical-literary course suitable only for an aristocracy" (Brubacher and Rudy, 1976, p. 290).

The debate and the tension were fueled by a speech delivered in 1837 at Harvard by Ralph Waldo Emerson, who promoted the idea of "adapting education to the individual" and "developing a distinctively American intellectual culture" (Brubacher and Rudy, 1976, p. 105). Eighty-one years earlier, the College of Philadelphia had adopted a more comprehensive curriculum by including coursework for those interested in "mechanic arts" as well as the learned professions (Brubacher and Rudy, 1976). Harvard continually led the movement to incorporate an elective system into the curriculum and thus better meet the needs of individual students. This system was an ongoing source of conflict, as the classicists thought it was lowering the educational standards of the institution.

Another attempt to revise the curriculum came from Henry Tappan at the University of Michigan. He set up a scientific curriculum as an integral part of the college and proposed further extending the traditional studies to include such areas as fine arts, industrial arts, and civil engineering. However, his rationale was fairly elitist, as he declared that the student who chose this "barely useful" course of study might become hooked on education and eventually proceed to the study of what was "ideal and beautiful" (Brubacher and Rudy, 1976, p. 108). Furthermore, to his seemingly liberal opinions about broadening the curriculum, Tappan added the notion that American colleges had for too long taught courses that belonged in lower schools and that admission standards were too low. He asked, "And of what avail could the learned professors and preparations of a University be to juvenile students?" He felt that admitting such raw, undisciplined students was a "palpable absurdity" (Brubacher and Rudy, 1976, p. 109).

Tappan's simultaneous striving for a comprehensive university with coursework designed to meet a variety of student needs and concern over a lowering of standards both summarizes this period of higher education and provides a framework for the decades to come.

The following would have made an appropriate university marketing release in the eighteenth century. It provides a representative picture of the philosophy, students, and curriculum of this early period.

The Currently Common College located in New England, U.S.A., is seeking young gentlemen of means and high moral character who, having been tutored appropriately in the classical tradition, desire to continue their study with others of like means and character. Our mission is to continue the education of young gentlemen to further develop their character and to strengthen the muscle of their minds. To accomplish this mission, our teachers provide lectures in Greek, Latin, and mathematics and listen diligently to student recitations.

Opening the Doors, 1862–1960

As the democratic nation evolved, the doors to higher education were increasingly opened to diverse populations.

What Is the Purpose of Postsecondary Education?

Between 1862 and 1960, the federal government became directly involved in the educational system at all levels. Its influence was felt in higher education as a result of several initiatives, including the Morrill Acts, equal opportunity legislation, and the GI Bill. This period also witnessed the development and rapid growth of the junior college. Together, these innovations expanded the perceived purpose of higher education, but this expansion did not occur without tension—both within colleges, as they developed distinctive units within their own walls, and between colleges, as institutions with very different missions vied for funding.

In 1862, the first Morrill Act was signed by President Lincoln, guaranteeing to each state thirty thousand acres of land per congressman to be sold for the purpose of funding colleges dedicated to teaching agriculture and the mechanic arts. This was followed in 1890 by the second Morrill Act, which reinforced the broadened educational mission and also prohibited the distribution of federal funding to states where discrimination persisted in higher education.

These acts significantly changed the focus of higher education and led to its increased democratization. States followed the directives by establishing A & M (agricultural and mechanical) universities, creating new colleges, or in many cases, increasing financial support to state universities in order to provide more technical training, mainly in the area of agriculture.

This new funding was controversial, especially in the Northeast, where private classical institutions were well established and viewed federal intervention in higher education as threatening and inequitable. It also led to a new debate regarding purpose: should the new training be designed with a pure or an applied science focus? In 1887, the Hatch Act provided support for the latter. This legislation brought higher education even more directly to the general public by establishing extension courses for farmers and setting up experimental agricultural stations at the colleges. The agricultural schools resulting from the Morrill Acts thus became the first vehicles for the popularization of higher education and the broadening of its mission.

It was not only from the areas of agriculture and mechanic arts that colleges and universities faced a challenge to the traditional purpose of higher education. Business leaders were calling for a curriculum that more directly prepared students for the professions. Richard T. Crane, a Chicago businessman, argued that "a college education, because of its classical and literary emphasis, was a worthless undertaking for any young man who wished to succeed in the business world" (Butts and Cremin, 1953, p. 370).

There was increased articulation between colleges and the secondary school system at this time, which also affected the role of higher education. In 1892, the National Education Association appointed a Committee of Ten to examine the curriculum of the high schools and the requirements for admission to college (National Education Association of the United States, [1893] 1969). The committee, a group of prominent college presidents, recommended that many of the subjects recently added to the previously classical postsecondary curriculum—for example, history and science—be taught at an earlier age so that students would have a more solid background and would be prepared to study in greater depth when enrolled in college. The introduction to the final report states, "When college professors endeavor to teach chemistry, physics, botany . . . to persons of eighteen or twenty years of age, they discover that in most instances new habits of observing, reflecting, and recording have to be painfully acquired by the students—habits which they should have acquired in early childhood" (p. 10).

Partly as a result of the Committee of Ten report, secondary schools became stronger and more standardized in the early twentieth century, and college leaders began to discuss the implications this held for the role of their institutions. Because students were now studying more subjects before entering college, it was suggested that the length of time a student spent in college be shortened. From this came the idea of a junior college within a four-year institution. The University of Chicago established such a two-year liberal studies division with the intent of creating a natural break for those not able to complete further study. A similar plan was created at the University of Minnesota, where 20 percent of the students in the two-year general college had failed elsewhere.

The notion of the junior college quickly became popular, and by 1917, seventy-six such institutions had been founded. The President's Commission on Higher Education provided support for the movement by affirming that "virtually 50 percent of the population has the ability to complete fourteen years of schooling, that is, through junior college and that nearly one-third has the ability to complete a college course in liberal arts or professional training" (Butts and Cremin, 1953, p. 522). For the first time, a minimum goal for college enrollment was established that would double the number of college students in the next thirteen years. Even though this was opposed by some college educators, who argued there were already too many students enrolled who could not do college work, it marked a new trend in American higher education. No longer was the purpose of college an exclusionary, elitist one.

As the junior college movement continued to develop in the first half of the twentieth century, it led to the proliferation of community colleges nationwide. Higher education became more of an expectation for the high school graduate; whereas in 1900, 1.6 percent of the college-age population enrolled in college, by 1960, that percentage had increased to 22.2 (Cohen and Brawer, 1982).

By 1960, colleges were no longer asking, What knowledge is of most worth? The new question was, What knowledge yields the greatest tangible benefit to individuals or to society? Indeed, mission and purpose were changing again to meet the emerging needs of a democracy.

Who Should Attend College?

Not only were the numbers of students enrolling in higher education during this period greater than in any previous time, but their faces were quite different. No longer was college the elitist training ground for wealthy males with no particular professional goal other than perhaps the ministry. Farmers and those wanting to be trained for business or engineering began to look for institutions that could meet their needs. Women began to further their education, often at all-female colleges, and following the Civil War, colleges were founded in the South expressly to provide an opportunity for the increasing numbers of black students seeking an advanced degree.

Even though preparation in the secondary schools was becoming more standardized, it was not assumed that the students should be grouped for a common plan of study, as they had been in the eighteenth and early nineteenth centuries. Instead, it seems that colleges did more to separate students on the basis of tested ability, goals, sex, and ethnicity. The admission requirements began to include the new College Entrance Examination, which enabled colleges to quantify differences between students more easily and to define their populations more precisely. Separate schools within colleges and universities were established to provide the curriculum for the new science, agriculture, and engineering students. These schools were considered by many to be inferior to their liberal arts counterparts and were chastised for admitting less qualified students. Even schools like Harvard created new degrees and certificates to accommodate less capable students (Eliot, 1969).

The junior colleges established within the universities were often used as termination points for those students who were not achieving. At the end of two years, they were counseled out. The community college systems that mushroomed were yet another sorting point. With their open-door admissions policies, they served as an accessible avenue for those denied admission elsewhere. They also provided an opportunity for further education to those with nontraditional goals, such as continuing education for self-improvement; training for a specific vocation; gaining credits for transfer to a four-year institution; and earning college credit while maintaining a home, family, and job.

Even though equal opportunity legislation had passed, and states were denied federal assistance if discrimination existed in their college admissions process, the policy of separate but equal was still followed, especially in the South. This led to the founding of colleges such as Tuskegee and Howard, which were developed to provide entirely new opportunities for black students. Because of the lack of well-established primary and secondary systems in the South, these black institutions provided instruction that would ordinarily have been considered below college level. In fact, they were more successful in their funding efforts when they held to a trade school curriculum rather than attempting to offer the traditional liberal arts. The state legislatures were so adamant about this that at one black school, the only way to offer Latin was to call it Agricultural Latin (Brubacher and Rudy, 1976).

Women who desired a college education at this time found themselves in a similar situation. They frequently attended colleges designed for women only, and because of the students' often inadequate secondary preparation, the standards in these early colleges were low. Many educational leaders were opposed to college training for women and felt that admitting them would lower the standards of universities in general, but the female students were insistent that they receive a classical education similar to that offered to their male counterparts. Women and black students alike felt that the validity of their college training and the opportunity for advancement hinged on a traditional curriculum.

Early Twentieth-Century Reflection

Even more discouraging was the deep-seated skepticism of the public with respect to the value of higher education for women. It was feared that such training would raise women above the duties of her "station." A man would not love a learned wife. Better far to teach young ladies to be "correct in their manners, respectable in their families, and agreeable in society. . . . They were such delicate creatures, so different in mental as well as physical make-up from men, that they would never be able to survive the prolonged intellectual effort" [Brubacher and Rudy, 1976, p. 65].

And likewise . . . the missionaries were warned by pessimists and opponents of education for blacks that they would soon reach a point beyond which the black's innate mental capacity would be unable to go. Some of the northern idealists, rejecting this counsel of despair, went to the other extreme of seeking to teach the freedmen, without adequate preparation, a full duplicate of the liberal-arts curriculum given in contemporary northern colleges. These attempts, of course, were ludicrous failures. The majority of the educational missionaries were far more realistic, however. Many of them realized that the illiterate former slave would have to be introduced gradually to higher learning. They began by establishing primary departments where the three R's could be taught. As soon as a few students were sufficiently advanced, "normal" and theological departments were instituted [Brubacher and Rudy, 1976, p. 75].

One of the more significant new groups to attend college during this period consisted of veterans returning from World War II. The GI Bill of Rights, written with the assumption that few would take advantage of it, inspired more than one million veterans to enroll in college by the fall of 1946 (Wyatt, 1992). These individuals, many of whom were married, had children, and were working, represented a whole new generation of postsecondary students. Often, they were the first in their families to even think about continuing their education beyond high school. With the funding that accompanied the veterans, colleges instituted guidance centers, reading and study skills programs, and tutoring services, primarily to serve the new students (Maxwell, 1979).

What Should the Curriculum Look Like?

Responding to Charles Eliot's lament in 1871 that freshmen entering Harvard exhibited "bad spelling, incorrectness as well as inelegance of expression in writing, (and) ignorance of the simplest rules of punctuation," the university developed an entrance exam that included a written composition. By 1879, 50 percent of the applicants to Harvard were failing this exam and were admitted "on condition." This situation led the college to provide extra assistance in order to prepare the students for college-level classes (Weidner, 1990, p. 4).

By the 1890s, educators at Harvard were describing a literacy crisis among freshmen and formed a committee to examine the composition and rhetoric offerings at the college. The Harvard Reports, as they came to be known, linked poor writing to a lack of clear thinking and placed the blame on the educational system at the lower levels. President Eliot criticized the lack of time given to the teaching of English in both the secondary schools and the colleges and acknowledged that "so little attention is paid to English at the preparatory schools that half of the time, labor, and money which the University spends upon English must be devoted to the mere elements of the subject" (Eliot, 1969, p. 100).

In 1907, more than half of the newly admitted students at Harvard, Yale, Princeton, and Columbia still did not meet the entrance requirements (Wyatt, 1992). As a result, these prestigious schools all added developmental courses to their curricula. The most common courses at this time consisted of remedial reading and study skills. By 1909, over 350 colleges were offering "How to Study" courses for underprepared students, and by 1920, 100 study habit books had been published.

A survey was sent to all state universities in 1929, asking if they provided remedial work in reading. Almost 25 percent of the respondents indicated that they tried to identify poor readers on admission, and slightly fewer responded that they then provided remediation (Parr, 1930, p. 548). Some of the schools made the remediation compulsory. At Ohio State University, for example, all "probation" students were required to take remedial reading. The instruction consisted mainly of drills involving eye movements, and tachistoscopes provided much of the training. One dean who returned the survey commented, "I am sorry that we have nothing to report as done, but I am heartily delighted that you are beginning work along this line. I don't know anything more timely" (Parr, 1930, p. 548).

At Indiana University, studies were begun to determine reading levels of students and whether "How to Study" courses made a difference. Book (1927) found that in the fall of 1926, only 27 percent of the entering freshmen could articulate the main point of an assigned passage. He concluded that "the reading ability of college freshmen should be accurately determined; that special remedial instruction should be given to all who are found to be deficient in this regard; and that this instruction should be given in a special orientation or 'how to study' course and given by an instructor who is specially interested in the work and well equipped to give the type of help which these students need" (p. 248). Such courses were offered at Indiana University using Book's 1927 textbook, *Learning How to Study and Work Effectively*.

The issue of reading instruction did not disappear. In fact, an even stronger cry went out in 1948, when William S. Gray called for college reading to be taught to all students. He recommended that instruction include both content and personal reading. An indication of how widespread the notion of college reading had become was the formation of a professional organization for the discipline, the Southwest Reading Conference (Wyatt, 1992).

Precollege courses increased in popularity during this period. In 1926, the University of Buffalo required that all entering students who fell in the lower ranks of their high school class enroll in a three-week study course that was held prior to the start of school. At the end of the course, a few students were "debarred" from admission to the university, and others who were considered "doubtful" were given a reduced academic load (Eckert and Jones, 1935).

Many black colleges throughout the South provided an excellent range of programs for high school students who were still not receiving adequate academic preparation from the elementary and secondary schools. The authors of a survey describing these offerings stated: "Such efforts deserve generous support for student expenses and institutional costs from foundations, state and Federal governments, and all individuals wishing to equalize opportunities for higher education among our young people. More important, since these varied efforts are now still in a formative stage, the opportunity exists to coordinate them as they develop to assure the widespread adoption of demonstrably superior practices and to make certain that the needs of all deserving students everywhere are met" (McGrath, 1965, p. 58).

These innovative programs for high school students included coursework in basic skills as well as seminars in science. Precollege programs lasting from one to fourteen hours a day for eight weeks at the Tuskegee Institute were designed to "obviate the need for remedial work after the student has entered college" (McGrath, 1965). One initiative, the Southern Teaching Program, Inc., brought Yale Law School students to thirteen black colleges to provide instruction during the summer.

Of the black colleges surveyed, only four reported that they provided no remedial instruction during the academic year. The programs described were required, often carried credit, and foreshadowed the variety that would appear nationwide starting in the 1960s and 1970s. Basically, five approaches were implemented to "rectify the deficiencies of incoming students": special courses, intensified sections of regular courses, tutoring, clinical work, and a reduced schedule of instruction. Interestingly, the clinical work, though the most expensive alternative, was the most popular among students because it was individualized and because they viewed it "more as an effort to improve themselves than as evidence that they are academically inferior" (McGrath, 1965).

It is evident that colleges were beginning to acknowledge their role in providing assistance to students who were not academically prepared. Some were willing to grant credit for the coursework and even hired a full-time staff and provided special training for those responsible for delivering the assistance (Barbe, 1951). Colleges offered the coursework from a variety of departments, including English, education, and psychology. Schools such as Harvard discovered that the title of the course affected the willingness of students to enroll. Once Harvard changed its "Remedial Reading" course to "The Reading Class," enrollment increased dramatically. From thirty reluctant freshmen per year, the classes began to attract hundreds of freshmen, upperclassmen, graduate students, and even professors from the law school (Wyatt, 1992).

The direction in which higher education was headed at the end of this era is reflected in Gleazer's plea to schools in 1970: "Meet the student where he is. I am increasingly impatient with people who ask whether a student is 'college material'. We are not building a college with the student. The question we ought to ask is whether the college is of sufficient student material. It is the student we are building, and it is the function of the college to facilitate that process" (p. 50).

The following would have made an appropriate university marketing release for this time period. It provides a representative picture of the philosophy, students, and curriculum:

> The Currently Common College located in Middle America, U.S.A., is seeking young gentlemen of European descent, a few young ladies of similar background, and a small number of Negro men who would like to study in the innovative field of science to become prepared for opportunities in agriculture. Our mission is to prepare individuals interested in a practical education that relates directly to vocational interests. Students may apply to the junior college of our university to determine if four years of study is appropriate for them.

Moving Beyond the Revolving Door, 1960–2000

With the enrollment of an increasingly diverse student population, colleges and universities needed to find ways to provide support services.

What Is the Purpose of Postsecondary Education?

"In spite of the identity crisis through which higher education was going, no comprehensive and coherent philosophy of its role emerged" (Brubacher and Rudy, 1976, p. 306). This philosophical vacuum was loudly lamented in the 1960s by the diverse voices that had been speaking out against the traditionalist approach to higher education. The concept of open admissions further challenged many of the assumptions that had gradually been losing status over the years, and the surge of "grass roots" colleges ensured that "educational diversity is a difference to be cherished" (Hall, 1974).

The voices of change were louder and clearer than in earlier periods, and the tension in the educational community grew accordingly. The debate over opening doors while maintaining standards entered the public domain with a roar. And this was not a debate for educators only; everyone seemed to have an opinion. College administrators often assumed the role of reformists, defending their institutions against those who charged that standards were declining.

The rapid growth of new types of colleges designed expressly to serve the needs of nontraditional students provides the best measure of higher education during this period. In 1970, there were more than one thousand junior and community colleges serving two million students. The critical issue facing these schools was how "to make good on the implied promise of the open door" (Gleazer, 1970, p. 48). Providing access was one thing; facilitating success was quite another. Gleazer suggested that these schools learn as much as possible about the needs of the community; that they meet the students where they were, and that they provide assistance to students to clarify their goals and identify their talents. This was quite revolutionary compared with earlier decades when the curriculum was fixed and the student was left to figure out just how to fit in and succeed.

A wide range of institutions challenged the former assumptions of higher education. College study was now considered more of a right than a privilege; it provided for social mobility and also offered a curriculum increasingly relevant to an individual's life goals, both professional and personal. Flexibility was built in as colleges began to recognize that the life circumstances of students had to be accommodated. Classes were scheduled for both daytime and evening hours, weekdays and weekends. Options for full-time and part-time study needed to be provided so that students could take several courses together or one course at a time to fulfill the requirements for a certificate or a degree. The latter could now be either a two-year associate's degree or the more traditional four-year bachelor of arts or science. The educational choices multiplied to meet the needs and demands of the public.

Cross's descriptions of some of the colleges offering alternative delivery systems demonstrate how the new, broader purposes of higher education were being met (Hall, 1974). These systems included work-study programs that connected the business world directly to higher education; TV colleges that extended coursework to both urban and rural populations; correspondence schools that allowed students to learn at their own pace in their own home; and schools that gave credit for life experiences. Schools were founded that reached out to specific populations that had previously been denied access to college. In Harlem, a no-cost night college opened that offered baby-sitting services as well as tutoring to students who were mostly unskilled workers. Schools for Native Americans, Chicanos, and blacks came into existence, with precollege programs that offered tutoring, basic skills, and counseling.

The Carnegie Commission, writing in 1973, described an "educational revolution" in the sixties, when colleges and universities moved from providing "mass higher education" to offering "universal access." The final report states: "The current transition to universal access to college involves the guarantee of a place for every high school student who wishes to enter higher education, the introduction of more remedial work, the adaptation to the interests of new groups of students regardless of age. . . . It is a transformation of fundamental historic proportions" (Carnegie Foundation for the Advancement of Teaching, 1973, p. 5).

Who Should Attend College?

For years we have been trying to make students fit colleges, rather than the reverse. When they have not fit, failure has been laid at the feet of the student, not the colleges (Hall, 1974). It would have been quite impossible to squeeze the "new" students, as Cross has called them, into the traditional mold of higher education. As colleges opened their doors wider and as the number of unskilled positions in the job market dropped—to 15 percent in 1979 (Cross, 1983)—individuals who had never considered a postsecondary education filled the seats of classrooms everywhere. During these decades, a major shift was also occurring with respect to high school graduation. Whereas in 1970, 75.4 percent of all adults had a high school degree, by 1993, 87 percent had one.

Cross (1971) described these students, who often ranked in the lowest third of their high school class, as being passive toward learning and bringing with them a fear of failure. The failure syndrome had been deeply embedded in them from years of nonachievement in the earlier grades, and the common result was passivity. Many of these new students were also the first in their families to attend college. They represented a wider range of socioeconomic levels and ethnic and cultural backgrounds than did earlier students. More women and adults entered the world of postsecondary education. Indeed, it is not unheard of today for a sixty-five-year-old grandmother to graduate from college. From 1972 to 1982, the number of adult learners aged twenty-five to thirty-four attending college increased by 70 percent while those over the age of thirty-five increased by 75 percent (King, 1985).

Nineteenth-Century Reflection Redux

These difficulties have to do with the age at which young men can get prepared for college, and therefore with the ages at which boys pass the successive stages of their earlier education. The average age of admission to Harvard College has been rising for sixty years past, and has now reached the extravagant limit of eighteen years and ten months. Harvard College is not at all peculiar in this respect; indeed, many of the country colleges find their young men older still at entrance. The average college graduate is undoubtedly nearly twenty-three years old at graduation [Eliot, 1969, p. 151].

As many of the new students entering college were either misprepared because they had not expected to pursue a postsecondary education or were returning to school after a lengthy hiatus, they often needed support systems to complete the transition to college. Hardin (1988) offered several assumptions regarding these students:

1. They may have been underprepared, but they were not incapable or ineducable.
2. The reasons for an earlier lack of achievement are complex.
3. These reasons could be overcome with the proper support system.
4. Given adequate time and opportunity, the new students could succeed.
5. These students needed assistance with social and personal concerns as well as academic needs.

In addition to the students already described, other populations started coming through the doors of higher education. Beginning with the Rehabilitation Act of 1973, students with disabilities were granted easier access to college and also given assurances of academic assistance (Hardin, 1988). Continuing to 1990, with passage of the Americans with Disabilities Act, access for the disabled became routine for all postsecondary institutions. Schools have been charged to provide "reasonable accommodation," and the number of disabled students attending college has grown steadily since the 1970s, in part because of increased support systems provided by the elementary and secondary schools. By 1994, 75 percent of disabled adults had completed high school (U.S. Department of Education, 1994), and 14,994 seniors took special editions of the Scholastic Aptitude Test (SAT) designed for the disabled.

Another significant population in terms of growth in higher education is that of international students and students for whom English is a second language. Academic assistance is frequently offered to them through formal coursework or more informal "conversation" groups to improve their communication skills as well as to promote a better understanding of the cultural differences they experience in the classroom. Tutors who speak a second language are frequently hired to provide supplemental support. This new population also brings a unique opportunity for reciprocal learning, as cultural diversity workshops abound and are often offered through the learning assistance unit.

What Should the Curriculum Look Like?

Over one thousand women's studies courses were offered in 1973 (Hall, 1974). These courses along with ethnic studies and others new to the traditional college curriculum continued to grow exponentially throughout the sixties and into the seventies. Students demanded relevant coursework, and universities accommodated them by expanding existing departments and often organizing new ones. Requirements were relaxed, and students were frequently allowed to construct their own academic programs. Along with this freedom of choice, however, came risk and the subsequent "opportunity to fail" (Cross, 1983). The open door often turned into a revolving door, with students dropping out and "stopping out" regularly. This led to a highly charged debate about the lowering of standards, often followed by the call to raise admission standards and close the doors of opportunity to the thousands of prospective new students.

Not everyone, however, believed in locking out the new students. With the eighties came attempts to combine access with excellence. Robert McCabe, president of Miami-Dade Community College, summed up one school of thought when he said: "It is clear that standards have declined in American education at all levels. . . . It is most important that we raise student expectations. . . . The college should assume responsibility for assisting individuals to succeed, and an ordered curriculum should be instituted to deal with reading, writing, and computational deficiencies first, so that all students benefit from attendance" (McCabe, 1983, p. 27). He further suggested that colleges hold to high standards not by excluding students but by requiring developmental coursework when test scores indicate the need. He advocated early advising, when the student would be apprised of strengths and weaknesses and directed into appropriate classes. He added that schools should develop systems that would allow variable time frames for course completion and that students who need assistance be given a reduced load.

The philosophy expressed by McCabe was also supported by other educators, such as Patricia Cross, who declared that many students needed assistance while overcoming their fear of failure (Cross, 1971). John Roueche (1978) advocated a more intensive, directed program of academic assistance. He was critical of the "Band-Aid" approach that gave a student in need of help a few remedial classes along with a full academic load. Instead, he suggested an integrated skills program that a student would complete *before* entering the regular curriculum.

The efforts of Miami-Dade Community College in Florida reflected the attempts during the eighties to hold to standards while providing the academic assistance needed by so many students. In a switch from the two earlier decades, the faculty at Miami-Dade developed a prescribed interdisciplinary general education core that all students were required to take. In addition, the school began to administer a test to all first-time students that assessed their skill levels in reading, writing, and computation. Using the test scores plus pertinent personal information, the school placed students in appropriate developmental courses, limited their academic loads, and restricted their enrollment in certain courses. Students who took part in this program were nine times as likely to graduate as those who did not participate (Roueche and Baker, 1987).

Miami-Dade's new programming was undertaken with the help of a grant from the Fund for the Improvement of Postsecondary Education, an indication of the growth of public support for such initiatives. In the fall of 1989, 74 percent of colleges and universities offered at least one remedial course and 20 percent awarded degree credit for these courses. Two-thirds of the institutions gave institutional credit and only one-tenth awarded no credit at all (U.S. Department of Education, 1991). The question was no longer, *Should* we provide learning assistance to the underprepared student? Rather, educators were asking, *How* should we provide learning assistance to afford the best opportunity for success to the underprepared student?

In addition, academic support units expanded to provide services for disabled students. These services included the taping of textbooks; accommodations in testing (for example, untimed tests, oral delivery and response, and computer-assisted tests); the provision of note-takers; and individualized supplemental instruction. Often, such services are multifaceted, as they attempt to address social and emotional needs as well as academic ones. Counseling components have been added to many college programs for the learning disabled, as have precollege transitional offerings designed to create support networks and to increase self-esteem. At Adelphi University, preliminary data indicated an 84 percent persistence for learning disabled students who participated in a holistic precollege program. This rate compared favorably with the overall persistence of 60 percent for the nondisabled students at the university (Yanok and Broderick, 1988).

A gradual change in the terminology of learning assistance programs indicated shifting perspectives on the underprepared student. While the term *remedial* was still applied to programs through the early sixties, it was often used interchangeably in the late sixties and seventies with the term *compensatory*. This became a popular term in education following equal rights legislation that funded programs designed to help students make up for earlier discrimination and poverty. According to Clowes (1980), "Compensatory education in higher education would take the form of remediation activities such as preparatory and supplementary work . . . all with a program to provide an enriching experience beyond the academic environment to counterbalance a non-supportive home environment" (p. 8).

It is interesting that Clowes included remediation within this definition of compensatory education, for all too often its meaning has not been clear. The term *remedial* has implied a more limited approach toward the student and has primarily described programs that focus on correcting specific skill deficits. It was reflective of a medical-model approach to learning assistance, in which "treatments" were prescribed for discrete symptoms, with little consideration given to the whole "patient" (Clowes, 1980). If evaluation showed that the treatments did not work, they were often repeated, the assumption being that additional time would make a difference.

Both terms, *remedial* and *compensatory*, have contributed to a negative connotation of the programs and students in question. They have focused attention on weaknesses and highlighted the differences between these students and those enrolled in the more advanced college curriculum. As learning assistance has become more acceptable and more integral to the well-being of higher education, a new term has come into use that reflects this shift in perspective.

The more current term, *developmental*, originally came from the field of college student personnel and was applied, beginning in the late seventies, to programs that took a comprehensive view of the individual student and sought to promote growth in both academic and personal areas. Behind the use of this term is a belief that a college or university should provide a comprehensive support system that meets students where they are and combines assistance in academic areas with personal counseling. Rather than focusing solely on weak skill areas, a developmental approach assumes that everyone has talents and is strong in some areas. By acknowledging these strengths while working to build up underdeveloped areas, developmental programs are able to establish a more positive tone with the student. One significant aspect of this shift in perspective is that *all* students are potentially developmental students: the talented mathematician may need help in writing an English essay; the fine musician may seek assistance with geometry; the overzealous high achiever may need time management skills and personal counseling.

Learning assistance, now increasingly approached from a developmental point of view, seems to have earned a permanent spot in higher education. Though some states are trying to relegate developmental education programs to two-year community colleges (Carriuolo, 1994), a great deal of effective programming is firmly in place among four-year institutions. Recent research has shown the effectiveness of these programs in terms of both persistence toward graduation and success in more advanced coursework: 48 percent of the students enrolled in developmental coursework at research universities graduate, and more than 90 percent of those who pass developmental English go on to pass college English. Similar statistics exist for developmental math and reading courses (Boylan and others, 1992).

These statistics, taken together with the increasing diversity of students in higher education and the democratic philosophy that emphasizes accessibility along with maintenance of standards, ensure that developmental education will be around well into the twenty-first century. The following commentary from Florence Cameron, a student who participated in a developmental program at National-Louis University in Chicago, provides an insight into the no-longer-new students who have settled into colleges across the country and whose growth and ability to contribute to society demonstrate the importance of access to higher education and of appropriate support systems:

> I can't begin to say how I have grown. I have gained a
> sense of confidence. When I first came to school, I was
> below the college's standards. By having the Center for

Academic Development available, I was able to come closer to the college level. My writing skills have improved tremendously. I feel I can achieve a bachelor's degree. I'll never forget the feeling of my self confidence in sitting down with my daughter. I knew I had a learning disability and was never encouraged in school, but by getting back to the basics, I was able to help my daughter. I know what's important in school, and now I know how to help her. In my work, I also have grown. For instance, I wrote my first minutes for a meeting [commentary quoted in a 1994 National-Louis University awards ceremony booklet].

The following would make an appropriate university marketing release in the twentieth century. It provides a representative picture of the philosophy, students, and curriculum from this period:

The Currently Common College located in Urban Area, U.S.A., is seeking individuals who would like to earn a degree while continuing to work. Incoming students have the option of applying for credit for life experiences that can be applied toward a degree or certificate program. Classes are offered in the evenings and on weekends at a site near you. Our mission is to provide an education that will develop the talents of adult learners and to ensure a support system that will facilitate that development.

Summary

It is evident that tension has been a part of postsecondary education throughout American history. Contributing to this tension have been the ongoing attempts to reconcile democratic ideals with a traditional educational system. The argument has revolved around how to maintain standards while opening the doors to an increasingly diverse student body. Educators discovered that it is not enough simply to open the doors of higher education; schools must be willing to provide the academic support necessary to maximize the potential of all their students.

Because the students enrolling in colleges and universities will continue to represent a broad range of talents and backgrounds, learning assistance and developmental education programs will be an integral part of the educational system for a long time to come. Chapter Two examines learning theories that provide a foundation for our work and help us to understand the diverse student needs that challenge us.

. . . .

2

Connecting Learning Theory to Practice

Throughout the history of our practice, we have been guided by principles that help us understand and, consequently, meet the needs of students. Various schools of thought have provided perspectives on how individuals learn and why they behave as they do. At certain times, we have been more influenced by one perspective than others, depending on what was currently being researched and chronicled. It is unfortunate that as new schools of thought develop, earlier ones are often discarded entirely. This chapter argues that for our practice to be most effective, it is imperative for us to be familiar with a broad range of theories and also to be willing to synthesize ideas from a variety of perspectives in order to provide an integrated approach to helping students achieve.

Theories can help explain the complexities of student behavior and show that it is not just a matter of chance or random effect. Collective knowledge about student performance in higher education comes from numerous sources, including hunches from personal experience as well as formal theories with extensive research bases.

According to Lewin (1951), there is nothing so practical as a good theory, and Cross (1981) has stated that although theory without practice is empty, practice without theory is blind. Both emphasize the importance of theory and research for professional behavior. (Chapter Seven explores this further, presenting a model for integrating theory with practice in learning assistance programs.)

This chapter examines five different perspectives and shows how they can guide us to help students. The behavioral, cognitive, social learning, motivational, and adult learning approaches have been chosen because of their extensive research bases and their potential for application to college student learning. We begin with a case study of Helen, an adult student experiencing academic and personal difficulties. Her situation is then used to illustrate specific concepts of each of the five approaches. The basic background of each perspective is sketched; this is followed by a description of practical implications and an outline of an action plan. In addition, the principles of the various individual approaches are synthesized and an action plan is presented that integrates all of them. Finally, the reader has the opportunity to examine another case study and prepare an integrated action plan using this discussion as a model.

Case Study

Helen is a twenty-five-year-old woman entering college for the first time. She is a full-time student majoring in nursing. Helen is a single mother with a five-year-old child. She works twenty hours a week as a nurse's aide, and her job has increased her desire to become a nurse.

In high school, Helen was an average student who was very socially active. Her family did not encourage her academically and offered no support to attend college. She did not study much and graduated in the lower half of her class. After graduation from high school, she married and gave no thought to attending college.

To make ends meet, Helen now lives at home with her parents; her mother helps with child care. Relations between Helen and her mother are strained, and she very much wants to move out and live on her own but cannot afford to. She sees the nursing degree as a way to get a good job and become independent; however, it will take at least four years and summer school to reach her goal.

The demands of her part-time job and the work required in her courses seem to be more than Helen can manage. In addition, she is frustrated living at home and is missing a meaningful social life. She is worried that she will not do well in her courses and is losing confidence in her ability to complete the degree.

Let us examine how we can provide the best assistance to Helen by reviewing each learning perspective in relation to her needs.

Behavioral Approach

Behaviorism is a theory of psychology that lies at the foundation of much educational practice. It originated with John Watson early in the twentieth century and is based primarily on three assumptions regarding the process of learning. The first is that learning requires an observable change in behavior. The second asserts that it is the environment, not the individual learner, that shapes behavior or causes any change. The third states that for learning to occur, appropriate stimuli must occur close together and be reinforced immediately.

How do these assumptions relate to Helen's case? One observable behavior change could be an increase in the time she spends studying. This is quantifiable and thus easy to validate. An external stimulus that could cause this change in behavior is a written study schedule developed for her by a learning specialist. To reinforce Helen's behavior when she adheres to the schedule and thus ensure that she will continue to follow it, the learning specialist could build in a system of rewards—for example, meeting a friend for dinner for an hour or taking an hour off to play with her child after several hours of study.

The concept of *connectionism*, or stimulus-response, is a component of behaviorism suggested by Thorndike (1913). It states that behaviors are connected to certain stimuli by the consequences of the behaviors. If a consequence is experienced as positive, the connection to the original stimulus will be strengthened. This idea has led behaviorists to postulate "the law of effect," which states that learning will occur and be remembered when positive effects follow a given behavior. A second law, "the law of exercise," states that significant learning will occur when this positive connection is repeated. Finally, "the law of readiness" asserts that learning is increased if the individual is ready for the connection to be made.

As Helen tries to follow the study schedule described earlier, it is important that she perceive the consequences to be positive and that she stick with the plan long enough to experience repeated success. Only if she is ready to see the connection between her action and the consequence will a more permanent change be effected.

The behaviorist B. F. Skinner shared Thorndike's interest in shaping behavior through a system of reinforcement. His concept of operant conditioning (Skinner, 1974) was based primarily on the power of behavioral consequences. He believed that if behavior was to be controlled and predicted, external conditions—or stimuli— would have to be appropriately engineered. Once the behavior had been modified according to the predetermined objectives, the behavior monitor—the instructor—would have to ensure that it was reinforced. However, if a behavior occurred that was undesirable, the monitor could extinguish it by simply removing any reinforcement that might have been present when it occurred. Skinner did not believe that punishment, or negative reinforcement, reduced unwanted behavior; rather, he suggested ignoring such behavior.

Skinner also asserted that an individual's personality is simply a consistent pattern of behavior that has been established through a series of reinforcements over time. Perhaps Helen's need for a social life developed in high school, when she was more successful with people than she was academically. Her social activities probably produced a more satisfying state for her than her grades and thus became a more potent reinforcer.

Implications

The behaviorist approach relies on observable changes in behavior in determining whether any learning has occurred. The instructor is responsible for providing external stimuli that will lead to successful consequences for the learner. This construct is often articulated through behavioral objectives that state exactly what the learner must do, under what circumstances, and what the successful outcome will be. The instructor is also responsible for reinforcing those behaviors that are positive so that they will be learned and, it is hoped, repeated.

This approach provides a solid foundation for programmed learning systems, computer-assisted instruction, competency-based learning, and tutoring programs. It leads to linear models of learning in which each step is outlined and mastered before the learner is allowed to move on to the next level. These models are very instructor-centered, as the instructor has the responsibility for monitoring and reinforcing each attempt at mastery. It is the student's rate of learning, however, that determines the pacing of any program based on behaviorism, and that is important in terms of meeting the needs of individual learners.

An additional and significant assumption that belongs to the behaviorist way of thinking is that almost everyone can learn if given the right conditions and enough time.

Action Plan

If Helen went to a learning specialist who applied a behavioral approach to learning assistance, the first step would probably be the administration of a battery of diagnostic tests related to the skill areas needed for success in her major field of study, nursing. In all likelihood, the tests would cover the basic areas of math, reading, and writing. Once the results were known, the specialist would develop a set of behavioral objectives that would lead Helen through a series of learning experiences designed to strengthen her weaker skills.

For example, if the reading test indicated that Helen needed assistance with comprehension, the following behavioral objectives might be written:

- Given an expository passage from a science text, the student will identify the main idea of the passage, with 70 percent accuracy.

- Given a list of scientific terms related to the field of nursing, the student will use each one in a sentence, with 70 percent accuracy.

- Given a list of facts and inferences from an article in an introductory nursing text, the student will distinguish fact from inference, with 70 percent accuracy.

Once the behavioral objectives have been discussed with Helen, the specialist will construct a series of learning activities. The activities will break down each objective into a set of sequential discrete skills designed to lead Helen toward mastery, which has been defined as a 70 percent level of accuracy. Activities designed to lead toward achievement of the first goal of comprehension might look like this:

- Reading a series of expository passages and listing the important details that have been included

- Articulating what the lists of details have in common for each passage and identifying that as the topic

- Specifying what it is about the general topic that is specifically being discussed and identifying that as the main idea

Helen would be given much practice with each of these activities and would not move from one to another without achieving mastery. Each one has been designed as a building block and therefore needs to be mastered before success can occur at the next level. Helen can proceed at her own rate, but it is important with this approach that regular appointments be made with the learning specialist. The specialist must continuously monitor and reinforce Helen's progress. When Helen is experiencing difficulty, the specialist must provide timely corrections and additional sets of learning activities for continued practice.

Helen may not achieve the written objectives in one term, but that is not important as long as she continues to engage in the activities regularly and to meet with the learning specialist.

Cognitive Approach

Cognitive theories of learning differ significantly from those of the behaviorists. Though a wide range of perspectives exists among cognitivists, there is an underlying framework that unifies and distinguishes them. This framework is based on the theory that learning involves a series of mental processes organized by the learner rather than by an external reinforcer. Learning does not have to be observable, and the locus of control is the individual learner.

What are some of the assumptions made by cognitivists regarding the process of learning? The first one is that learning is an active process rather than a passive one. Individuals are constantly receiving information from their environment and taking action to organize it for storage in their memory system. Second, cognitivists believe that individuals think about problems until they gain the insight that will lead them to a solution. They are driven by the need to reduce the ambiguity that exists until a solution is found. This leads to a third assumption, namely, that the motivational drive is an intrinsic one and will lead to personal satisfaction when the learning is achieved. (Compare this with the behaviorist belief that motivation comes solely from external reinforcement.) The fourth cognitivist assumption is that to solve any problem, learners must have access to pertinent pieces of information that define the problem. Learners will gain the insight needed for the solution only if they have the opportunity to arrange and rearrange the pieces.

Again, this presents a marked contrast with the behaviorist belief that learning occurs after a series of discrete steps in which pieces of information are processed hierarchically.

For Helen, the cognitive approach would have her more actively engaged in the process of solving her problems. She could be encouraged to keep a journal to record her thoughts as she receives new information about the challenges of achieving success in college. Reading over her entries on a weekly or biweekly basis might lead her to reflect on successful experiences and could help her discover solutions for some of her problems.

The cognitive view of how learning occurs is most notably characterized by theories of developmental stages and by the information processing and schema theories that flow from them. The work of Piaget, Perry, and Belenky serves as a conceptual framework for understanding the nature of cognitive stages or levels of readiness for learning. Piaget (1966) was the first to propose that there are distinct stages of cognitive development and that they emerge at specific ages. He believed that cognitive abilities develop sequentially and are hierarchical—that is, one ability must be fully developed before the next can function effectively. Piaget identified four stages of learning in children: sensorimotor, preoperational, concrete operations, and formal operations. These stages normally occur during predictable age frames and move the individual from manipulating the environment for the purpose of learning to thinking in the abstract. According to Piaget, this last stage, formal operations, should occur around the age of fifteen and represents the highest level of cognition. Individuals no longer need to "see" the discrete elements of an issue; they can consider the elements by reflecting on the whole.

The notion of schema—the way an individual mentally organizes information—originated with Piaget, who contended that learning takes place through assimilation or accommodation. Assimilation occurs when learners take in information for which they already have a knowledge base, or schema, available. This base has been created over time as learners have taken in and stored information. Accommodation, by contrast, implies that the learner can find no existing schema with which to connect the incoming information, so either existing schemata must be modified or new ones created. According to Piaget, the ideal learning situation occurs when the individual has some background knowledge to connect to the incoming information but at the same time must alter his or her existing schema to accommodate new ideas. This creates a challenge and will most likely assist the learner in maintaining a balance between what is known and what is unknown and must be learned. Piaget considered this desire for balance a major source of motivation.

Whereas Piaget associated the concrete operational stage with the age of twelve or thereabouts, a study reported by Lucas (1990) found that most first-year students at two-year colleges functioned at this level. The finding has implications for instructional delivery in postsecondary education. For instance, in Helen's case, it would be important to determine her cognitive level. It would also be important, keeping in mind Piaget's concepts of assimilation and accommodation, to provide her with assistance for which she has some schema already established. For example, Helen probably has already internalized a fairly complicated time management plan as she has juggled child care with her work schedule. The specialist can show her how to build on what she has already managed successfully by adding the new dimension of schoolwork.

In the early seventies, after conducting interviews with students at Harvard University, Perry suggested that there were nine stages of cognitive development (1970). Perry, like Piaget, considered the nine stages to be sequential and hierarchical. His stages proceed from dualistic (where thinking forms around clear dichotomies of right and wrong, known and unknown) through multiplicity (where individuals begin to form personal opinions) to relativism and commitment (where learners are able to construct their own conceptual systems).

Although Perry described college students as operating at the higher cognitive levels, Cameron (1984) conducted research with community college students and found that 63 percent of entering students who were at least twenty-two years old were functioning at the dualistic stage. Again, this has important implications at the postsecondary level. At the dualistic stage, students view knowledge as something that comes from an external authority; there is a set of facts they do not have but must acquire. (It corresponds with what Freire [1970] has referred to as the banking concept of teaching, namely, that students are considered to be empty vessels into which knowledge must be deposited by someone else who has it.) At this overly simplistic level of cognition, the student is not ready to challenge or synthesize ideas—tasks that are often routinely assigned to college students.

If, through testing or interviewing, it is determined that Helen is thinking at the dualistic level, the specialist must gradually give her the confidence and the know-how to question some of her existing notions about education. Helen may be too willing to let the learning specialist prescribe a set of behaviors for her, rather than having the self-confidence to come up with her own solutions. Perhaps through journal activity she can be guided to see the significance of her own thoughts.

One final variation of a developmental stage theory that may be significant in Helen's case comes from the work of Belenky, Clinchy, Goldberger, and Tarule (1986), who conducted research with women. Through an interviewing process in which they originally tried to fit the women's responses into Perry's cognitive scheme, they developed a set of five perspectives through which they suggest women filter their thinking processes. Their set of perspectives follows a sequence similar to Perry's (though less structured and not necessarily hierarchical) as they move from "silence," where the individual perceives herself to be voiceless and less knowledgeable than an external authority, to "constructed knowledge," where the individual creates a personal knowledge base and system of thinking.

Belenky, Clinchy, Goldberger, and Tarule have used this set of perspectives to frame an ideal instructional process that they describe as *connected teaching*. They suggest that teaching is a process that is shared between student and teacher and that instruction should be carried out through "public dialogue." This ensures that students do not remain voiceless and that they are respected for both their own knowledge and their experiences. The instructor becomes somewhat like a midwife, assisting students in accessing new knowledge and relating it to prior experience. If Helen is at the voiceless stage, she needs to be carefully led from there to a point at which she becomes confident that her own ideas have value. This could be accomplished through a journal or guided discussion sessions with a learning specialist. For example, at the start of an individual session, Helen could be asked to write down one successful experience she has had during the past week and to reflect on what made it successful. After ten minutes of internal reflection and writing, the discussion could begin by using her thoughts as a catalyst for additional problem solving. Eventually, Helen will see the value in her own ideas and will develop them more independently and spontaneously.

In addition to the various developmental stage theories that help define the cognitive approach are information processing theories that are linked to the formation of schemata. Loftus and Loftus (1980) have provided a computer analogy that helps clarify what information processing is all about. The computer takes in information, manipulates it, and then produces something. This process is dependent on what has previously been stored in its memory system and the directions it receives from the software being used. The operation seems to happen automatically when the appropriate systems are engaged. Likewise, the human mind receives information, manipulates it, and uses it to produce individual thinking and behavior.

As information is received from the environment, individuals must decide what to do with it. Like the computer, they proceed on the basis of what has already been stored in memory and what the current situation seems to require. On the one hand, they may decide that the information needs to be stored for a short time only, in which case they will not take action to save it. On the other hand, they may decide that they will need this information in the future and consequently need to take action now to store it for a longer time. In this latter case, they will transfer it to their long-term memory system. When they process the information for this type of storage, they need to organize it in a meaningful way in order to find it later. This is analogous to computer files: when they are not properly organized, even though they contain all the desired information, they may be difficult or impossible to access. At this point, learners try to chunk the information into meaningful categories so as to create organized files. Learners also search their long-term memories to find other files with which to connect the incoming file of information.

As learners search for existing files, referred to as schemata, they will go through Piaget's process of assimilation if they find any that connect in a meaningful way to the incoming file. At that point, they may simply add the new information to the old, increasing the size of the established schema. If they cannot find an existing file, they must create a new one for the new information, thereby making what Piaget calls an accommodation.

Rumelhart and Norman (1978) have discussed learning in terms of information processing. Norman (1982) has described learning as "purposeful remembering." This concept of learning fits the process that was described earlier as the learner actively searched for a meaningful storage system in order to have access to information whenever it was needed. In addition, Norman has categorized various types of learning that occur within the framework of information processing; he calls them *accretion*, *structuring*, and *tuning* (Hergnhahn, 1988). Accretion—the most common, according to Norman—occurs when the learner receives information that can be added to preexisting schemata. It is important to note that even when there are existing schemata, they may change somewhat whenever items are added. Structuring, which Norman considers to be the most difficult mode of learning, occurs when the individual can find no match between incoming information and preexisting schemata and consequently must decide how to organize it in a meaningful way. This may include reorganizing existing schemata in order to accommodate new information or creating an entirely new file. Tuning, the third mode of learning, occurs as the learner moves from the level of novice to that of expert. For this movement to be successful, the learner must become adept at accessing particular schemata quickly and accurately. This implies that schemata are regularly being refined as they are organized and reorganized to ensure efficient access.

As far as Helen is concerned, she is probably involved in both accretion and structuring. The new information she is taking in every day may fit into a preexisting schema, but more likely she is modifying and creating schemata at a fairly rapid pace. This may be frustrating to her, as she has a clear-cut goal—to become a nurse— and she may have thought that college would provide a more immediate tuning level of learning, where she would simply refine her skills as a nurse's assistant.

Implications

The cognitivist approach assumes that for learning to occur, the student must take an active role. If that is to happen, students must have access to previous knowledge that they have stored in a systematic way so that they can connect it to new information. The role of the instructor is to determine how much the student already knows and then to present new information that will connect to existing schemata. Thus, personal experiences and the ways they have been perceived and organized in the learner's mind are important in the learning situation.

In addition to knowing where students fit in terms of prior knowledge, the instructor must have at least a general understanding of the cognitive level at which students may be processing information. Students cannot be expected to synthesize information if they are processing at either a concrete operational level or a dualistic one. What they need is a set of basic concepts around which they can begin to create schemata; subsequently, they can be led into making comparisons and then gradually into analyzing and synthesizing. Likewise, they may not be able to actively participate in a class discussion or collaborative learning situation unless the format is highly structured. Indeed, they may become angry if they perceive that the instructor is "abdicating" a conventional role and expecting students to learn from one another in collaborative situations.

Action Plan

A learning specialist using the cognitive approach with Helen may start with an open-ended interview at the first session, to gain a general idea of her level of thinking. By asking her questions like those listed below, the specialist can more effectively organize a plan for guiding her from one level to another. In addition, the specialist can decide how best to present new information so that Helen can link it to preexisting schemata.

Sample Interview Questions

- How do you feel about yourself as a learner at this university? What is your role as a student in the college classroom? Is this role different from your role as a student in high school?

- Describe your experience in high school. What was the most meaningful part?

- What was the most frustrating part? Please explain.

- What do you like best about being a nurse's aide?

- Why did you decide to enter college at this time?

- What do you think will be the most difficult adjustments you will have to make at college? Please explain.

An analysis of Helen's responses guides the specialist in making an informal assessment of her level of processing information. The specialist then has a better understanding of Helen's awareness of herself as a learner and her perspective on university expectations. The specialist may then, in regularly scheduled dialogues, draw out Helen on how she plans to reach her long-term goal of becoming a nurse. The following strategies could be developed through their sessions:

- Increasing Helen's awareness of her particular approach to learning and her ways of adjusting to a range of instructor styles

- Sharing strategies for organizing new content and for creating connections to her personal experience and to her practice on the job

- Affirming Helen's basic competence and ability to succeed by drawing from her the strategies that she has successfully applied elsewhere and showing how these can be applied in the academic setting

- Developing active learning behaviors with Helen that assist her in asking questions in class, linking new information to prior learning, and subsequently synthesizing ideas across courses

Gradually, Helen will become a more active, independent learner. She will proceed through several developmental stages as she becomes more proficient and confident as a student.

Social Learning Approach

The social learning approach, most commonly associated with Bandura (1986), emphasizes *observational learning, modeling,* and *generalization.* It provides another framework for understanding Helen's situation while developing a plan to help her achieve.

The basic tenet of observational learning is that individuals acquire knowledge by observing actions and events around them. Observational learning is more than looking and imitating what is seen. In fact, a person may learn by observing something and never imitating it. For example, as a nurse's aide, Helen may observe a nurse incorrectly administer a medication and witness the patient's adverse reaction. She does not have to repeat the action to learn from it. Thus, observational learning may be either positive (learning what to do) or negative (learning what to avoid).

In observational learning, people from whom one learns are called *models.* A special group of models consists of those we *choose* to imitate. These individuals tend to be highly respected and thought of as competent, attractive, or powerful. They may be personally known (a parent, teacher, or counselor) or not (a character from film, television, or literature). Without intending to do so, these models can teach values and attitudes and affect patterns of behavior. Even creativity may be stimulated by modeling: an individual may observe a variety of models and draw from each of them particular styles or characteristics.

When one lacks effective models, the opportunity to learn positive behaviors may be thwarted. In Helen's case, for example, she failed to identify a model teacher or counselor in high school and instead imitated the social behaviors of her peers. In her own family, there were no academically motivated models from whom she could learn, and she lacked a significant figure who could promote her self-confidence in learning and encourage academic achievement.

In observational learning, individuals may have models from whom they learn through imitation and ultimately *generalize* what has been learned to similar situations. For example, Helen may observe a nurse she admires comfort and care for a dying patient. As the nurse actively listens to the patient, Helen learns the importance of unconditional acceptance and will be able to generalize this to her own experiences with other patients.

Another aspect of social learning theory is Bandura's (1986) concept of *reciprocal determinism*, which postulates constant inter-action and influence between the person, the environment, and behavior. In Helen's situation, her environment of financial depen-dence and impoverished social life affects her behavior, and she her-self influences her behavior and environment through her lack of self-confidence and overall frustration. A change in one of these (behavior, environment, or person) will produce a change in the other two. All of these factors have significant implications for developing an intervention plan to assist Helen.

Implications

The overriding difficulties Helen is facing include

1. Loss of confidence in her ability to achieve her degree

2. A sense of being overwhelmed by the demands of school, work, and home

3. Loss of ability to concentrate because of her worries

4. Lack of a fulfilling social life

How can social learning theory provide a guide for helping Helen address these concerns?

Given the importance of models, it would be important for Helen to identify someone whom she could emulate as she pursues her degree. Potential models might include a teacher in her acade-mic program who, like Helen, had significant obstacles to overcome in her past and achieved in spite of them. Maybe there is a nurse at Helen's job who could assume this role. Perhaps there is another student in Helen's program who is achieving and could be seen as a role model.

Since social learning theory emphasizes the importance of the interaction among the person, the environment, and behavior, each of these factors needs to be assessed when developing a plan to help Helen achieve.

Action Plan

The first step in providing learning assistance would be an assessment of Helen as she is interacting with her environment. An initial session would probe the characteristics of her home, work, and school settings to identify the specific conditions encouraging and impeding her learning. Helen would be guided to identify both the positive and the negative forces in her environment and would be helped to choose one positive force to cultivate and one negative force to address.

For example, at work there is a nurse whom she respects and who seems to take a special interest in her. To further this relationship, Helen could see if this person would be willing to give her some individual time and help her review some of her course material. Or she could suggest that they find time to meet over coffee and become better acquainted. This could lead to an ongoing relationship that would foster some modeling behavior. It could also address Helen's concern about needing to socialize more.

At home, one of the negative factors impeding Helen's academic progress is the mounting stress between her and her mother. Helen may need to rework things at home with the help of the college counseling center.

Specific strategies for improving concentration and study skills would also be part of the action plan, though these would not particularly be related to the principles of social learning theory. The main emphases in the social learning approach would be, first, the attention given to the environment and Helen's interaction with it, and second, the search for a role model with whom a relationship could be cultivated.

Finally, Helen would be encouraged to observe other effective learners. What distinguishes these learners from those who are struggling? What specific behaviors do they exhibit that make them effective? Meeting and talking with other students who are achieving could begin to give Helen the direction she needs.

Motivational Approach

One of the best-known theories explaining the dynamics of human motivation is that of Maslow. Maslow's theory (1970) postulates that behavior is initiated out of a desire to meet basic human needs. Humans are seen as fundamentally good and motivated to behave so that basic needs are fulfilled. Maslow held that human needs are arranged hierarchically according to potency and priority. The "lower" needs are stronger and take precedence over the "higher" ones. The hierarchy of needs in Maslow's theory comprises, from lowest to highest, *physiological* needs (for food, water, sleep), *safety* needs (for shelter, clothing, freedom from danger), *love/belonging* needs (for friends, family), *esteem* needs (for respect, admiration), and *self-actualization* needs (for development of one's potential).

This theory represents an optimistic conception of human behavior. It focuses on the natural tendency toward growth, excellence, and satisfaction, and the hierarchical need structure allows for the interpretation of behavior along a continuum. For example, higher-level needs are often unfulfilled because lower-level needs are unmet. When a person has unmet needs for food, water, and shelter, most of the individual's energy is spent on fulfilling those needs to the exclusion of others such as the needs for friends, respect, or admiration.

Helen is struggling with needs at the most basic level, as well as others along the continuum. To meet her physiological and safety needs, she is dependent on the support of her parents. She is unhappy living at home and is worried about how and when this will ever change. When these basic needs are cause for concern, it is difficult to concentrate on academics.

In addition, even though Helen is living among her family, her belongingness/love needs remain unfulfilled. Tensions at home have caused a rift between Helen and her parents, and lack of regular contact with friends has left her social life impoverished. She desires a meaningful relationship with a member of the opposite sex but does not participate in social situations where she would be likely to meet someone. The sense of being somewhat isolated has affected her concentration and contributed to academic difficulties.

Feeling good about oneself and believing in one's unique importance and value are what characterizes high self-esteem. When one has high self-esteem, one sees oneself as intelligent, capable, energetic, and motivated to achieve. Helen's dependency on her parents has affected her self-esteem and given her occasion to doubt herself as she pursues her academic goals. A compounding factor is her lack of academic success in previous educational settings. She does not have a repertoire of academic successes to boost her confidence now and is plagued by self-doubt.

None of the basic needs in Maslow's hierarchy are being fully met, which makes it impossible for Helen to strive toward self-actualization or realization of her full potential.

Implications

Maslow's theory emphasizes the importance of fulfilling basic internal needs in order to live happily and achieve one's goals. Contrary to the behavioral approach, Maslow's motivational approach stresses that an educator or counselor attempting to help someone achieve must have an understanding of the individual's feelings.

Given Helen's low self-esteem, unfulfilled need for belongingness and love, and worry about safety as she remains dependent on her parents, the approach best suited to the situation, following Maslow, would involve personal counseling. Counseling sessions would focus on Helen's unmet needs, and she would be guided to discover ways of meeting them. Even though the levels of need are arranged hierarchically, all levels can be addressed simultaneously. There is an interactive effect across the various levels, and working solely on one level would reduce the likelihood of achieving results in the others. Therefore the following action plan includes a concerted effort to address all of Helen's needs.

Action Plan

The learning assistance provider with basic counseling skills would begin to explore Helen's areas of satisfaction and dissatisfaction. This could be done in a number of ways. An initial meeting would involve a discussion of her current situation, including the areas that are most unfulfilling. The learning assistance session would be designed to help Helen gain insight into the reasons for her frustration. In subsequent meetings, Helen and the counselor would work toward some resolution of her problems, with specific plans for addressing them. For example, Helen could develop with her counselor a timeline for decreasing her dependence on her parents. Specific steps along the timeline would be identified so that she could see progress toward her goal of independence.

The counselor might also use a survey instrument to help Helen more clearly identify her own problems. The Mooney Problem Checklist (Mooney, 1950), for example, could help her focus on the specific areas of need. Even though this checklist was not based on Maslow's theory, it is organized in such a way that the areas examined can be easily related to the Maslow hierarchy (Silverman, 1993). A survey instrument gives a focus to the counseling session, permitting use of Helen's own responses as guides for the conversation.

Throughout the session, Helen would be guided to develop a series of steps to fulfill her unmet needs. She would be encouraged to become increasingly conscious of her feelings and how they connect to her performance. She would be urged to focus as much as possible on her successes and shown how she can build on them rather than continually dwelling on her problems. The goal of learning assistance would be to help Helen see how having her needs met will help her function better as a student. Highlighting the connection between need fulfillment and academic achievement and guiding Helen to actively work on fulfilling her needs is the central core of the action plan.

Adult Learning Approach

Lindemann (1961) introduced the term *andragogy* (the art and science of helping adults learn) to the United States in 1927, when he first articulated his thoughts on what adult education was all about. Although additional perspectives have been added since that time, Lindemann's assumptions still serve as the basic foundation for adult learning theory. They include the following: education is life itself, not a preparation for it; its focus is nonvocational; learning occurs best through situations, not subjects; and the learner's most significant resource is experience. Lindemann highly valued the learner's experience and the importance of discovering new meanings by discussing and interpreting past experiences. He also believed that adults are more likely to learn when the learning is immediately relevant than when they are presented with formal subject matter.

How do these assumptions relate to Helen? According to an adult learning approach, it is significant that Helen has voluntarily chosen to make a major change in her life and is therefore motivated. Moreover, her needs include more than the acquisition of new knowledge related to nursing; she must also learn strategies for coping with a new life-style. According to Brookfield (1987), one distinctive purpose of adult education is to provide the learner with a set of analytical procedures that can be applied to a variety of settings. Clearly, Helen needs to develop such strategies.

While Lindemann formally introduced the notion of andragogy, it was Knowles (1990) who popularized the andragogical model for educational purposes. His basic premise is that learners want to be more independent and self-directed than our formal educational system allows. Children are taught to be highly dependent on the teacher, and this orientation is nurtured throughout the individual's educational career. Knowles contends that learners need to be guided toward independence and self-direction earlier because this is part of the natural maturation process. In Helen's case, she has probably been conditioned to depend on teachers, and now she needs to be guided toward more independent decision making.

Knowles has put forth several assumptions regarding the adult learner that expand on Lindemann's original framework. First, learners have a strong need to know the rationale for what they are being taught. It is not enough to learn for the sake of learning; there needs to be an explanation of the significance of the activity. Second, adults have a need to be seen as self-directed; this is linked to their self-concept. They have been responsible for themselves in all other aspects of their lives, and now that they have chosen to participate in a formal learning situation, they do not want to be treated as dependents. A third assumption is related to the role of the learner's prior experiences. The adult brings a wide range of experiences to the learning situation, and these must be seen as a vital resource. Adults are defined by their life experiences, which should be used as a foundation for further learning. Not only will their experiences help their own learning, but the experiences can be utilized to enhance classroom discussion, collaboration, and problem solving.

The last three of Knowles's assumptions relate to what motivates the adult learner. He believes that adults are motivated primarily by an inner drive, and that increased satisfaction and self-esteem will provide a continual source of motivation. Knowles contrasts this internal motivation with that of younger learners, who seem to need more external praise and reinforcers (such as grades). In addition, adults are ready to learn because it is usually a life situation that brought them into school. Most probably, they need to learn new skills or strategies for coping with a change in their lives. As a consequence of this need to cope or adjust, their orientation to learning is life-centered or problem-centered as opposed to subject-centered. Rather than learning sets of facts, the adult would prefer to learn through problem solving or case studies, where ideas are directly applied to real-life situations.

Knowles's assumptions supply a framework for thinking about the characteristics of adult learners and how to refine our instructional practice, but we need to use them in conjunction with a more theoretical perspective that examines the adult learning process.

Mezirow (Mezirow and Associates, 1990) suggests that at the heart of adult learning is critical reflection, a self-examination and assessment of one's assumptions and beliefs, which leads to perspective transformation. He talks about learning perspectives as cognitivists talk about schemata; they are sets of assumptions built up over time, through which new experiences are filtered and understood. They are uncritically acquired at an early age and become frames of reference for all subsequent learning. Mezirow believes that through critical reflection, adults experience a transformation of these previously established perspectives. And as old beliefs, opinions, and attitudes lose their apparent validity, individuals may begin to question their own identity. He suggests that through this process of reflection, learners' perspectives become more inclusive and integrated.

Mezirow describes three types of perspective "distortions" that critical reflection may correct. The first is epistemic: the adult learner needs to look critically at concepts that have been accepted and internalized without question as representing right or wrong, good or bad. The second distortion is sociocultural, resulting from generalized beliefs about specific population groups. The third distortion is psychic and includes assumptions that produce anxiety and block certain behaviors. Critical reflection on any of these types of belief may be highly stressful, especially if it occurs—as is often the case in adult learning—simultaneously with a major life transition. Mezirow recognizes the significance of this stress and suggests that the educator should provide emotional support and collaborate as a colearner in the learning situation. The instructor acts as a mentor in assisting the learner to examine entrenched assumptions. Mezirow suggests that critical reflection can be best facilitated through a reflective dialogue in which the learner is guided to assess the consequences of prior assumptions, to identify and explore alternatives, and then to test the validity of new sets of ideas.

For Helen, the idea of critical reflection is significant, as she probably needs guidance in reexamining her belief systems regarding the role of formal schooling, interpersonal relationships, and herself as a student and a professional.

Implications

Brookfield (1986) has suggested a set of principles of effective practice for adult education that synthesizes the various approaches to adult learning and can provide a foundation for an action plan for Helen. Underlying his principles, and implicit in both Knowles and Mezirow, is the premise that education is a transactional process, with the teacher and learner continually engaged in negotiating priorities, method, and criteria for evaluation.

One important element in Brookfield's scheme is the requirement that the learner's participation be voluntary. In Helen's case, she has made the initial decision to return to school; now she must take the first step toward obtaining assistance. As she can stop at any time, the assistance she receives must be directly relevant to her needs and connected to her experiences. Brookfield also emphasizes the importance of respecting the learner; adult learners bring many years of experience to the learning situation, and their feelings of self-worth can hinge on how that experience is valued. Along with respect comes a greater delegation of responsibility for the process to the learner. The teacher assumes the role of a facilitator who fosters collaboration with the learner. Together, they negotiate the learning objectives and activities.

Brookfield also asserts that praxis is central to the learning situation; learner activity and reflection must be built into the process. The foundation for critical reflection is thus established, and learners move toward greater empowerment as they gradually feel more capable of self-direction.

Action Plan

The learning specialist who develops a plan for Helen based on an adult learning approach can assume that she is internally motivated, as she has voluntarily sought assistance in addition to making the initial decision to enroll in college. These events are occurring at a point in her life where she is making major transitions, both personal and professional. An action plan for Helen must relate directly to the entire situation with which she is attempting to cope. During the initial session, the specialist can guide a discussion that encourages Helen to reflect on the reasons she is entering college at this time in her life. The specialist can also help her think through the consequences of her decisions: the application and (it is hoped) acceptance to the school of nursing, increased demands on her time, possible increased dependence on her parents for child care, decreased time with her child, and fewer opportunities for recreational socializing. Once these consequences have been identified by Helen, she and the specialist can collaborate on setting priorities, outlining appropriate activities, and setting criteria to evaluate success.

As they analyze some of the problem areas that Helen is encountering, the specialist can identify resources within the school, and possibly the community, for Helen to turn to as she seeks solutions. For instance, the office of student affairs might be able to provide her with information on child care or housing situations with other single mothers that would enable her to experience more independence. The school of nursing could give her information on specific entry requirements following her core coursework, and an interview with the dean and/or current students might provide additional insight to help her prepare herself.

A key element of this information-gathering phase will be reflection by Helen on what she discovers. This can be done through journal writings that she shares with the learning specialist on a weekly basis. During these sessions, Helen should be encouraged to evaluate the information and discuss how it may differ from her preconceptions. If it does differ significantly, she will then need to think through the new set of consequences that it holds for her and how best to deal with them.

Another activity that would be helpful for Helen would be participation in a support group. By joining a group of students who share similar concerns, she can gain from hearing the experiences of others and from articulating her own. Not only will this increase her self-esteem, but it may provide a context for the socialization that she misses. Initially, the learning specialist would lead the students in discussions, role-plays, simulations, and case studies, but this facilitation role would gradually diminish as the students became more proficient and confident in leading their own sessions.

Helen may also need individual or small-group tutoring sessions to strengthen her skills in the areas considered important by the school of nursing. If there is an entrance exam or screening test in a particular content area, Helen might request that a workshop be organized to review that area or to provide strategies for test taking or reducing test anxiety.

As Helen's collaborator, the learning specialist will probably need to provide emotional as well as academic support on a regular basis but must always be prepared to refer her to professional counseling if her emotional needs become too great.

An Integrated Action Plan

Helen's case has been viewed from several different perspectives—behavioral, cognitive, social learning, motivational, and adult learning—(summarized in Table 2.1), but practitioners may find that using only one of these is limiting. Aspects of each perspective may seem appealing and appropriate. An eclectic or integrated approach is often the choice for those seeking the best practice. An integrated approach reduces the probability that any one aspect of Helen's problems will be overlooked. Furthermore, if one strategy proves ineffective, the integrated plan will have a variety of others from which to choose, each with a foundation and rationale to support it. The result of using a variety of perspectives is a richer, more complete, and more effective action plan representing the best practice in the field. Here is an example of an integrated approach to addressing Helen's needs.

Summary of Helen's Situation

- Frustration with personal problems (isolation, tensions at home, self-doubt)

- Need for encouragement

- History of weak academic performance—lack of skills and strategies

- Lack of confidence

- Struggle for independence

Using the overview in Table 2.1, the detailed integrated plan shown in Table 2.2 can be developed.

It is clear that the best plan for Helen includes strategies that have their foundations in multiple perspectives. The integrated plan outlined here is a comprehensive approach to helping Helen achieve success. Note that her academic and her emotional needs are being addressed simultaneously. This is a key element of any developmental education or learning assistance program.

Now that you have seen how an integrated learning assistance plan of action can develop, it is your turn to design one.

Table 2.1. Learning Assistance for Helen: An Overview of Approaches.

Approach	Cause of Difficulty	Action Plan
Behavioral	Lack of basic skills	Diagnose skills
	Lack of positive reinforcement	Develop behavioral objectives
	Lack of opportunity to practice	Give opportunity for extended practice
		Give regular feedback and reinforcement
Cognitive	Prior emphasis on passive learning	Determine developmental stage of learning
	Reduced access to prior knowledge	Administer learning styles inventory and analyze it
	Lack of self-awareness (metacognition)	Assign a learning journal
		Provide active learning experiences
		Teach active learning strategies
Social Learning	Lack of significant academic role models	Identify role model/mentor
	Problematic home environment	Evaluate home and social environment
	Impoverished social life	Provide counseling for personal relationships

Table 2.1. Continued.

Approach	Cause of Difficulty	Action Plan
Motivational	Unmet basic needs for safety, love, belonging, esteem	Administer evaluation with checklist, survey, and/or interview
		Suggest personal counseling to address unmet needs
		Form or assign to support groups
Adult Learning	Lack of self-direction	Encourage self-direction
	Lack of prioritized goals	Detail and prioritize goals
	Weak support system	Provide resource information
		Build on past experiences

Table 2.2. Detailed Integrated Plan for Helen.

Assessment	Approach
Diagnose skill levels with tests (reading, writing, math)	Behavioral
Determine developmental learning stage (surveys, inventories)	Cognitive
Assess personal relationships and support system (personal interview)	Social learning; motivational; adult learning
Review all assessment findings with Helen	

Strategies	Approach
Develop a learning plan together	Cognitive; adult learning
Set short-term objectives; identify activities for achieving them	Behavioral
Prioritize goals	Adult learning
Introduce Helen to an adult learning support group	Social learning; adult learning
Provide frequent and consistent reinforcement in the support group	Behavioral
Use tutors to help build skills	Social learning; behavioral
Teach coping strategies to deal with learning conditions not well matched to assessed learning style	Cognitive
Have Helen keep a learning journal to record and reflect on her learning experiences	Cognitive; adult learning
Arrange for Helen to meet regularly with the nurse at work to discuss her program, get tips and encouragement, and observe the nurse in action	Social learning; adult learning

Case Study

Ben is a thirty-six year old male returning to college after eighteen years in the workforce. He first enrolled in college as a high school graduate but dropped out the first year because of personal responsibilities: his father died that year, and Ben was the sole support for his mother and younger sisters. He found employment at a factory near home, where he was able to work forty hours a week plus overtime yet still take care of family matters.

Recently, Ben's youngest sister married and assumed the care of their mother by taking her into her new home. Ben was a good student in high school and has frequently been promoted at the factory. He has been told that with a college degree he could move into the management ranks at the factory, but until now, he felt that he had too many family responsibilities. The factory owner has recently offered to help finance Ben's return to college, and Ben has decided to give it a try.

He is very concerned that he will not fit in with younger college students. He will attend classes in the evening while continuing to work full-time during the day. He has not taken a course in eighteen years and has had little time for outside reading or other academic pursuits. He has never had a great deal of interest in business management coursework, the area for which the factory is willing to provide financial support.

When he first started college, he was planning to major in psychology, as he has always had an interest in people's behavior. He considers his greatest strength to be in the area of relating to people and has doubts about his ability to succeed in traditional business courses.

As you design an action plan for Ben, consider him as an individual and then take components from each perspective that best fit his needs. To get started, it might help to review Helen's case and the action plans that follow each of the five perspectives. Exhibits 2.1 and 2.2 are outlines of forms you can use to design the action plan.

Exhibit 2.1. Summary of Ben's Situation.

- _____

- _____

- _____

- _____

- _____

Learning Assistance for Ben: An Overview of Approaches

Approach	Cause of Difficulty	Action Plan
Behavioral		
Cognitive		
Social Learning		
Motivational		
Adult Learning		

Exhibit 2.2. Detailed Integrated Plan for Ben.

Assessment	Approach
_____	_____
_____	_____
_____	_____
_____	_____

Strategies	Approach
_____	_____
_____	_____
_____	_____
_____	_____
_____	_____
_____	_____

Summary

In this chapter, a case study demonstrated how an integrated approach to learning assistance is the most desirable one, as it ensures a plan of action that is comprehensive. Familiarity with basic principles from various perspectives is important. It enables the practitioner to combine those elements from each one that are most relevant for a particular student. No one perspective is broad enough, and this chapter has suggested that there are principles from at least five areas (behaviorism, cognitivism, social learning theory, motivational theory, and adult learning theory) that can be combined to produce an effective plan.

Part II

. . . .

Creating an Integrative
Approach for Practice

I n this part, we take a pragmatic look at the current state of our practice. The section begins with general guidelines and principles for effective programs. It then examines specific programs to see how these principles have been applied. It concludes by describing a new model for effective practice that integrates the theory suggested in Part One with the practice detailed in Part Two.

Chapter Three outlines how to organize and manage a successful program. It does not suggest that one formula fits all, but it does assert that there are general principles to be considered across a wide range of programs. After this general overview of operations, Chapter Four moves on to the more specific component of assessing students. Assessment, which is essential to any learning assistance support, is viewed as a process in which students and professionals act as partners. Care must be taken to choose the appropriate instruments and utilize the results as effectively as possible to facilitate student achievement. Another key factor is the tutor. The tutoring component of any learning center is complex in its organization and management. The discussion of this subject, in Chapter Five, confines itself to the *training* of tutors. Tutor training is a strong correlate of student success, and it must have a firm theoretical foundation if it is to be optimally effective. This chapter presents seven perspectives that, in combination, form such a foundation.

Chapter Six offers the reader the opportunity to see how the principles that have been described have been applied in four different types of programs. It becomes apparent that a range of possibilities exists for developing and maintaining an effective program.

Chapter Seven details a new model for effective practice that flows from the general principles and guidelines for program development previously reviewed. Chapter Six described how these principles could be applied in four extremely diverse programs. Chapter Seven utilizes all this information to construct a model that includes theory, research, principles, and practice in a cyclical process. It is a framework for the development of new programs or the strengthening of established ones.

3

Organizing and Managing
a Successful Program

Knowing historical precedents and understanding how theory connects with practice are important underpinnings for professional activity. What came before helps define what is yet to come. The theories that support our activities guide us to revise and refine our work. The role of history and theory is primary and sets the stage for developing an organized and well-managed program.

There is no one formula for developing and managing a successful learning assistance program. The particular characteristics and needs of each individual institution drive the organization of programs, the format of service delivery, the overall management and operation of the program, and the methods of program evaluation. However, this does not mean that each successful program develops in a vacuum devoid of basic principles of organization and management. We know a great deal about how to operate successful programs.

In this chapter, we look first at the importance of the institution's mission and relate it to the program and its goals. Then we focus on the importance of administrative leadership and personnel, with particular attention to staff selection, supervision, development, and appraisal. Policies and procedures for the overall operation of the program are addressed, as well as record keeping and data collection as they relate to accountability and program evaluation. Finally, program funding and fiscal management are discussed, and basic principles of program evaluation are described in the context of the program's mission and goals.

Programs are of many different kinds. Keimig (1983) has outlined a hierarchy of programs, with remedial courses at the base, followed in order by learning assistance for individual students, course-related learning services, and comprehensive learning systems. This chapter will not attempt to discuss each type of program but will present basic principles and guidelines that may apply to all.

Mission Statement and Program Goals

Successful programs begin with a well-defined mission statement and a set of program goals addressing specific areas. What constituency does the program serve? What objectives does it aim to achieve? How does the mission of the program fit with the overall mission of the institution?

Every institution of higher education has a written mission statement that sets forth the purpose of the institution and details the values and ideals it seeks to promote. A successful learning assistance program must fit with the mission of its institution. The following excerpts from an institutional mission statement indicate how such a statement might guide a program in developing its own mission and goals.

> The university endeavors to develop in the lives of students, faculty and staff, the spirit of searching for truth and living for others. . . .
> This university exists to preserve, extend, and transmit knowledge and to deepen understanding of the human person. . . .
> In addition to developing professional expertise, [the university] emphasizes ethical behavior and recognition

of the dignity of each individual [Loyola University Chicago, 1993].

The mission statement of a learning assistance program should fit with the institutional mission so that it serves to promote and advance the purpose of the larger organization. The following program mission statement dovetails with the institutional mission statement just quoted.

> In keeping with the mission of the University, the Learning Assistance Center exists to serve the individual needs of students as they pursue the attainment of a degree and develop into intellectually mature persons. Students are served along a broad continuum ranging from one tutoring session to a combination of ongoing multiple forms of support (tutoring, individual learning assistance counseling, workshops, and support groups). All students are treated with respect for their need to seek assistance and to maintain confidentiality regarding their academic and personal concerns. The Center subscribes to the belief that each individual is unique and requires a personalized approach for achieving in the University. Every effort in providing learning assistance is characterized by the respect for and appreciation of individual differences [Loyola University Chicago Learning Assistance Center, 1995].

The goals of a learning assistance program are a natural outgrowth of the mission statement. Whereas the mission statement puts forth the overall purpose and direction of the program, the goals are more specific; they include both short-term and long-term objectives that are student-centered, staff-centered, and program-centered. The following goals are those of a learning assistance program modeled from the quoted program mission statement.

Program Goals

1. To help all students achieve academically to their fullest potential

2. To assist students to become more independent, self-confident, efficient learners so that they will be better able to meet the university's academic standards

3. To provide a place where faculty can refer students who need help

4. To offer consultation and resources to faculty concerned about improving student learning

5. To provide an opportunity for graduate students to learn about the field of learning assistance in preparation for careers in higher education

6. To provide continuous opportunity for staff to grow and develop professionally

7. To evaluate all activities and use evaluation results to improve services

Administrative Leadership

Effective leadership is essential to a successful program. The head of a program needs to possess many competencies and qualities and has the dual challenge of managing people and programs. The following characteristics of an effective administrator are organized into five categories: program planning and implementation, communication and institutional relations, staff management and supervision, ethics, and overall leadership effectiveness.

Program Planning and Implementation

- Defines and articulates the program's purpose and objectives so that they are supportive of the institution's mission statement

- Develops a system to facilitate the smooth and orderly operation of daily activities

- Establishes a comprehensive evaluation system to determine the strengths and weaknesses of the program

- Creates ways to respond to institutional needs as they arise

Communication and Institutional Relations

- Uses both oral and written language to successfully communicate with all institutional constituencies

- Resolves conflicts as they arise with other areas of the institution and within the program

- Interacts effectively with faculty and staff and participates in interdepartmental dialogues

- Actively participates on institutional committees and other planning groups

Staff Management and Supervision

- Recruits well-trained and enthusiastic personnel

- Orients staff to prepare them for their roles

- Clearly defines performance expectations and sets standards for achievement

- Encourages and motivates staff to achieve

- Provides ongoing educational and developmental opportunities for staff to grow professionally

- Offers constructive and frequent feedback on staff performance

- Successfully confronts problematic staff performance

- Facilitates resolution of conflict among staff

Ethics

- Makes decisions with the priority goal of serving students

- Protects the confidentiality of student files and records

- Enforces policy that limits access to records to those who "need to know" and protects student rights to informed consent

- Ensures that staff members are treated equitably

- Manages funds and allocates resources fairly

Overall Effectiveness

- Shows awareness of personal management style and its impact on staff and decision making

- Connects behavior to theories of leadership and motivation

- Uses a variety of strategies to motivate staff and reduce stress

- Clarifies goals, prioritizes tasks, and delegates responsibility

The role of the skilled administrator is complex. It includes many nuances and competencies that are often absent from the educational training and experience of individuals thrust into the leadership role. Those anticipating a transition into administration may find helpful the following six suggestions offered by White (1981).

1. *Request an orientation period.* It may take several weeks to talk with selected management personnel and observe what is going on in related departments. Gather as much information as possible

about the requirements of the position and ways to interact with other administrators.

2. *Identify a mentor.* Find someone in the organization who is recognized as a successful administrator and whom you can respect and trust. Initiate regular meetings to discuss the problems and possibilities of your position.

3. *Form a core staff.* Be patient, as inherited staff may be wary and resistant to change. Gradually build trusting relationships with staff and enlist cooperation for change.

4. *Develop rapport with the boss.* A respectful and trusting relationship includes the negotiation of boundaries for autonomy and authority. Clarify expectations and maintain regular communication.

5. *Seek out training.* New administrators need to become educated in the theory and practice of management. It is recommended that opportunities for training be negotiated when the job is taken on.

6. *Seek constructive feedback.* No one begins a new position without making errors or needing to make adjustments. Asking staff and peers to respond to ideas and management activities is an important part of becoming an effective leader.

Strategies for becoming an effective administrator and leader involve many different approaches and styles. There is no one set of personality traits that constitutes the profile of an effective leader. In fact, it is not personality or behavior alone that defines effectiveness but the interaction of personality and style with situational factors. The skilled administrator is conversant with a variety of management theories and adapts his or her behavior to meet the demands of the situation. It is not within the scope of this text to present and discuss different management theories, but they include (1) McGregor's Theory X and Theory Y (1983), that is, centralized, unilateral decision making as opposed to consultative and participatory activities; (2) Hersey and Blanchard's situational leadership model (1982), which comprises four leadership styles (directing, coaching, supporting, and delegating); and (3) House and Mitchell's path-goal leadership theory (1980), which outlines the difference between task-oriented behaviors and maintenance behaviors. New administrators are encouraged to learn different theoretical approaches to management and use them as they develop their own individual styles.

Program Personnel: Selection and Evaluation

Professionals in the field of learning assistance and developmental education come from many different backgrounds. It is not uncommon to find learning assistance staff from such diverse areas as counseling, educational psychology, reading, English, mathematics, and history. This diversity is desirable and gives strength to a program. However, there must be a core of shared knowledge and expertise to define the learning assistance professional. The Council for the Advancement of Standards for Student Services/Developmental Programs (1986) offers the following list of recommended courses relevant to the development of learning assistance professionals:

Adult development theory

Learning theory

Counseling theory and techniques

Administration and interpretation of diagnostic tests

Learning disabilities and special education

Cognitive processes

Design and presentation of group workshops

Group leadership and dynamics

Curriculum and supervision

Administration and management

Program evaluation

Instructional methods and media

Educational technology and computerized instruction

English as a second language

Human relations training

Professional staff should have experience working with college students and higher education personnel and expertise in coordinating efforts between academic and student affairs. They should either have taught at the college level or have familiarity with college teaching and the design and implementation of instruction. In addition, it is important that staff have ongoing professional development activities to help them grow and stay current with information in the field.

Learning assistance programs are also staffed with paraprofessionals, who are often crucial to the programs' operations. Tutors, for example, are part of the paraprofessional staff. All such staff members need to receive adequate training and supervision. It is certainly not expected that paraprofessionals approach the level of expertise of professional staff, but the more knowledge they have about college student learning and ways to enhance it, the more effective they will be in their roles.

Managing both professional and paraprofessional staff is an important function of the program administrator. It is the responsibility of the administrator to set performance standards and establish a performance appraisal system that gives frequent and timely feedback, identifies problems and training requirements, and offers encouragement and motivation.

Methods for evaluating staff performance commonly include written narrative appraisals, trait checklists, and comparative rankings. Narrative appraisals detail specific strengths and weaknesses;

impressions are often supported by descriptions of critical incidents. Though this type of appraisal is helpful and may offer direction for staff development, it does not allow for comparisons between staff members that could be used in decisions on such matters as salary increases and promotions. In addition, language used in narrative appraisals is often subject to arbitrary interpretation. For example, descriptors like "excellent" or "satisfactory" can have widely variant meanings.

Trait checklists offer the opportunity to evaluate staff performance along a rating continuum. The advantages of checklists are that they can be completed relatively quickly and they yield a numerical rating that can be used for purposes of comparison. Of course, like narrative descriptions, they are also subject to supervisor bias. Comparative rankings show the spread of staff performance from highest to lowest on several global criteria. One such criterion might be "developing and implementing creative workshops." Despite the usefulness of this appraisal method, supervisors are often resistant to making overt comparisons between staff members.

No matter which appraisal method is used, it is important to involve staff in the process. The following procedures are suggested for promoting such involvement (Austin, 1981; Harper, 1986; Lewis and Lewis, 1983).

1. *Access to criteria.* Written job descriptions and methods of performance evaluation should be made available to staff *before* performance reviews.

2. *Frequent reviews.* Reviews should occur more than once a year and include both informal and formal evaluations. Frequent meetings between supervisor and staff member help promote clear communication and understanding of expectations.

3. *Staff self-evaluation.* Performance appraisal should be a shared process. Before a formal evaluation meeting, the staff member should produce a self-evaluation to be shared with the supervisor.

4. *Written evaluation preceding review.* Prior to the actual per-formance review meeting, the staff member should receive a writ-ten appraisal. This allows for reflection before the actual face-to-face meeting.

5. *Mutual feedback.* The meeting between supervisor and staff member should allow for mutual sharing of impressions and reac-tions. In addition to discussing the staff member's strengths and weaknesses, the supervisor can solicit feedback about management style and administrative effectiveness.

6. *Staff member's written response.* After the formal review, the staff member should have the opportunity to respond in writing and have the response included in the personnel file.

7. *Separation of performance review from personnel decisions.* Deci-sions on matters such as salary, promotion, training, and termina-tion are best made after the formal review meeting.

Supervising and appraising staff members leads to planning for staff development, which should be an ongoing activity. Even the most highly competent staff need continuing opportunities for growth and professional enhancement. Staff development activities include opportunities to attend conferences, to participate in spe-cial educational seminars, to take courses, and to listen to invited guests and speakers. As much as possible, staff members should be involved in the planning and implementation of staff development activities, taking an active role in the design of their own profes-sional growth.

Record Keeping and Data Collection

Successful developmental education programs are accountable for their services. They know how many students they serve, can describe them demographically, and can answer questions about their performance and the effects of help rendered. Tutoring ser-vices, for example, are organized so that daily contacts are recorded and grouped by academic subject. In addition, student grades in courses tutored may also be collected and analyzed for interpretation. At any point, a request for a usage/outcome report can be met expeditiously.

Just as there is no one way to successfully manage a program, there is no one record-keeping or data collection system that can be applied to all situations. However, selecting the items that will be monitored must be done with great care. Maxwell (1991) lists ten items that are important for a learning assistance center:

1. Extent to which students use the program

2. Extent to which users are satisfied with the program

3. Grades and grade point averages of those who use the program

4. Year-to-year retention rates of students in the program

5. Pre- and post-test scores of those who used the program

6. Faculty attitudes toward the program

7. Staff attitudes toward the program

8. Impact of the program on the campus as a whole

9. Grades in follow-up courses

10. Course completion rates

Deciding which data to collect and organizing them for ready retrieval are the important first steps toward effective program evaluation. Before beginning an evaluation effort, it is important to write a clear description of the program and to establish a database including records of student characteristics, use of the service, program outreach activities, and program and staff policies (Maxwell, 1991).

Small programs may find that keeping paper-and-pencil records is sufficient. However, larger, more complex programs need to develop some kind of computerized tracking system to collect and organize data. Learning assistance programs need to use the resources of the information technology department on their campus, where staff may be available to assist with the development of a data collection system. Computer programs already in place in the institution for organizing student data may be applicable to learning assistance usage data. If not, information technology personnel have the expertise to design specialized programs. Alternatively, some published computer software may be useful.

Funding and Fiscal Management

Learning assistance programs are funded in many different ways. Some programs depend entirely on "soft money" obtained from outside sources. Some are fully supported within the institution. Some depend on student fees. Others are financed through a combination of these methods. Sources of funding often determine the stability of a program. For example, programs supported entirely by institutional funds tend to be more stable than those receiving money from outside agencies. Once an institution accepts the responsibility for maintaining a program, it becomes a recognized part of the institution's operating budget and is not seen as external to its function. Programs dependent on outside funding are often more volatile, needing to reapply for support on a regular basis and to provide extensive reports detailing use of funds and program results.

No matter where the funds come from, they need to be managed prudently. Higher education is always subject to financial cutbacks, and the wise administrator must find ways to economize as much as possible. Learning assistance programs that do not offer courses for credit and thus do not contribute to the institution's income with tuition dollars are particularly vulnerable.

Preparing an operating budget is one of the program administrator's responsibilities, and projecting needs for the year ahead is often challenging. For example, projection of costs for tutoring necessitates predicting student demand in particular subjects. The demand may vary from year to year, fluctuating with curricular changes and student preparedness. The program administrator needs to be aware of institutional changes—such as those in enrollment characteristics and instructional requirements—that are likely to affect student demand for learning assistance. This information is crucial for projecting needs and having resources to meet them.

The program's budget administrator must be a keen financial manager. Since most learning assistance programs are not revenue producing, they are often at risk for resource reduction. Daily decisions concerning distribution of funds need to be made with care and consideration for the continued growth and development of the program without sacrificing its viability.

Program Evaluation

Effective administrative leadership, competent professional staff, useful data collection, and sound fiscal management are necessary components of a well-organized program. But the key to a program's continuing achievement and success is a disciplined approach to program evaluation. Ongoing evaluation provides the basis for improvement and promotes awareness and innovation.

Deciding what to measure and how to measure it is the first step in beginning a program evaluation project. To assist in decision making, Keimig (1983) proposed a hierarchical approach, stating that decisions about what to measure and how to measure it can be organized into four levels. These four levels are arranged according to their potential for improved learning and instructional change. For example, at the lowest level, there is no systematic evaluation of students' long-term learning. At the next level, evaluation is limited to only one academic term. Moving up the hierarchy, in the subsequent level, changes are monitored throughout one course and into a course that follows it. Finally, in the highest level, follow-up studies are conducted, and long-term effects and changes are analyzed. In Keimig's hierarchy of decisions, five variables are considered and assigned to one of these four levels. The five variables are institutional context and outcomes, student outcomes, academic standards and grade point average (GPA), ongoing evaluation, and structure of the developmental program. For example, when Keimig's model is applied to a consideration of program structure, remedial courses are at the lowest level for effecting improved learning while comprehensive learning support systems are at the highest.

Keimig's framework is useful for deciding on the complexity and comprehensiveness of an evaluation project and is recommended as a basis for making important judgments about just what to include in the evaluation venture.

It is not the purpose here to fully explore program evaluation and its application to learning assistance programs. The subject is extensive and is covered elsewhere (Maxwell, 1991) in significant detail. However, an overview of program evaluation methods and criteria is presented here to provide guidance for further reading and exploration.

Methods of Program Evaluation

The two most common distinctions among methods are *quantitative* versus *qualitative* and *formative* versus *summative*. Qualitative methods are distinct from, but not incompatible with, quantitative methods. One difference between these methods is in their underlying philosophies about the world. The quantitative stance, which has been prevalent in education, adopts a natural science view of investigation. This view is reductionist in that it limits inquiry to a relatively small area where questions and hypotheses are formulated in advance; investigation is directed toward quantitative information that will answer those questions and test the hypotheses. In the field of education, for example, outcomes are measured quantitatively with test scores, grade point averages, and years of persistence. The notion here is that statistically significant changes tell us all we need to know about educational progress.

Qualitative evaluation, also known as naturalistic inquiry, is an investigative approach that does not formulate questions or hypotheses but searches for "truth" through information that emerges from the inquiry. The qualitative paradigm has been used extensively in the fields of sociology and anthropology and is now being applied to educational settings. Two major methods used in qualitative research are (1) participant observation, whose levels range from "complete participant" to "participant as observer" to "complete observer," and (2) interviewing, whether by means of a formal conversational interview, a general interview guide (a list of sequentially ordered topics), or a standardized open-ended interview.

Information gathered through qualitative methods is recorded by means of detailed note taking or tape recordings and then studied in depth for emerging themes and ideas. In contrast to the quantitative approach, hypotheses are drawn from the investigation rather than formulated beforehand. Table 3.1 summarizes the attributes of these two methods (Cook and Reichardt, 1979).

Quantitative methods have much to offer program directors who need to convince faculty and administrators of the value of their programs. Outcome measures such as higher retention figures, improved test scores, and increased grade point averages are often indispensable for verifying a program's effectiveness. However, quantitative evaluation does not always produce results that reflect the total growth and development of students as witnessed by those most closely involved with them.

Qualitative evaluation is the method for investigating all those areas that we feel have profited from special efforts but are not quantifiable (see Table 3.1). Most learning assistance programs have goals for affective development, such as building academic self-esteem, maintaining motivation for college study, and encouraging goal-directed behavior. The evaluation of these program goals is best accomplished through qualitative methodology. Patton (1980) provides a useful checklist for deciding which situations are appropriate for using qualitative methods (see Exhibit 3.1).

Table 3.1. Attributes of the Qualitative and Quantitative Paradigms.

Qualitative Paradigm (Advocates use of qualitative methods)	Quantitative Paradigm (Advocates use of quantitative methods)
Phenomenologism and *Verstehen* (understanding from within): "seeks to understand human behavior from the actor's own frame of reference"	Logical positivism: seeks the facts or causes of behavior with little regard for the subjective states of individuals
Naturalistic and uncontrolled observation	Obtrusive and controlled measurement
Subjective	Objective
Close to the data: the "insider" perspective	Removed from the data: the "outsider" perspective
Grounded, discovery-oriented, explanatory, descriptive, and inductive	Ungrounded, verification-oriented, confirmatory, reductionist, inferential, and deductive
Process-oriented	Outcome-oriented
Valid: "real," "rich," and "deep" data	Reliable: "hard" and replicable data
Ungeneralizable; single case studies	Generalizable; multiple case studies
Holistic	Particularistic
Assumes a dynamic reality	Assumes a stable reality

Exhibit 3.1. Appropriateness of Qualitative Methods in Evaluation: Partial Checklist.

1. Are different participants in the program expected to be   Yes   No
   affected in qualitatively different ways? If so, is there
   a need or desire to describe and evaluate individualized
   client outcomes?

2. Are decision makers interested in elucidating and   Yes   No
   understanding the internal dynamics of programs—
   program strengths, program weaknesses, and overall
   program processes?

3. Is detailed in-depth information needed about certain   Yes   No
   client cases or program sites—for example, particularly
   successful cases, unusual failures, cases that are critically
   important for programmatic, financial, or political reasons?

4. Is there interest in focusing on the idiosyncrasies and   Yes   No
   unique qualities of individual clients or programs,
   as opposed to comparing all clients or programs
   on standardized, uniform measures?

5. Is the intent to inform decision makers about details   Yes   No
   of program implementation—what clients in the program
   experience, what services are provided, how the program
   is organized, what functions staff perform?

6. Are program staff and other decision makers interested   Yes   No
   in the collection of detailed, descriptive information
   for the purpose of improving the program? In other words,
   is there interest in formative evaluation?

7. Is there a need for reports on the nuances of program   Yes   No
   quality—that is, descriptive information about the quality
   of program activities and outcomes—as opposed to
   simple numerical data?

8. Will the administration of standardized measuring   Yes   No
   instruments (questionnaires and tests) be significantly
   more obtrusive than the gathering of data through
   natural observation and open-ended interviews? In other
   words, will the collection of qualitative data generate
   less reactivity among participants than the collection of
   quantitative data?

A combination of quantitative and qualitative methods makes for a stronger evaluation. Whenever possible, these different methods should be used together, one reinforcing the other.

The second distinction among evaluation methods is between formative and summative. A formative evaluation is one that is ongoing throughout the program. It is conducted by the program staff, and the results are usually not shared with other administrators. A formative evaluation is often conducted for the purpose of "fine-tuning" and to make internal decisions about the program and its function. A summative evaluation is conducted by program staff or the program director at the end of a project and is concerned primarily with outcomes or how well the overall effort achieved its objectives. The summative evaluation is usually of interest to policy makers who are in the position of determining the continuance or expansion of a program.

Choosing Program Evaluation Methods

Program evaluation methods are chosen according to the purpose of the exercise. Before embarking on an evaluation project, it is important to clearly define the purpose for which the evaluation is to be used. For example, if the objective is to convince administrators that the program needs to be continued and enhanced, a summative report including significant quantitative information is necessary. On the other hand, if the goal is to make adjustments in a program without requesting funding or external support, a formative approach using both quantitative data and qualitative responses from program participants is more appropriate. Sometimes, of course, a comprehensive approach may be required, which will address more than one objective. In such a case, both quantitative and qualitative data will be gathered, and a summative presentation of the results given.

How often should programs be evaluated? This depends on the needs of the institution and the resources available for the evaluation project. Annual or semiannual reports are very helpful in demonstrating the viability of a program and offering opportunities for refinement. All too frequently, however, staff are overextended serving students, and program evaluation projects get pushed aside. The inherent danger in this is that programs may continue for years without their administrators knowing what is working and what is not or which program goals are being achieved and which ones are in jeopardy. Under such circumstances, a director may be hard pressed to justify individual activities of a program or the existence of the program itself when called on to do so.

It is recommended that a program evaluation, no matter how small, be conducted at least once a year. Some institutions have graduate courses in program evaluation, and students from such courses may be valuable resources for this activity. If not, staff members may work in small teams on different tasks, with their results summarized in a single report at the end. If no one on staff has expertise in conducting evaluations, someone may be brought in for a brief in-service workshop to get things started. The program administrator must make evaluation a priority and be accountable for its completion.

Pitfalls in Planning Program Evaluations

One of the most common barriers to completing evaluations is attempting to evaluate too much. Successful evaluations start small, one step at a time, perhaps focusing on only one or two program goals. If resources are limited and time is at a premium, this approach is especially advisable. Attempting to evaluate everything can be overwhelming and often results in evaluating nothing.

It is important, then, to set priorities and decide which program parts are most in need of evaluation. For example, continued funding for tutoring might be in question. Before funding reductions occur, it would be imperative to evaluate the tutoring program and communicate the results to those in control of financial allocations. Other priorities could be set with defined timelines so that evaluation activities are staggered over time to maximize the likelihood of completion.

Another common concern in conducting evaluations is lack of attention to program goals. Evaluators must be aware of what the program is trying to accomplish and connect evaluation activities to the program's particular goals. Goals must be clearly articulated and communicated before any program evaluation initiative can begin. For example, is the purpose of tutoring to provide relief and assistance to faculty, to help retain more students in the institution, or to assist students in passing the most difficult courses? When the purpose or goal of tutoring is stated, it can then be evaluated in a meaningful way.

Preparation and Use of the Evaluation Report

Evaluation reports must be timely, brief, and focused. They need to be written clearly and concisely for an audience that may not be familiar with the program or the issues related to it. Knowing the audience is very important when preparing the written report.

Reports that are overly statistical tend to be boring and often languish unread in files or on shelves. Whether the goal is to provide information for making program adjustments or to determine future viability, the report must be read and reactions must be solicited. It is recommended that the written report begin with an executive summary that consolidates the key points and findings for quick review and reflection. The reader may continue into the body of the report for more details as desired. The body of the report may take many different forms. Case studies may be used to illustrate some findings. Charts and graphs may be utilized for summarizing quantitative information. Direct quotations are often effective in illustrating qualitative data. A combination of formats tends to make the report more interesting and readable.

No matter what format is used, the report should include a set of recommendations based on the findings of the evaluation effort. The purpose of an evaluation is to provide guidance for decision making, and recommendations are stimuli for discussion and deliberation.

The presentation of the evaluation report can also take many forms. The written report may simply be sent to selected staff and administrators, but it is recommended that there also be planned opportunities for interaction and discussion. These may occur at a meeting scheduled particularly for this purpose or at a series of discussion sessions where different parts of the report are presented. Visual aids such as overhead transparencies and videotaped examples can also enhance the presentation.

The individuality of each program helps determine the process of the evaluation effort, the purpose for which it is designed, the probability that it will be completed, and the way in which the final product is communicated. However, no matter how programs differ, the basic principles outlined here are applicable to all.

Summary

Well-organized learning assistance programs reflect the institution's stated mission and have clearly defined goals. Effective administrative leadership is essential, and program personnel must meet minimum standards of competence. Staff performance must be evaluated regularly, and personnel should be actively involved in this process. Successful programs have organized record-keeping and data collection systems, adequate funding, and sound fiscal management procedures. Finally, a disciplined approach to program evaluation characterizes all successful programs and should include both quantitative and qualitative elements organized into readable and useful evaluation reports. Next, Chapter Four addresses the idea that successful programs are dependent on the effective assessment of students.

4

Assessing Student Needs

The uniqueness of each learner requires that we know as much as possible about his or her specific needs. A well-organized and well-managed program must therefore include ways of gathering detailed information about individual learners who require help.

Students who seek assistance do so for a variety of reasons. Some come to address serious academic difficulties that are impeding their progress or may even have put them in jeopardy of academic dismissal. Others arrive in good academic standing but experience isolated areas of frustration often related to specific learning weaknesses or poor preparation. Anxiety about performance is frequently mentioned and can be identified as a barrier to success. Still other students present specific disabilities and require academic accommodations such as extended-time testing, readers, note-takers, or special tutoring. Some students experience academic distress because of incidents such as a death in the family or personal illness. Given this wide variety of circumstances, it is the task of the learning assistance professional to help determine just what is needed to advance academic achievement for a particular learner. The process of assessment is indispensable for accomplishing this.

What is meant by *assessment*? How is it different from *evaluation*? For our purposes, assessment is used to refer to the appraisal of individuals and evaluation to the appraisal of groups or programs. In this chapter, we are focused on determining the needs of *individual* students and their academic strengths and weaknesses so that effective intervention can be made to enhance learning. The discussion of assessment in this chapter is aimed at the professional who has little familiarity with the underlying concepts of formal assessment procedures. Though for some readers the treatment of the topic may seem elementary, for others it may be challenging.

There are many ways to assess individual learning needs, and the process of gathering information is complicated by numerous issues. What instruments are best used to collect different types of information? What role do students play in assessing their own needs? Is formal or informal assessment better? How valid and reliable are the results of assessment efforts? Can bias in testing be eliminated? For what purpose will the results be used? How can we avoid misusing tests in the assessment process?

We will begin by looking at the process of gathering information, then move on to the selection of assessment instruments. Next, some of the misuses of tests are presented, and a four-part plan for conducting an assessment is outlined. Finally, a specific case study is given to illustrate a way of organizing, analyzing, interpreting, and presenting assessment results.

Gathering Information

Collecting information on student needs may be done in a variety of ways. These are typically divided into *formal* versus *informal* approaches, with a combination of both yielding a more representative body of material. Formal assessment includes the use of tests, inventories, checklists, and surveys, some of which may be standardized and yield results that can be compared to the responses of other students.

In contrast to formal methods, the informal assessment, though subject to guidelines, is more loosely structured and not as dependent on prescribed directions and scoring procedures. Informal assessment involves the collection of information through conversation and/or observation. For example, a personal, social, and educational history would be part of an informal assessment, along with observation of the student during a real learning activity.

It is critical that the student participate in the assessment process. This participation involves the student's own hunches about what factors are contributing to his or her difficulties. In addition, the student must confirm whether causes suggested by more formal means of assessment are indeed present in the situation. Without the active role of the student, there is no effective assessment process. An interview guide for collecting information from the student is very useful.

Selecting Assessment Instruments

The marketing of educational tests, surveys, and inventories is big business, and the learning assistance professional must be aware of their distinguishing elements and the purposes for which they are designed. Not all developmental educators are familiar with the theory and practice of tests and measurements, but it is important to understand at least four basic aspects of testing and to use this knowledge when making selection decisions: (1) norm-referenced versus criterion-referenced tests, (2) the fallacy of unbiased tests, (3) test validity, and (4) test reliability.

Norm-Referenced Versus Criterion-Referenced Tests

If the purpose of an assessment is to determine the performance of a student in relation to others on a particular learning task, a norm-referenced test is most appropriate. Norm-referenced tests rank student performance on a scale from most to least proficient. Examples of norm-referenced tests include standardized college entrance exams like the Scholastic Aptitude Test (SAT) and American College Test (ACT) as well as some typical academic achievement tests.

However, if the purpose is to discover whether the student has achieved specific goals and objectives in a learning activity, a criterion-referenced test is the instrument of choice. Knowing the purpose of the assessment is crucial to the selection of appropriate instrumentation. The following chart (Wergin, 1988) provides a useful comparison of norm- versus criterion-referenced tests.

Norm- and Criterion-Referenced Measurement

	Norm	Criterion
Purpose	Discrimination/ selection	Diagnosis mastery
Determinant of items	General objectives	Specific objectives
Test composition	Sample from large pool of items	Complete coverage of objectives
Scores	Variability desirable	Variability irrelevant
Interpretation	Relative standing	Student performance

Classical test theory is the basis for norm-referenced tests, which rest on the assumption that human behavior is distributed along a bell-shaped curve. This assumption leads to the expectation that any sampling of human behavior will reveal a small number of individuals at the top and bottom of the distribution and a large number in the middle.

Criterion-referenced tests, by contrast, do not compare students with one another. They demonstrate the degree to which a student has mastered content according to a set of standards.

The goal of the assessment determines the choice of the test. If the goal is to select the most proficient students, a norm-referenced test is recommended. If the goal is to ascertain whether students have mastered a set of specific competencies, the criterion-referenced test is indicated.

The Fallacy of Unbiased Tests

There is no such thing as a totally fair or unbiased test. Standardized or formal tests are sometimes thought to be more objective than informal measures, but volumes of research on test bias against minority populations tell a different story (Wigdor and Garner, 1982; Reynolds and Brown, 1984). Furthermore, well-trained test takers can learn how to navigate a standardized test with specialized test-taking techniques, but they may not be able to demonstrate knowledge in other ways.

Instead of searching for a test without bias, one should direct one's energies to the real challenge of minimizing error in interpretation. For this to be accomplished, the selected test needs to be evaluated for both validity and reliability.

Test Validity

There are three main types of test validity: *content*, *criterion-related*, and *construct*.

Content validity is a matter of how well the test items sample a defined set of tasks. When a test has content validity, it adequately measures the content of a body of knowledge. For example, in a standardized achievement test, establishing content validity might entail selecting test items on the basis of material in textbooks or consultation with subject experts.

Criterion-related validity shows the ability of a test to predict an individual's performance. For example, to predict someone's achievement in the first year of college, one might use a comprehensive exam as the measure or criterion. A test that samples content knowledge covered in the freshman year would be developed and administered to a group of high school seniors. Then, at the end of these students' freshman year in college, their earlier test results would be correlated with their final grade point averages. A high correlation between the test taken in high school and performance at the end of the freshmen year would establish criterion validity for the test.

Construct validity is a characteristic of tests that measure a particular trait ("construct") such as reading proficiency, intelligence, critical thinking, or personality type. The construct must be defined, then test items are developed to measure it. Construct validity is the extent to which different items on the test measure the same thing; it is also the degree to which a test correlates with other instruments attempting to measure the same construct. For example, the construct of "intelligence" may embrace verbal ability only, or it may encompass nonverbal abilities as well. The Wechsler Adult Intelligence Scale (WAIS) (Wechsler, 1972) has a construct of intelligence that includes both verbal and nonverbal factors. Some other intelligence tests include only nonverbal factors. When the construct of intelligence is defined so differently on two tests, they should not be compared with each other.

The extent to which any particular test has content validity, criterion-related validity, or construct validity is a crucial factor in test selection. Standardized tests are usually evaluated for validity; however, informal measures often are not. Assuming test validity without actually verifying it is precarious and can lead to faulty interpretations of student learning.

Test Reliability

A test is reliable or dependable if subsequent administrations yield consistent results. But this idea of consistency between later and earlier administrations is not totally clear because "consistency" must be defined. Does reliability imply perfect consistency or agreement? No. Test reliability means approximate agreement between different behavior samples or test administrations; it also means that the scores are relatively free from errors of measurement. Factors that give rise to errors of measurement include student guessing, student fatigue, or characteristics of the test itself, such as test length, wording of items, or even trick questions. A "reliable" test, when repeated a large number of times, yields results that are in agreement to an acceptable degree, and any differences between the scores are not attributable to errors of measurement. In general, if a test is valid, it is also reliable; however, the opposite is not always true.

Misuses of Tests

Learning assistance professionals need not be specialists in the fine statistical intricacies of test construction. However, they must be familiar with the basic concepts if they are to effectively use and interpret tests. The American Institute for Research lists "five common misuses of tests"—a further indication that judicious and ethical use of assessment instruments must be actively pursued.

1. *Acceptance of a test title for what the test measures.* Only full knowledge of the items can reveal what is being measured. . . . failure to examine the manual and the items carefully in order to know the specific aspects . . . to be tested (memory, vocabulary, type of reasoning) can result in misuse by virtue of selecting an inappropriate test for a particular purpose or situation.

2. *Ignoring the error of measurement in test scores.* Every test score contains an error of measurement. . . . It is a misuse of any test score or any observation to accept it as a fixed, unchanging index. . . . It is impossible to say with certainty that an individual's observed score gives his "true" performance . . . about which inferences are to be made.

3. *Use of a single test score for decision making.* Misuse of tests occurs when scores are not considered and interpreted in the full context of the various elements that characterize . . . the general education environment. . . . A test score represents only a sample from a limited domain and does not include the variety of factors that might influence that score.

4. *Lack of understanding of test score reporting.* There is substantial misunderstanding . . . of the meaning of test scores. . . . More is involved than a single number indicates. Forty-five items answered correctly out of fifty easy items has a substantially different meaning than forty-five items answered correctly out of a sample of fifty difficult items from the same domain. . . . The misinterpretation of grade equivalents is even more common. A grade equivalent is the score that was exceeded by 50 percent of the group at the specific time when the test was given. It does not represent a standard to be attained. It does not represent the grade in which the student should be placed.

5. *Attributing cause of behavior measured to test.* It is common . . . to confuse the information provided by a test score with interpretations of what caused the behavior described by the score. A test score is a numerical description of a sample of performance at a given point in time. A test score gives no information as to why the individual performed as reported. Claiming that it does, whether intended as a positive attribute or a criticism, is tantamount to test misuse [Gardner, 1989, pp. 1–2].

The Assessment Plan

When gathering information in the assessment process, it is important to have a plan. There is no magic formula for conducting an effective and ethically sound assessment, but having a plan and being aware of the important components and limitations of tests and other behavior observations helps to produce a more accurate and reliable body of information. The following four-step assessment plan indicates the areas to be addressed. Each step in the plan is based on guiding questions that give direction and provide structure.

Step One: Enunciate the Purpose for the Assessment

This may seem obvious; too often, however, learning assessments are initiated with little or no articulation of purpose. If the purpose of the assessment is to make a decision about a course placement, the procedures and instruments selected must be chosen for this purpose alone. However, if the purpose of the assessment is to obtain a more detailed analysis of the student's learning strengths and weaknesses in order to develop interventions that will improve learning, the assessment plan will be distinctly different. It is not unheard of for placement test results to be used to develop a personalized learning intervention program; this is what must be avoided if the student is to be served well.

An assessment may have more than one purpose—for example, making placement decisions, designing individualized learning plans, or even developing approaches to foster personal and social growth. In such cases, different means and criteria must be chosen for each purpose.

Step Two: Select the Measures and Data-Gathering Methods

After determining the purpose of the assessment, the next step is to decide how to collect information and by what means. How much background information is already available from student records and documents? Has other testing been completed elsewhere? If so, how recent are the results, and are they appropriate? How much time is available now for more informal and formal testing? What instruments are useful for gathering the data?

Generally, the more varied the sources of information, the more likely the assessment results are to reveal the student's learning needs. The assessment process needs to include more than one way of gathering information. For example, if the purpose of the assessment is to make an appropriate course placement decision, the background information might include previous courses completed and the grades achieved, as well as results from a recent placement test.

During this step, time devoted to preparation is important. One might begin with a personal student interview to gather necessary background information. After the interview, pertinent data may be collected from other sources. Educated choices may then be made about what exactly needs to be evaluated, and which instruments would be most appropriate for the purpose. For example, if the purpose of the assessment is to discover why a student is having difficulty in courses with heavy reading assignments, it would be important to first review the student's reading history and explore the availability of any recent reading test results. Next, specific reading tests might be selected for an updated assessment.

Step Three: Organize, Analyze, and Interpret Results

Once tests, surveys, forms, checklists, and informal means of assessment are selected and administered, the data collected must be organized, analyzed, and interpreted. Methods of doing so vary greatly; however, one assessment plan is presented at the end of this chapter as a model.

It is important that a written report of the assessment results is prepared. Simply collecting data will serve no purpose unless it is reviewed and presented in some systematic, reproducible form that can be read by those who are actually working on improvement of student learning. The case study at the end of this chapter includes a written report illustrating a way of organizing, analyzing, and interpreting data for effective use.

Step Four: Make Recommendations for Action

No assessment is complete without recommendations. Collecting data merely for the purpose of labeling a student or confirming a hypothesis is, in the authors' view, unethical. When students are asked to complete surveys, checklists, or tests, it must always be with the clear understanding that the information is leading to a plan of action.

Case Study

The following case study illustrates the four-step assessment plan.

Joe is entering his third semester at a major university. He is the star quarterback on the football team and aspires to play professional football on graduation. Since entering college, his academic performance has been marginal despite regular class attendance and effort given to studying. As a member of the football team, he is on scholarship and is required to spend a great deal of time practicing and playing.

In high school, Joe put forth an average amount of effort and was considered a satisfactory student; he never suspected he had learning problems. In college, he is majoring in computer science even though he is not particularly strong in math. He chose this field because it interests him and offers good career opportunities if his dream of playing professional ball does not materialize.

Because of his marginal academic performance, the threat of being on academic probation, and his concern about remaining eligible to play ball, Joe was referred by the coach for an assessment to determine the reasons for his low achievement. Speculations about Joe's difficulties have included the possibility of a learning disability, failure to utilize effective study strategies, insufficient time given to studying, weak background in math or reading, and low motivation for academics.

The following shows how Joe's assessment is conducted following the four-step plan.

Step One: Enunciation of Purpose

The purpose of the assessment is to answer the question, Why is Joe having academic difficulty despite regular class attendance and effort expended studying? Many speculations have been put forth to account for his weak performance, but none have been verified. To determine how to best help Joe improve academically, this assessment seeks to appraise basic skills in reading and math, inventory the use of learning and study strategies, and assess learning style preferences. Motivation for academic study as a contributing factor in achievement will also be investigated. In addition, the possibility of a learning disability will be explored and a referral for diagnostic testing will be made if necessary.

Step Two: Selection of Measures and Data-Gathering Methods

Since the purpose of this assessment is primarily to screen for possible learning problems, the measures and methods used are not extensive. Time and resources are limiting factors, so four areas are tested with the following instruments: (1) learning styles (Canfield Learning Styles Inventory, 1988), (2) use of learning and study strategies (LASSI, Learning and Study Strategies Inventory, Weinstein, 1987), (3) math skills (Descriptive Tests of Math Skills of the College Board, 1989), and (4) reading (Descriptive Tests of Language Skills of the College Board, 1989). In addition, a personal interview is conducted to explore further issues related to school performance. Readily available student records and documents are collected, which show that Joe has never before had a formal learning assessment.

In the first meeting, the specialist reviews Joe's academic history and the reasons for the assessment. Joe is assured that the results of the assessment will be used only to determine how to help him improve academically. No negative consequences such as dismissal from the university or sanctions related to football will be outcomes of this process. It is essential to establish trust in the assessment process and gain the full cooperation of the student. Because testing often has negative connotations, it is important to dispel any notion that the assessment results will be used in any punitive way.

During the personal interview, arrangements are made for the administration of tests and surveys. Dates are set and a timeline is established for both the administration of testing instruments and final reporting of the results. As only four instruments will be used in this case, the assessment will take place in two sessions, and one of the measures, the Canfield Learning Styles Inventory, will be taken home for completion.

In this case, all of the instruments are formal measures possessing the required validity and reliability. Additional informal methods, such as observations of Joe while he is studying or interviews with his teachers and tutors with Joe's permission, may be added at a later time.

Step Three: Organization, Analysis, and Interpretation of Results

The following summary is presented to illustrate how the results of this assessment might appear in a written report. The information is organized in two parts: results and interpretation. Recommendations will follow in the fourth and last step of the assessment process, where findings are translated into action.

Results

The Canfield Learning Styles Inventory showed that Joe prefers to work in activities directly related to real-world experience. He has no strong preference for either social or independent approaches, and instruction involving practical applications, site visits, and labs creates the closest match.

His highest area of interest is "inanimate," indicating his preference for working with things—building, repairing, designing, or operating. His preferred mode of learning is "direct experience," that is, in hands-on situations. He has very little preference for learning activities involving reading or working with words or language.

The conditions for learning that are most preferred include "competition" (desiring comparison with others and needing to know how he is doing in relation to others) and "detail" (wanting specific information on assignments). The conditions that he likes the least are "independent" (working alone and determining his own study plan) and "instructor" (wanting to know the instructor personally and student and instructor having a mutual understanding and liking for one another).

On the reading comprehension test, Joe correctly answered 31 out of 45 items correctly. This placed him at the 41st percentile of entering college-level students. His weakest area was in reading for the main idea, where he answered 8 of 15 items correctly. His strongest area was in drawing inferences, where he answered 12 of 17 items correctly. Overall, Joe's reading comprehension is in the low average range for entering college-level students.

On the arithmetic skills test, Joe answered 32 of 35 items correctly. This placed him at the 85th percentile for students who have had at least one semester of algebra.

Ten areas of study practices and attitudes were assessed on the Learning and Study Strategies Inventory. Of these, only two were in the average or above-average range: use of time management principles and concentration. All other areas fell below 50 percent. For example, Joe answered that he has low motivation, diligence, self-discipline, and willingness to work hard on academics. He further indicated that he lacks skills in information processing and reasoning, selecting main ideas and recognizing important information, and test-taking strategies. Overall, except for time management and concentration, Joe's self-report responses show that his motivation and study skills for college-level work are lacking.

Interpretation

Joe presents himself as someone with relatively low motivation for college study but is willing to put forth effort to succeed. He lacks, however, the basic study strategies that would enhance his learning. He is not troubled by lack of concentration but prefers learning situations that involve hands-on experiences. Subject areas such as philosophy, literature, and history that are required in his academic program are not taught from a practical applied standpoint. It is anticipated that these abstract subjects will be of little interest to Joe and would require a significant amount of motivation if he were to concentrate and succeed.

In addition, Joe is not a particularly strong reader. Though it does not appear initially that he has a specific reading disability, this is not to be ruled out. He is weak in reading for main ideas, and given the large amount of reading generally required in his coursework, this is likely to pose a significant challenge.

Joe basically sees himself as an individual who is capable of getting average or low average grades—a perception consistent with his current performance. Given his lower motivation for college study and his higher motivation for football and applied learning experiences, this is not surprising. Were it not for his desire to play intercollegiate football, another academic setting emphasizing technical and applied studies might be better suited to his learning style preferences and motivations.

Step Four: Recommendations

The following recommendations flow from the data and the interpretation presented in the report:

1. Joe should meet regularly with a learning assistance counselor to learn and apply effective learning strategies for reading and test taking. Whenever possible, he should choose courses that offer learning environments more closely aligned with preferences for application of knowledge.

2. Joe should receive tutoring in subjects requiring heavy reading assignments. He should work with tutors to practice reading for the main idea and important details. He should utilize specific study strategies with courses requiring heavy reading and abstract reasoning.

3. Joe should seek career counseling to determine possible alternatives to a major in computer science. While this major does relate to learning preferences for real-world experiences, it requires a very high level of abstract reasoning and is theoretically focused.

4. If academic performance does not improve after the above recommendations are implemented, referral for diagnostic testing would be indicated, to determine the possible presence of a learning disability.

Summary

Because of the diversity of the students we serve and the uniqueness of each individual, it is crucial that student needs be identified
with assessment procedures that are valid and reliable. Both formal
and informal assessment methods are important and can be combined to yield valuable information on the basis of which interventions can be planned. When assessment instruments are being
selected, four basic principles of testing must be understood: (1) the
difference between norm-referenced and criterion-referenced tests,
(2) the fallacy of unbiased tests, (3) the distinctions between different types of test validity, and (4) the meaning of test reliability.

Every assessment activity should be guided by a plan that
includes (1) stating the purpose of the assessment, (2) selecting
measures and data-gathering methods, (3) organizing, analyzing,
and interpreting results, and (4) translating findings into recommendations for assisting the learner. Students are at the center of
the assessment process and must always be active in validating the
assessment results and determining how they will be used. Only
when students are partners in the process can the results be used
effectively to promote academic achievement.

Chapter Five explores what tutors need to know about the individual characteristics of the students they help. It also explains the
importance of tutor training.

5

. . . .

Training the Tutors

This chapter focuses on how to educate tutors to better understand the students they serve and to adapt their approaches to different learner needs. It is not the purpose here to fully describe tutoring programs in general. Although this topic is worthy and of interest, it lies outside the scope of the present text.

One recent research finding showed that when tutoring is delivered by trained tutors, it is the strongest correlate of student success; however, when tutors are not trained, there is no correlation with academic performance (Boylan, Bonham, and Bliss, 1992). This is a powerful endorsement for mandatory tutor training and points to the importance of including it in every tutoring program.

This chapter discusses tutor training under three headings: (1) using theory to construct a tutor training program, (2) connecting theory to specific tutor training activities, and (3) choosing essential tutor training content, that is, the topics on which tutors are to be trained—for example, rapport setting, helping students with disabilities, or fostering student independence. The development and management of a training program deals with the size of the training groups, the role of the facilitator, the frequency of training sessions, and the actual organization of tutors into training groups. As there is no universally applicable formula for running a tutor training program, the specifics of developing and managing such programs are not addressed here. Instead, emphasis is placed on content, so that prospective trainers will have a basis for constructing training formats pertinent to their own settings and circumstances.

Using Theory to Construct a Tutor Training Program

What is meant by tutor training? Orientation sessions at the beginning of a term? Instructions for completing forms? Strategies for problem situations? All of these and more. The foundation of a good tutor training program is a well-articulated philosophy containing a combination of perspectives, including college student development, sociolinguistics, metacognition, motivation, counseling, group dynamics, and adult learning. Each of these perspectives is presented as it pertains to the tutoring relationship and inclusion in a tutor training program.

College Student Development

College student development is an eclectic perspective that combines the viewpoints of several cognitive theorists (Erikson, Piaget, Perry, Kohlberg, and Chickering). These theorists view human behavior through one or more of three basic prisms: (1) differences among individuals, (2) differences in environments, and (3) predictions about behavior when particular types of individuals interact with certain kinds of environments. It is not the intention here to summarize each theorist's view but to present the tenets of college student development in terms of different cognitive theories and to show how these ideas are useful in tutoring and tutor training.

The tenets of college student development are focused variously on holism, humanism, pragmatism, and individualism (Delworth, Hanson, and Associates, 1980). The *holistic* view promotes education for the whole person, stressing the importance of attending to both affective and intellectual needs. The tutor using this perspective understands how past experiences of failure relate to self-confidence and can ultimately affect academic performance. When a tutor takes a holistic view, the interaction with students is more personal and leads to an emphasis on the learning process.

The *humanistic* perspective is one that emphasizes the unique qualities of the person, specifically human freedom and potential for personal growth. Rogers (1961) and Maslow (1970) represent humanism in their optimistic views of human development. Maslow assumes people are largely rational and conscious and can control their basic urges. Rogers promotes the importance of the self concept and emphasizes a person's subjective view of the world. For instance, according to Rogers, feelings about one's intelligence, abilities, and attractiveness are believed to have more influence over behavior than any objective reality. A tutor needs to know, for example, that academic achievement is related to feelings of capability and must learn how to conduct tutoring sessions to help promote such feelings.

A *pragmatic* approach involves attention to objective facts and outward behavior. In a tutoring situation, the pragmatic view would lead to an assessment of actual performance in a course, with attention to a detailed evaluation of previous tests or papers. A pragmatic tutoring strategy would involve the use of active learning strategies to overcome past difficulties and improve academic achievement.

The last tenet of college student development is that of *individualism*. This is the belief that no two individuals are exactly alike and that differences among persons are significant factors in human behavior. The tutor who embraces individualism knows about individual learning styles and what effect style has on performance. A tutor's awareness of individual differences leads to the development of a repertoire of tutoring approaches and appropriate application to different tutees.

Sociolinguistics

Sociolinguistics is the study of verbal (and certain classes of nonverbal) communication in a cultural context. Using sociolinguistic theory, MacDonald (1991a) developed a coding procedure to identify and describe the communication patterns used in the tutoring process and found that there are two basic patterns of tutor-tutee interaction: informational and initial. The *informational pattern* occurs when the tutor and tutee are conveying information to each other. In the informational pattern, the tutor provides information that leads the tutee to competence by encouraging reciprocal communications.

In contrast, in the *initial pattern*, the tutor uses initiations, utterances intended to cause a verbal or nonverbal response. They begin or introduce new topics and may be questions, statements, or commands. Whereas communications in the informational pattern are characterized by periods of interaction in which information is shared back and forth, initiations start an interaction in which replies are short and concise: for example, the tutor asks, "What do you think will be on the test," and the tutee responds, "I don't know." In the informational pattern, reciprocal explanations are longer and more detailed. Tutor and tutee can engage in teaching and learning in this pattern when the initial pattern is no longer effective. The tutor can explain concepts to the tutee and provide background, new information, and examples. MacDonald stresses the need to train tutors in these two patterns, and he provides an interaction guide called the "tutoring cycle" to help the tutor monitor and direct the session. The twelve steps in this cycle direct the tutor to pay close attention to each part of a session so that the interaction is well planned, focused, and complete.

Metacognition

Metacognition refers to an awareness of one's own process of thinking and learning. According to Costa (1984), metacognition is "our ability to plan a strategy . . . to be conscious of our own steps and strategies during the act of problem solving, and to reflect on and evaluate . . . our own thinking." In addition to self-awareness, metacognition may also include learners' beliefs about the nature of a task; such beliefs may affect performance. For example, if a student believes that memorization is the best way to approach a task, learning is likely to be mostly passive and lacking active problem solving (Lochhead, 1985).

Tutors themselves sometimes lack awareness of their own learning strategies. Without realizing it, they are often involved in passive learning, devoting excessive amounts of time to reading, rereading, and memorizing. To help others become better learners, tutors need to become aware of active learning strategies, some of which they may never have used themselves.

The development of metacognition involves both a heightened awareness of how one learns and a greater knowledge of specific learning strategies. The latter include active reading and note taking; systematic approaches to organizing large amounts of material; methods for regular periodic review; and techniques for reducing anxiety and building confidence. Self-understanding is strengthened by knowledge of individual learning styles, and this is an important component of the tutor training program. As tutors become aware of their own specific learning styles, they notice similarities and differences between themselves and others and see that tutoring must be conducted in a variety of ways. This part of tutor training is often the most stimulating, as the tutors learn how their styles match or conflict with those of their instructors. Specific training activities for presenting both active learning strategies and individual learning styles are described later in this chapter.

Motivation

It is not sufficient to know different strategies and to appreciate individual learning styles. There is still the question of motivation to be considered. What makes some students persist in the face of continuing adversity whereas others give up?

The tutor needs to be familiar with factors that enhance and inhibit motivation to learn. For example, Maslow's hierarchy of needs, as described in Chapter Two, is an important framework that helps explain why some students may be more motivated to learn than others. Tutors are better able to help others when they understand how basic unmet needs for safety and security affect a student's ability to concentrate and perform academically. For instance, a student who lives in an environment filled with the threat of violence is likely to have difficulty focusing on academics and may need to pay more attention to reducing the threat than to conquering course content.

Concepts of *extrinsic* and *intrinsic* motivation are also significant in illuminating the learning process. Is the student more motivated by such extrinsic factors as grades and praise or such intrinsic factors as a personal feeling of accomplishment and pride in learning something new? If the tutor can answer this question, he or she is more likely to select strategies that lead to success. Tutors should also be familiar with theories of self-efficacy and attribution. A student may have high *self-efficacy,* or confidence in his or her ability, in writing but low self-efficacy in math. These beliefs are powerful in that they tend to affect motivation and ultimate levels of performance. *Attribution* is the phenomenon of ascribing causality to one factor or another. Each student has a characteristic way of explaining his or her failures, and this pattern of attribution is what the tutor needs to observe. Like self-efficacy beliefs, attributions also contribute to motivation and performance. Knowing a tutee's attributions for success or failure can help a tutor adjust strategies and be more effective.

We are not proposing that tutors become experts in the fields of psychology and learning. There is not enough time to accomplish this, and most tutors are not preparing for a professional career in tutoring. However, we are advancing the idea that in addition to competence in academic areas, tutors need to have some basic familiarity with concepts associated with successful learning. The more they understand these ideas, the more effective they will be as tutors.

Specific guidelines to help tutors identify factors contributing to negative motivation or a perception that the task cannot be completed, as well as strategies for enhancing positive motivation, are provided later in the chapter.

Counseling

Even though tutors are not seeking to become professional counselors, it is important that they know how to establish rapport, to listen, and to respond. The tutoring experience is often the only one in which the tutee feels unthreatened and comfortable enough to honestly address academic concerns and frustrations. Meetings with instructors are helpful, but some students find them intimidating because the instructor, unlike the tutor, is in a position of power.

To be an effective tutor, it is essential to have good rapport with the tutee. Knowing how to establish such rapport, how to listen and respond, is not innate. It is a learned art and becomes refined only with practice. Arkin and Shollar (1982) use the term *tutor-counseling* when referring to tutor behaviors that facilitate rapport. They suggest an approach from Rogerian psychology that emphasizes "nondirective listening," a process in which the tutor establishes empathy by hearing what the tutee says from the tutee's point of view. Nondirective listening is followed by reflecting, in which the tutor verifies that his or her interpretation of the tutee's verbal and affective message is accurate.

Like a counselor, the tutor must view the student as a whole person. Arkin and Shollar stress the importance of a holistic approach that sees the tutee as someone with needs, goals, and desires—someone with strengths and weaknesses whose learning has both intellectual and affective components.

The counseling perspective guides the tutor to use basic attending, or listening, skills. The following five components are integral to active and effective listening (Ivey, Gluckstern, and Ivey, 1982).

Basic Attending Behavior

The tutor maintains eye contact by looking at the tutee from time to time but not staring. This sensitive eye contact communicates attention and concern. In addition, the tutor adopts a comfortable body posture, leaning slightly forward but keeping a relaxed and easy posture that conveys interest. Finally, the tutor speaks in a normal, friendly tone, encouraging the tutee to communicate and paraphrasing the tutee's messages to verify understanding as necessary.

Minimal Encouragement and Paraphrasing

Three types of encouragers are useful in the tutoring session: (1) silence is a nonverbal message that can convey genuine acceptance and encouragement; (2) empathic responses, such as "I see" or "Uh-huh," along with head nods, let the tutee know he or she is being heard; (3) probing responses, such as "Tell me more" or "Give me an example," encourage the tutee to continue.

Paraphrasing is another way to respond effectively and give attention. Basically, the tutor gives back the essence of what he or she thinks the student has just said. The tutee's exact words are not repeated, but the idea is restated. The following is an example of paraphrasing:

TUTOR: So, how are you doing in statistics?
STUDENT: I don't understand these new formulas.
TUTOR: This new material is unclear to you.

When paraphrasing is used, the student knows the tutor is listening and is encouraged to continue.

Reflection

A tutor can help a student identify the source of a problem by reflecting the tutee's feelings. For example, if the tutee is discouraged and losing motivation, the tutor might say, "It sounds as if you feel you can't go on and don't know how you're going to finish this assignment." Statements of reflection show the student the tutor is listening and communicate empathic understanding.

Questioning

There are two types of questions—open and closed. Closed questions usually deal with specific points of information ("Are you a math major?") and are answered with simple yes or no responses. Open questions lead the student to talk about the situation and usually begin with "What," "How," or "Why" ("What part do you understand best?" "How do you like this course?" "Why do you think this assignment is unclear?"). Closed questions tend to limit responses, while open questions tend to stimulate discussion.

Summarizing

At the end of a session, a tutor needs to help the tutee to see what has been accomplished and to look ahead. By restating or reviewing the substance of the session, the tutor gives reinforcement, guides the student to draw conclusions, and helps the tutee to see what to do next.

The counseling perspective emphasizes acceptance and respect for the individual while promoting personal growth. The way one speaks to the student is central to the interaction. As in the sociolinguistic approach, words are deliberately chosen to achieve a goal. In tutor-counseling, knowing the difference between "I" messages and "You" messages is an example of this. Simply stated, "I" messages focus on the speaker ("I'm frustrated that I haven't helped you understand better"), and "You" messages center on the listener ("You don't know the main points in the chapter"). The tutor-counselor knows that "I" messages are preferred because they reduce defensiveness, encourage honesty, identify behavior and its consequences, invite exploration, and define limits. The concept of "I" and "You" messages is simple, but the effort to use "I" messages more frequently is not. Role-playing activities in tutor training are good opportunities for developing this skill. For example, tutors may be given a set of "You" messages ("You didn't come prepared for the session"; "You missed the last appointment and didn't call") and practice changing them to "I" messages ("I'm concerned that I can't help you if you didn't prepare," or "I wonder if there's a reason why you missed last week and didn't call").

Group Dynamics

Related to counseling but posing some different concerns is the challenge of working with students in groups. With an increased need to contain costs and an increased appreciation for the power of sharing learning strategies, more and more tutoring is being conducted in the group format. However, tutors who work with students in groups need some fundamental background and understanding about the special nature of this interaction. In group tutoring, students present disparate learning styles, varying degrees of competence, and differing needs for support and encouragement. Managing a group tutorial to meet different student needs requires special expertise.

MacDonald (1993) proposes five categories of concern related to group tutoring:

1. Being aware of the specialized roles individuals take on in a group—mediator, leader, scapegoat—and how these roles affect the tutor-tutee relationship and group cohesion (Bales, 1979)

2. Identifying students' needs, to determine if differing needs among group members will preclude the group format from working in a particular instance

3. Developing a workable plan and timeline so that all group members are aware of the session goals and cooperate to achieve them

4. Using jump-starting and other techniques for keeping groups on target and refocusing as necessary

5. Providing for effective floor management or promoting opportunities for each group member to participate so that one or two students do not dominate the session to the exclusion of others

Tutors who conduct group tutorials need to be aware of these concerns and have opportunities to address them in training.

Adult Learning

More and more adults are entering higher education, and the particular needs of these learners are pertinent concerns for the tutor. Information about the characteristics and needs of adult learners is extensive and complex and cannot be fully explored in these pages. Instead, a representative concept of adult learning, andragogy (Knowles, 1990), provides useful background for tutor training.

The andragogical perspective on adult learning is a philosophical stance based on the fundamental beliefs that (1) the individual learner is the primary focus, (2) the goal of learning is to promote personal growth and realization of the individual's potential, (3) autonomy and self-direction are important components of adult learning, and (4) the individual has the power to persevere against social, political, cultural, and historical forces (Merriam, 1993). This view of learning focuses on the empowerment of the individual and leads to particular approaches to instruction. For example, the andragogical view emphasizes the role of the individual in making decisions about what and how to go about a learning task. If the learner's need for autonomy and self-direction is assumed, details of assignments may be negotiated rather than prescribed, with the learner taking an active role in the decision making and the teacher functioning with less authority.

The stance of andragogy prompts the tutor to mediate the session while letting the adult learner determine the direction of assistance. The tutor must become comfortable taking a back seat and allowing the student to exercise autonomy and independence. The following conversation between tutor and adult tutee is an example of such interaction.

TUTOR: So, what do you need help with?

TUTEE: I'm uncomfortable with the assignment. The professor wants a standard research paper, but I think I could do this better with an interview and discussion.

TUTOR: Have you asked if that's an option?

TUTEE: He's rather unapproachable. I don't feel comfortable asking him.

TUTOR: I know what you mean. Sometimes it just seems easier to try to do it as assigned. [*After looking at assignment*] I think you may have a good idea here. I'd encourage you to see if you could do it your way.

TUTEE: I don't know. He's kind of intimidating.

TUTOR: Let's try it out. I'll be the professor and you ask me.

In this interaction, the tutor validates the student by listening and openly accepting the student's idea. Knowing the importance of independence and autonomy in adult learning, the tutor provides encouragement and supports the tutee in at least pursuing another option. Without an understanding of this adult learning principle, the tutor might have dismissed any alternative approach and insisted on working with the student on the task as assigned.

Connecting Theory to Tutor Training Activities

The seven different perspectives discussed here—college student development, sociolinguistics, metacognition, motivation, counseling, group dynamics, and adult learning—provide a foundation for developing a series of tutor training activities. Because tutoring is effective only when combined with tutor training, it is important to provide a well-integrated tutor training program tied to a base of knowledge about learning. The suggested tutor training activities that follow are organized within the framework of the seven views of learning that have been presented, so that they fit together in a systematic fashion and reflect what we know about the learning process. Each activity is related to one of the seven perspectives; however, it is possible that more than one view can apply to a specific activity. The suggested activities are merely representative and are intended to provide the reader with a foundation on which to design new and creative ideas.

Activity: *Discovering learning styles and their educational impact* (perspectives: college student development and metacognition). Have tutors complete learning style inventories and discuss the results. Have them develop mini tutoring plans for different learning styles and present them to each other.

Activity: *Analyzing communication* (perspective: sociolinguistics). Select tutoring sessions to be videotaped or role-played. Tutors identify examples of informational and initial patterns of interaction in the sessions. (Material in MacDonald's *California Tutoring Project* [1991b] offers specific examples for use in this exercise.)

Activity: *Active learning—concept mapping* (perspective: metacognition). Introduce the strategy of representing content in a graphic display, selecting the most important ideas and organizing them in a connected way in a visual schema. Provide models and demonstrate the process. Then have the tutors read a piece of content and design their own maps, sharing them with each other and discussing the relative merits of this technique.

Activity: *Goal setting* (perspective: motivation). Introduce the concept of goal setting (short- and long-term) and identify the characteristics of successful goals. Present a set of goals and have the tutors evaluate them according to the criteria. Pair tutors and have them develop their own weekly goals using the criteria for effective goal setting. Discuss how this activity is useful in a tutoring session.

Activity: *Active listening* (perspective: counseling). Develop a set of statements typically heard in tutoring sessions ("I don't understand why we have to know all these dates. Who cares if it was 1864 or 1875?" or, "I understand it perfectly in class but never seem to get it right on the tests"). Divide tutors into groups and have them practice active listening and reflecting by acting out the statements. Tutors identify feelings first, then pinpoint the problem, noting any nonverbal clues, and finally paraphrase the whole interaction.

Activity: *Keeping control of the group tutorial* (perspective: group dynamics). Present the five key concerns related to group tutoring (MacDonald, 1993). Assign roles to the tutors (mediator, leader, scapegoat), and construct a scenario to be enacted. Have tutors take turns in the different roles and in being the tutor for the session. Analyze the interactions.

Activity: *Analyzing a case study of the adult learner* (perspective: adult learning). Present an adult learner scenario such as the following:

> Susan is a single mother returning to school. She is thirty-five years old and has not been in school for fifteen years. She is carrying five courses and works part-time twenty hours per week. She is doing well in three courses (math, natural science, and communication) but is having great difficulty in English composition and literature. Most of the problem lies in writing papers. She develops blocks and cannot seem to get started. She puts off the papers until the last minute and then freezes. Now she has two compositions and a character summary due. She has come to you for help.

Use the following questions to guide a discussion: What would you do in this session? What would you ask the student to do for the next session? What would you plan for the next session? How would active learning be part of your session?

These tutor training activities are examples of a wide range of experiences that help develop effective tutors. The emphasis here is on designing exercises that reflect what we know about learning from a range of theories and perspectives. The trainer and tutor need to be conscious of both how and why a particular activity promotes successful learning.

Tutor Certification

The College Reading and Learning Association certifies tutoring programs at three different levels. Programs applying for certification must complete a verification process that examines the amount and duration of tutor training, modes of training, areas or topics covered in training, required tutoring experience, tutor selection criteria, and tutor evaluation criteria. Information on how to obtain certification is available from the association.

Why have a tutoring program certified? One reason is to provide a form of external validity for the program that can be demonstrated to staff and administrators in the institution. When a program is judged competent by an outside reviewing agency, it may receive a degree of credibility not available in any other way. Another reason for certification is to provide tutors with an incentive for ongoing training as they progress through the three levels and to offer them a tangible external form of commendation that could be useful in their future careers. Finally, and perhaps most importantly, certification provides the opportunity for a tutoring program to examine itself and reach a higher level of expertise in its service to students.

Choosing Essential Tutor Training Topics

Every tutor training program must cover certain essential topics, including the following.

The Tutor's Role

The difference between tutoring and teaching is often the first topic covered in a tutor training program. All too often, tutors incorrectly envision themselves as "mini-professors"—content experts who can teach students what they failed to learn in the classroom. Instead, it is important to train tutors to see themselves as facilitators and promoters of active learning who help students become more independent learners. Effective training shows tutors how to encourage risk taking, guessing without fear of error, and exploring subject matter through a variety of different study strategies. Tutors must be shown how to handle situations where they do not know the answers and to use those situations as productive learning opportunities.

Tutors need to know that they are not saviors and cannot work miracles. They must realize that the responsibility for learning rests with the tutee. The tutor exists to support, encourage, motivate, and guide the tutee with study strategies and content clarification. One tutor summarized the role of the tutor using the letters of TUTOR, as follows: *T* for talk and listen, to establish a good rapport with the tutee; *U* for understand the student's goals, being careful not to impose one's own; *T* for tutor as guide, not teacher; *O* for organize the sessions so that one is in tune with upcoming events and changes in the tutee's course requirements; *R* for reflect on the sessions to learn what really works for each individual tutee (Kramer, 1993).

In addition to pointing out that tutors are not substitute teachers, it is important to emphasize that tutors are not professional counselors either. When tutees present personal concerns that may interfere with learning, tutors must know how to listen and respond, but they do not function as counselors or therapists attempting to interpret situations and resolve issues. In such cases, it is important that tutors know how to make relevant referrals to other resources.

Referrals

When tutors are faced with situations beyond their scope of expertise, they must know where to turn for help. For example, it is not uncommon for tutees to share personal concerns that are seriously impeding their academic progress. These concerns might include roommate problems, family or personal illnesses, divorce, or other challenges. Tutors need to know how to respond when these concerns are presented and how to be empathic listeners. They must clearly communicate their lack of training and expertise to handle concerns outside the academic realm, but they must also give support and encouragement. Tutors who are knowledgeable about resources like the counseling center, health center, and university ministry are prepared to guide the student appropriately. However, it is not enough just to know the resources. Tutors must also know *how* to make the referral. When suggesting that a tutee seek help elsewhere, they must avoid any appearance of a lack of caring or concern. This is a delicate task and an important component of tutor training.

Policies and Procedures

Tutors must not only have a clear understanding of their roles, their limitations, and the occasions when referrals are necessary. They must be aware, too, of all of the policies and procedures that govern the tutoring program. How are appointments made? What is the process for drop-in tutoring? What are the responsibilities regarding paperwork and tutor session notes? How does the overall communication system work among tutors, tutees, and the managerial staff so that everything runs smoothly? Typical tutor training programs begin with orientation sessions where much of this basic information is conveyed. In addition, tutor training manuals that include written policies and procedures along with other pertinent information are commonly used and are very helpful.

Special Populations

Tutoring programs attract a diverse group of students. Some students seek tutoring because they want to gain confidence and be more efficient learners. Others come because they need to address serious academic difficulties. Still others seek assistance because of special needs. Tutors meet with student athletes, those on academic probation, students with disabilities, adult learners, and students from many backgrounds and cultures. Successful training programs include sessions on student diversity and special needs. For example, tutors learn about various types of learning disabilities and how to adjust approaches for the students affected by them. They learn that a student's cultural background can affect academic performance; for example, a female student may be discouraged from pursuing a particular major or career because of social barriers in her community. Tutors working with students who are visually or auditorily impaired learn that specialized computers and advanced technology are essential for academic achievement. In all, well-trained tutors have some basic information about the wide variety of students with whom they are likely to interact. Learning about the needs of special student populations is essential for effective tutoring.

Ethics and Academic Integrity

Many issues of ethical behavior are likely to arise in tutoring sessions. The most common are making sure the student's work is his or her own and not that of the tutor, maintaining confidentiality so that details of the session are not shared with others without the student's permission, being neutral when complaints about faculty are aired, and recognizing and honoring the limitations of the tutoring function so that students are not promised unrealistic outcomes. Tutors need opportunities to discuss these ethical issues, both in general and in relation to specific incidents, and to resolve problems in consultation with each other and their supervisors.

Supervision

No matter what form tutor training takes, there must be a format for regular supervision. Many programs assign tutors to individual supervisors, who may be professional staff members or veteran tutors with experience and training as supervisors. Tutors need to know they can bring concerns and issues to someone who will help them. This may occur in regular group meetings with other tutors and a supervisor, or it may take place in one-on-one sessions with the training director. Even experienced tutors need ongoing supervision, and it is recommended that all tutors, regardless of their level of experience or expertise, receive some form of supervision as long as they are tutoring. Periodic feedback sessions are important to the ongoing development of tutor proficiency and should be an integral part of every tutor training program.

Tutor Recognition

Education and supervision are only part of the tutor training picture. Tutors need to be recognized for their service and competence. Most tutoring programs are able to pay only minimal wages, and sometimes tutors work as volunteers. It is therefore important to honor tutors for their contributions to improved learning and academic achievement. There are many ways to accomplish this. Some programs identify a tutor of the month, with a public display for all to see. Others hold formal tutor recognition ceremonies where faculty and others are invited to acknowledge tutor accomplishments. Articles about tutoring and features about tutors may be published in the student newspaper. Whatever the format, tutor recognition is critical and not to be overlooked. When tutors are appreciated and recognized for their hard work and contributions, they become more bonded with the program, continue longer in their roles, and function more effectively.

Evaluating Tutor Training Programs

There are many ways to evaluate training programs. Tutors may be solicited to respond to surveys about their training experience. Tutees may be asked to evaluate the effectiveness of their tutors and given specific questions relevant to training topics. Whether the evaluation takes the form of surveys, questionnaires, or interviews is determined by time, resources, and other relevant factors. No matter the form, some type of evaluation is central to effective training programs. Evaluation results guide future planning and contribute to training program improvements. The National Association for Developmental Education produced the *NADE Self-Evaluation Guides* (Thayer, 1995), which is recommended for this purpose.

Summary

Tutor training is essential to tutoring effectiveness. When designing training programs, it is important to connect training activities to theory. Although training programs are necessarily diverse and specific to individual institutional settings, the core topics of all tutor training are the tutor's role, referrals, policies and procedures, special populations, ethics and academic integrity, supervision, and tutor recognition. Finally, all effective tutor training programs use evaluation procedures that guide future planning and give direction for improvement efforts.

Chapter Six takes a look at some actual programs to illustrate ways in which effective practice is realized in four different settings.

6

Taking a Look at the Real Thing

Four Programs

Throughout Part Two, the principles and guidelines described have been those that can be applied across a broad range of programs. However, the general concepts underlying organization and management, student assessment, and tutor training need to be considered in the context of one's own institution and program. This chapter provides specific examples of how these ideas have been applied to programs in a variety of contexts.

Over the years, learning assistance programs have been implemented with a wide variety of organizational and instructional designs. Effectiveness has been claimed for many types of programs. Clowes (1992) contends that "successful remediation is not directly related to program design. The program purposes, students, institutions, curriculum and the faculty are each too diverse to allow for easy solutions" (p. 469). Indeed, there can be no rigid design for the delivery of learning assistance. Programs must be developed to fit their own unique settings; their goals and objectives must support those of the larger institution. Recent research, however, has identified several components related to academic success that may be helpful to program planners. A survey conducted by the National Center for Developmental Education (Boylan and others, 1992) found eight components that were present to varying degrees in effective programs. Of these components, student assessment, tutoring, and academic advising and counseling were described as "commonplace" services by the researchers. The most powerful finding from the study was the presence of tutor training in the tutoring component of successful programs. Though the study did not attempt to establish a causal relationship between components and program effectiveness, it did establish that most successful developmental programs offer a wide variety of services.

Although it is difficult to maintain that specific components must be included to ensure program success, current research of the kind just described provides a good starting point for reflection. An additional resource is the NADE Self-Evaluation Guides developed by the National Association for Developmental Education (Thayer, 1995). Neither the current research nor the NADE guides assert that particular components must be included in an effective learning assistance program; rather, they provide the practitioner with a foundation from which to build a unique program that is most appropriate for local needs.

In addition to the specific components already mentioned, there are two more general characteristics that can help to provide an overall framework for program design. Keimig first identified them in her "Decision Guide for Effective Programs" (1983, p. 4), and Tomlinson (1989) referred to them when she asserted that "from a global perspective, successful programs are found to have two characteristics in common: comprehensiveness in their support services and institutionalization within the academic mainstream" (p. 41). A program is comprehensive when it provides services to meet the needs of a wide variety of students; it is institutionalized when it has been integrated into the overall culture of the school and is not viewed as a separate, isolated unit.

Keimig (1983) suggested a hierarchy of "learning improvement" programs that helps us operationalize the two concepts of comprehensiveness and institutionalization. Her hierarchy (introduced in Chapter Three) includes four levels of programming, with isolated basic skills courses representing level one. This level is "least likely to effect long-term academic achievement and persistence" (Keimig, 1983, p. 21). Level-two programs are those that include level one but with the addition of learning assistance for individual students, delivered primarily through tutoring. According to Keimig, the main criticism of this approach is that it generally occurs *after* student failure rather than as a proactive attempt to prevent failure and that because it does not employ systematic outreach it may not attract those who most need help. Level three in this hierarchy of learning assistance includes levels one and two but with the added component of course-related support services. These are integrated into the coursework through assignments or small-group exercises and offer supplemental opportunities for content review. This level assumes that any student may need additional time and effort to master course content and that this is attributable more directly to the objectives of the course than to any deficiencies in the student. Level four represents programs with "comprehensive learning systems." They are designed to include a variety of services that meet the overall needs of a wide range of students. These needs may be affective as well as cognitive and skill based.

This chapter describes learning assistance programs that have been developed at four very different types of postsecondary institutions: a community college, a proprietary and technical school, a four-year private research university, and a four-year public research university. Even though the mission statements of these institutions are distinctive and the programs reflect a variety of components and organizational structures, the reader is urged to focus on the extent of comprehensiveness and institutionalization of each program. These characteristics and the means of maintaining them vary from one program to another, depending on the mission and climate of the larger institution.

In addition to the fact that they operate in different types of institutions, the programs selected here differ in terms of the administrative units that manage them. Those at Loyola University Chicago and the University of Illinois at Chicago are housed within student affairs. The programs at Oakton Community College and DeVry Institute of Technology are part of academic affairs.

Because program models are reviewed from a variety of institutional types and administrative frameworks, it should be possible for readers to relate to the one(s) that most closely resemble their own or that they are most likely to encounter. This chapter does not advocate emulation of any one of the programs described; rather, it describes a range of programs and program components that have a history and have been shown to be effective within their institutions. The reader is invited to examine each program and to use the categories provided to raise questions and to make decisions about which components would lead most effectively to comprehensiveness and institutionalization in his or her own setting. To facilitate this personalized analysis and application, Table 6.1 presents a graphic comparison of all the programs, allowing readers to readily decide how to review the material of this chapter. They may choose to review only those programs that apply directly to their own work or to review all four and select portions of each for further reflection. In addition, a worksheet at the end of the chapter provides readers with an opportunity to apply the material in a variety of ways. For the novice in the field, the worksheet can serve as a preliminary outline for establishing a learning assistance program or as a lens through which to gain understanding of a program. For the more experienced practitioner, the worksheet can serve as a means for reviewing or evaluating an established program.

Loyola University Chicago: Learning Assistance Center

"One of the president's goals this year included a statement about bending the rules if it was important and if they needed bending. That is a goal that our Learning Assistance Center really takes to heart; we're not rigid, and we don't always go by the rules in the book. If a student needs a special accommodation, we try to provide it" (Lisa Kerr, learning assistance counselor, Loyola University Chicago).

Table 6.1. Comparison of Four Program Models.

Institution	Type of Institution	Administrative Framework	Center/Services
Loyola University Chicago	4-year urban, Jesuit research university; 15,000 students	Student affairs, student services unit	Learning Assistance Center: tutoring, academic support groups, workshops, individual counseling sessions
University of Illinois at Chicago	4-year urban, state supported research university; 40,000 students	Student affairs, counseling center, Center for Academic Excellence	Academic Skills Program: coursework, workshops, supplemental instruction
Oakton Community College	Open-admissions community college; 11,000 students	Academic affairs, curriculum and instruction division	Instructional Support Service: testing, workshops, coursework, tutoring, special services, non-native services, academic skills lab
DeVry Institute of Technology	Proprietary; distinctive technical focus in baccalaureate program; 25,000 students	Academic affairs, general education division	Academic Support Center: tutoring, testing, coursework, mini-course sessions, computer-assisted instruction

General Description of Institution

Loyola University Chicago is an urban Jesuit university with over fifteen thousand students from across the United States and from sixty-one foreign countries. It has existed for over a century and stresses excellence in what it considers the complementary areas of research and teaching. Loyola maintains four campuses in the Chicago area and one in Rome, Italy. Within the university, there are nine schools, including several for graduate and professional training. At the undergraduate level, all of Loyola's schools offer a common core of liberal arts and sciences. The undergraduate population of Loyola is a combination of commuters and students who live on campus in residence halls. The majority is middle class, of traditional college age, and white; 60 percent of the student body is female. Regularly admitted students typically score at least 24 on the American College Test (ACT) and are ranked in the top 25 percent of their high school graduating class. If their score is below 24 on the ACT, and their rank is lower than the top quarter of their high school class, students may still be considered for admission. If admission is denied because of low test scores, a student may be eligible for the Learning Enrichment for Academic Progress (LEAP) program, which was developed and is administered by the Learning Assistance Center.

In addition to its regular undergraduate departments, Loyola has a part-time division for adults who are returning to school. Loyola's mission statement emphasizes the importance of developing the whole student. Respect for the human person characterizes Jesuit education, which encourages students to develop their intellectual, emotional, physical, creative, moral, and spiritual dimensions.

Loyola's mission also reflects its Jesuit commitment to "knowledge in the service of humanity." The word *service* appears repeatedly in the mission statement and is reinforced through the president's annual statement of goals, which consistently stresses the importance of serving the needs of others.

This is where the Learning Assistance Center connects directly with the institutional mission and goals. The written mission of the center states: "The Learning Assistance Center exists to serve the individual needs of students as they pursue the attainment of a degree and develop into intellectually mature persons. We strive to serve these students along a broad continuum ranging from one tutoring session to a combination of ongoing multiple forms of support (tutoring, individual learning assistance counseling, workshops and support groups). Every effort in providing learning assistance services is characterized by the respect for and appreciation of individual differences" (Loyola University Chicago, 1995). In addition to the direction set forth in the written mission, there is a requirement that the center's director (like all unit heads) prepare an annual statement detailing how the unit serves the president's goals for the year. This provides a further opportunity to demonstrate how well the Learning Assistance Center contributes to the university's overall mission.

Evolution of the Learning Assistance Center

Learning assistance officially began at Loyola in 1981, when one staff member, a learning assistance coordinator, was hired by the Counseling Center. There was no actual learning center; tutoring services for a limited number of content areas were simply provided by several tutors. The tutors at the time were neither trained nor supervised, and some were actually volunteers. The learning assistance coordinator helped students individually and organized tutoring.

Services were provided in this manner until 1984, when the Counseling Center hired an additional secretary with a part-time responsibility to the learning assistance program. In 1986, this individual became the tutoring coordinator. By this time, the staff had grown to two full-time members and one graduate assistant. Several years later, the learning assistance coordinator was named director of the program, and learning assistance began to take on more specific parameters within the overall Counseling Center. Gradually, more staff were hired to deliver learning assistance on other Loyola campuses and to special populations such as adult learners, student athletes, and students with disabilities. By 1994, the staff consisted of a director; three full-time learning assistance counselors; one part-time counselor; one counselor and an educational assistant for student athletes; one half-time coordinator for students with disabilities; a tutor coordinator; sixty tutors; a full-time secretary; and two graduate assistants.

The rapid growth of staff in the learning assistance program reflects the expansion of its services. This unit that originally offered only a minimal amount of content-specific tutoring now provides services for all students and faculty. Much of the evolution is the direct result of requests from the university. For instance, when the athletic department recognized that its student athletes needed additional assistance, it requested a learning assistance counselor, and funds were provided to hire one.

In another case, when the federally funded Educational Opportunity Program was dismantled, the Learning Assistance Center was asked to propose a program for underprepared students that could be permanently integrated within the university. This was the origin of the LEAP program, which continues to be one of the most visible components of the center. Also, as the needs of students with disabilities became more apparent, a staff member was reassigned from within the university to spend half of her time in the learning assistance program, coordinating services for these students.

At Loyola, the Learning Assistance Center is viewed by the administration as the appropriate unit to deliver services that provide academic support to students. When a need arises, or a special population is identified, the center is contacted for its expertise. Support is then made available from the institution, through additional staff or space.

The issue of space was not always a simple one for the program. When learning assistance originated at Loyola, it was located in one small office within the Counseling Center. Students had to search for it by presenting themselves initially to the personal counseling receptionist. This was often problematic because it added an extra "label" to those seeking help. The space was gradually expanded to meet the needs of the staff and students, and eventually it became distinct from the Counseling Center, with its own separate entrance.

In the midst of its growth, however, it was threatened with a move to a basement space at the outer edge of the main campus. The entire staff of the Learning Assistance Center prepared a lengthy memo based on data from the *Exxon National Study of Developmental Education* (Boylan and others, 1992) and other research that showed the negative consequences of such a move. They documented the program's effectiveness with student retention data and stated their intention to seek support from others in the university in order to secure better space if necessary.

This immediate response by the learning assistance staff, with their accessible, relevant data detailing the effectiveness of their program, had a favorable result. Instead of moving the center to a basement, Loyola awarded it additional prime space in the central classroom building where it had been housed.

Although most of the programming has evolved to the point at which the main objective is to maintain high quality, there are two areas that the Learning Assistance Center would like to develop further. The first is the Achieving Collegiate Excellence Seminar (ACES) program for students on probation. This was originally designed as a support group that met weekly with a learning assistance counselor to discuss concerns and successful study strategies. The groups frequently have not materialized because of difficulties in scheduling and also because these are the students who "have to be coerced. They haven't been to see us before; they're the reluctant students in the first place" (Kerr, 1994).

In an attempt to make the program more effective, the learning assistance staff met with the deans and collaborated on a formal referral system that now requires the probationary student to enter into a contract to go to the Learning Assistance Center and schedule an individual appointment. Following the initial appointment, the learning assistance counselor signs the contract and articulates a set of recommendations for the student. The staff are hopeful that this collaborative effort and a more formalized system will lead to a more effective program for students on probation.

An interesting issue arose during the meeting with the deans. They initially argued that only those students whose grade point average (GPA) had fallen to 1.75 should be required to pursue learning assistance. They felt that it should not be required of those who were just below the 2.0 GPA cutoff for probation. The staff representatives from the Learning Assistance Center maintained that they could probably make a greater difference to those students who had not fallen quite so low.

The second area to be further developed is that of the faculty liaison committee. Initially, this group was formed to create visibility and to provide positive marketing for learning assistance. The center's director invited each department within the university to appoint a faculty member as a representative. By the end of its first year, the committee had evolved into one to which faculty could come and consult the learning assistance counselors about students who were experiencing academic difficulties. The staff of the Learning Assistance Center would like to explore ways to increase the effectiveness of this group.

Philosophy That Guides the Program

The Learning Assistance Center does not subscribe to any one specific theory of learning or instructional delivery system. The director has always emphasized the idea that open discussion at staff meetings provides room for many perspectives. Sometimes opinions differ not only on a principle of learning but also on the appropriate instructional strategy to apply. When this occurs at a weekly staff meeting, all the staff members engage in an open dialogue. This promotes an integrated approach to the delivery of learning assistance and takes advantage of the multiple areas of expertise represented by the staff.

The goals of the program reflect a perspective on learning that is applied not only to the student who is experiencing academic difficulty but to all students and faculty. They support the concept that faculty and students need to share the responsibility for learning. The goals also address the affective as well as the cognitive needs of the students served. The following five goals form the framework of the program:

1. To help all students at Loyola achieve academically to their fullest potential

2. To assist students to become more independent, self-confident, efficient learners so that they will be better able to meet the university's academic standards

3. To provide a place where faculty members can refer students who need help

4. To offer consultation and resources to faculty concerned about improving student learning

5. To provide an opportunity for graduate students to learn about the field of learning assistance in preparation for careers in higher education

Administrative Structure and Program Organization

The Learning Assistance Center is a component of the student affairs unit at Loyola University Chicago. This unit is headed by a vice president who serves as the administrator for areas related to student services, which has four departments: the Learning Assistance Center, the Career Center, the Counseling Center, and the Student Health Center. The directors of these centers report to the dean of student services. The following chart provides a summary of this administrative structure.

Vice President of Student Affairs
Dean, Student Services

| Learning Assistance | Career | Counseling | Student Health |
| Center | Center | Center | Center |

Within the center itself, there are three layers of staff. First, there is the director, who manages all of the learning assistance programming and reports directly to the dean. The director, in addition to hiring and supervising staff, assumes the role of mentor for two graduate assistants each year. She also develops a yearly detailed budget and communicates the center's financial needs to the dean, who allocates moneys that have been earmarked for the student services unit by the vice president.

The second layer of personnel, the full-time staff, includes three learning assistance counselors who provide individual sessions for students and serve as the initial contact for individuals who want assistance but who are unsure of their needs. These counselors also provide supervision to small groups of peer tutors and lead them through training workshops. There is an additional counselor assigned full-time to student athletes, who delivers learning assistance in the center as well as in the gym at scheduled times. The tutor coordinator, responsible for the overall operation of tutoring services, and the secretary complete the layer of full-time personnel.

The third layer, that portion of the staff working on a part-time or temporary basis, includes one learning assistance counselor, one half-time coordinator for students with disabilities, and two graduate assistants who serve for one academic year. In addition, there is an educational assistant for student athletes and approximately sixty peer tutors per year. The following chart summarizes this internal structure.

Director, Learning Assistance Center
Full-Time Staff

| Learning Assistance Counselors (3) | Learning Assistance Counselor for Student Athletes | Tutor Coordinator | Secretary |

Part-Time Staff

Learning Assistance Counselor	Educational Assistant	Coordinator for Students with Disabilities	Peer Tutors (60)	Graduate Assistants (2)

Staff meet on a weekly basis and engage in professional development at least once per academic term. Often, individual staff members present workshops based on their own expertise and interest areas. At other times, outside faculty and administrators are invited to provide workshops. These workshops often become collaborative sessions, as the outside faculty come seeking additional strategies for implementing their ideas. For example, a history professor described how she was using cooperative learning in her classroom. Following her description, she sought ideas from the learning specialists, whom she acknowledged as the experts in the area of instructional delivery methods.

The basic requirements set by the center for student tutors include a minimum of sophomore standing, a GPA of 3.0 or higher, and three letters of reference from faculty at Loyola. Training for tutors follows one of two paths, depending on the expressed needs of the tutor. Because the center has met the standards of the College Reading and Learning Association (CRLA) for levels one through three of tutor certification, Loyola tutors have the option of choosing training activities that will lead to formal certification. They can enroll in the three-credit-hour course "Individualized Instruction and Collaborative Learning," which is offered through the school of education each fall term and taught by the director of the Learning Assistance Center. In addition, tutors can watch videotapes designed to model good practice in tutoring situations, and they can participate in small-group workshops led by the learning assistance counselors. These activities are all designed to meet the CRLA criteria so that tutors have the opportunity to advance through the three hierarchical levels of expertise.

Services Available to Students

The Learning Assistance Center offers services to students in four general formats: individual counseling sessions, workshops, content area tutoring, and academic support groups. One of the larger of these components is individual sessions, which are delivered by the learning assistance counselors. This type of session is often initiated when a student comes into the center wanting assistance but is unable to identify a specific content area problem. The secretary then schedules an appointment with a learning specialist, who meets with the student to diagnose learning needs and recommend an overall plan. The plan may include further individual sessions with the specialist to review study strategies and to discuss referral to tutoring, personal counseling, career counseling, or academic advising.

The center offers a menu of workshops that is developed each year by staff members according to their areas of expertise. The menu is sent to all faculty and is distributed to various student groups—for example, residence halls and fraternities. When a faculty member requests a workshop, a meeting is scheduled with a counselor and a presentation that is content-specific is developed for delivery in class.

Individual tutoring for specific coursework is available weekdays, some evenings, and Saturdays; both drop-in and appointment tutoring is available. All Loyola students are entitled to receive tutoring for one hour per subject per week. About nine hundred students are seen for tutoring each year.

Academic support groups are designed for specific student populations. There are four ongoing support groups. The first is the Achieving Collegiate Excellence Seminar, which was developed as a weekly meeting for all students on probation. This program, discussed earlier, is currently being restructured to facilitate greater participation. The second group is Bridging Exemplary Students of Tomorrow (BEST), which was designed to serve Asian-American students on probation. The group was created because one of the learning assistance counselors had a particular interest and expertise in this area. The third group, Athletic Learning Assistance Program (ALAP), is structured to meet the needs of student athletes.

The fourth and largest academic support group is Learning Enrichment for Academic Progress. This program was designed for students whose ACT scores are below the minimum required for regular admission to Loyola but who graduated in the top quarter of their high school class. It regularly accepts forty-five to fifty students who attend an intensive summer session before their freshman year. This session consists of four mini-courses representing the core liberal arts and sciences curriculum and is taught by full-time Loyola faculty. Daily study strategy sessions led by learning assistance counselors follow the classroom experiences and continue weekly throughout the fall term. At the end of that term, students receive three hours of credit and a grade for successful completion of all the requirements. Persistence for the first year is higher for LEAP students than for comparative groups of regularly admitted students.

Program Evaluation

The center evaluates its services on a regular basis for the purpose of self-assessment and quality assurance. Whenever students receive services from the center, they are asked to sign a card that grants permission to send them an evaluation form at the end of the term. Questionnaires are then sent to all students who have agreed to be contacted. The director reads all the forms that are returned and then distributes them to the appropriate staff members.

In addition to this overall evaluation, students in the LEAP program are closely monitored for persistence, GPA, and graduation data. A computer-generated data report is obtained twice yearly. At the end of each term, individual students are tracked for academic achievement. The learning assistance counselors send personal notes congratulating them on their progress.

One interesting consequence of collecting data and disseminating evaluation reports occurred at Loyola in 1994, when the

Learning Assistance Center held a tenth anniversary celebration for the LEAP program. Extensive data showing the effectiveness of the program was shared. However, one set of figures indicated that for the previous two years, the persistence rate for LEAP students had declined. The university president, in his first year at Loyola, expressed concern over this data and asked for an explanation. Turning to their well-organized, accessible database, center staff were able to investigate and document, case by case, why the students had left the institution. The reasons included a wide range of personal problems unrelated to school—most significantly, financial concerns. Because the first year of the program almost always includes full funding in the form of grants, not loans, the school simply became too expensive for many students the second year. Identifying these issues may lead to a more extensive review of students admitted to the program and/or the addition of a more focused counseling component related to the problem areas.

Physical Layout

The Learning Assistance Center is located on the first floor of a highly trafficked classroom building in the middle of Loyola's main campus. It occupies newly renovated space that contains five private offices and a separate tutoring center. When the space was reconfigured, the center director was given several options, which were weighed in light of confidentiality needs. Five offices were designed with solid doors, allowing the director and the learning assistance counselors to conduct private sessions. These offices are located along one hallway behind the main reception area.

Ideally, there would have been two more private offices for the tutoring coordinator and the counselor for student athletes, but financial and space constraints prohibited this. These two staff members have their offices in the tutoring center, which is down the hall from the main reception area. The tutoring program is located in a large open space, with cubicles that are formed by partial walls providing semiprivate conditions. The separation of the tutoring program from the counselor offices allows students to come in for individual sessions and be assured of relative privacy; however, the learning assistance counselors feel a separation from the tutors that they would like to overcome.

The Learning Assistance Center is enjoying its newly constructed separate entrance. Formerly, when students came for assistance, they entered the same reception area as those coming for personal counseling. The two centers have different philosophies regarding the appropriate environment for their services. The Counseling Center requires a quiet, clinical setting for its reception area, whereas the Learning Assistance Center is suited to a less reserved and more interactive setting.

University of Illinois at Chicago: Academic Skills Program

"We're in the Counseling Center, but we're so different; we go in totally separate directions. Our program is very focused on coursework and content rather than concerned with the development of the whole student. That's much more a student affairs kind of approach and our course-based program has not adopted that philosophy" (Karen Quinn, coordinator, Academic Skills Program, University of Illinois at Chicago).

General Description of Institution

The University of Illinois at Chicago is an urban, state-supported institution with approximately twenty-five thousand undergraduates and another fifteen thousand graduate students. It is a four-year institution where research and graduate education have historically provided a significant focus. The university is currently expanding its urban mission by participating in the Great Cities Initiative. This project promotes a partnership with the city of Chicago: the university supports research related to urban issues, and the city uses the university as a major resource.

This urban focus also drives the recruitment of students. Each year, approximately 2,800 students enter for the first time. Most of the university's undergraduates commute and are either from the city or have recently made Chicago their home. Many are first-generation college students, and often a second language is spoken in their home. Others have graduated from the city's public schools or are transferring from local community colleges. The transfer population is large and is frequently retained more effectively by the university than the traditional freshmen. The freshman is typically eighteen years old, whereas the transfer student has an average age of twenty-two.

Students are admitted directly into a specific college at the university. Because requirements differ from one college to another, admissions criteria are flexible but include ACT scores, high school rank, and letters of reference. Students who do not meet the basic criteria may be considered "differentially qualified" and admitted on a provisional basis. Although these students are encouraged to participate in support programs, they are not required to do so. Similarly, though all entering freshmen are required to take placement tests, they are not forced to enroll in the developmental coursework that may be indicated by the results of those tests. Depending on their program, they may be strongly advised to take a particular course, but no learning assistance is mandated.

Evolution of the Academic Skills Program

The Academic Skills Program began in 1979, when a director was hired to coordinate coursework in the area of basic skills. Prior to this, one faculty member who had a joint appointment in the School of Education and the Counseling Center delivered this type of academic assistance through workshops that were held on an ad hoc basis. In 1979, however, moneys became available to the university for learning assistance and programs that were specifically designed for minority groups. Two other programs were started simultaneously: a Latin American recruitment and educational services program, and an educational assistance program.

The three programs were separate, but the Academic Skills Program was designed to be the instructional unit for all three. Any instruction that was delivered was coordinated by the director of academic skills. The other two programs placed heavy emphasis on advising and recruiting students. At first, there were only a few offerings, taught by one staff member; now there are seventeen separate courses delivered by a staff of nine.

Though the coursework proliferated, there was a lessening of support from the university in the 1980s, when the school's overall mission focused more on graduate education. In the 1990s, however, there has been a renewed interest across campus in the undergraduate population. This interest stems primarily from an administrative concern over freshman retention rates and what needs to be done to increase persistence. There is currently a mandate to provide support for all student groups across all university programs.

The institution has looked regularly to the director of the Academic Skills Program for guidance regarding student retention as well as other universitywide issues. Because the program is housed in the student affairs division and is unique in that it serves the entire institution, it is seen as a unit that understands issues across campus and can be depended on to facilitate objective analyses of issues. In 1994, the program director served as chair of a universitywide task force looking into academic retention issues and coauthored the recommendations presented to the administration.

Another example of how the program has evolved to become a resource to the entire university community occurred when the placement test for reading and writing was revised. Working with the Testing Center along with the English department and College of Education, the Academic Skills Program assumed a leadership role in developing an internal assessment measure. Again, the director was a coauthor of the new test, and the developmental course instructors helped to validate the internally normed scores.

The director predicts that although the future may bring some changes to the program, the coursework will remain at basically the same level. If, however, a universitywide freshman orientation course is supported by the administration, its design and implementation will most likely fall to the Academic Skills Program and add to its curriculum. The one area where there is likely to be a significant change is that of funding. More and more, the depth and breadth of the services offered by the program will depend on the ability of the unit to gain additional funding, either from within the institution or from outside agencies.

Philosophy That Guides the Program

The Academic Skills Program does not have a specific mission statement, but its philosophy was summarized in a document coauthored by its director:

> The Center embraces the guiding principle that intellectual and professional learning are facilitated by social interactions and communication with students, faculty and administrators in a variety of flexible, diverse and adaptive instructional settings. Learning at the Center is collaborative, student-centered, and domain specific. This concept of learning acknowledges research which supports that
>
> - students work best within the context of a community of scholars;
> - successful learning must be centered on the specific academic needs engendered by students' engagement with coursework demands;
> - thinking, literacy and study strategies differ across disciplines;
> - students come to higher education with individual differences in interests, cultural background, motivation, and abilities;
> - every student, even the most gifted, can profit by exposure to Academic Skills instruction [Bentley, Quinn, and Piokowski, 1993].

This rationale for an expanded academic support unit reflects the university's overall perspective on the learning environment, both in the language it uses and in its conceptual framework. For instance, it acknowledges the role of research in defining learning; the university places a high value on the importance of research. It also emphasizes the strong linkage between "successful learning" and the "academic needs" brought on by "coursework demands." Student achievement is defined here in academic terms only; there is no reference to the affective needs of the students. This is in total accord with the university's perspective.

The statement also points out how learning is "domain specific" and that strategies differ across disciplines. This affirms the power held by the individual schools and programs across the university and acknowledges a willingness to provide assistance for a range of academic needs. Also, by referring specifically to "every student, even the most gifted" the statement is truly inclusive of the entire university community, from undergraduate to graduate student.

Administrative Structure and Program Organization

The Academic Skills Program is a component of the student affairs unit at the university. This unit is headed by a dean who reports to the vice chancellor. The program is housed in the Counseling Center, along with the Testing Center and the Clinical Counseling Division. Within the Counseling Center, the Academic Skills Program is a subdivision of the Center for Academic Excellence. The following chart summarizes the overall organization.

University Vice Chancellor

Student Affairs

Counseling Center

Center for Academic Excellence   Testing Center   Clinical Counseling

Academic Skills Program

The Academic Skills Program has a coordinator who is also the assistant director of the Center for Academic Excellence. The program has no specific budget, but the coordinator is responsible for staffing the courses that are offered. Mainly on the basis of this need, she requests funding from the Counseling Center director, who decides how to distribute funds across the entire center. The director comes from a clinical counseling background, a fact that frequently affects funding priorities within the unit.

The staff members are instructors who are distinguished primarily by the number of months they teach during the academic year. The structure is as follows:

Academic Skills Program Coordinator

Academic Professionals (4)   *Lecturers (4)*
12-month contract   9-month contract

Graduate Students (2)   *Secretary (60 percent-time)*

Since the foundation of the Academic Skills Program is formal coursework, all staff members teach classes. One of the academic professionals also coordinates the supplemental instruction program, and everyone is expected to conduct workshops across campus when they are requested.

The professional academic staff members may choose nine- or twelve-month contracts each year. The lecturers, however, are faculty members and are bound by the universitywide nine-month faculty contract. The difference in status among the staff is the result of a merger between the Academic Skills Program and another unit in the university where the instructors held faculty status. This is a distinction that the program coordinator would like to eliminate by seeking faculty status for the entire staff.

Professional development occurs on a regular basis, either in a workshop format or individually as staff members confer with the coordinator. In addition, each instructor is observed once a year and given feedback by the program coordinator. Plans are under way, however, to develop a peer evaluation system. Says the coordinator: "I think more learning goes on when peers observe one another. When I come in, there is too much defensiveness and explaining what went wrong and why" (Quinn, 1994).

Services Available to Students

The Academic Skills Program is a course-based support system with seventeen courses in its curriculum. The courses are offered for three hours of administrative credit, and students receive grades that count toward their GPA for the term in which they enrolled in the course. Students whose initial test scores indicate a need for developmental coursework are strongly advised by their program advisors to enroll. None of the courses are required, but they are listed in the university catalogue, from which all students may choose to register.

The courses cover a range of skill areas from "English for Speakers of Other Languages" to vocabulary enrichment to study strategies to academic reading to academic and professional writing. Many of the courses are limited to twenty-five students and primarily serve the freshmen and sophomore students at the university. The course with the largest enrollment, 221 students in the fall of 1993 (Quinn, 1994), is "Study/Learning Across the Disciplines." This course is designed to teach practical strategies for success in college. It is linked directly to discipline-based coursework and is taught through both lecture and small-group learning activities. The course is typical of the curriculum in that it is based very strongly on the academic expectations of coursework across the university.

Supplemental instruction is the second type of service offered by the Academic Skills Program. It is regularly organized for one or two classes on campus. The effects of the supplemental instruction efforts have been very positive, with average grades exceeding those of the classes from which students have come. The Academic Skills Program sees this as "an important retention initiative at UIC. Additionally, the training and supervising of SI leaders provides an important and unique in-service teacher-training experience for graduate students" (Bentley, Quinn, and Piokowski, 1993).

Program Evaluation

The director evaluates the program's services each term by requesting information on students who have enrolled in its coursework from the Testing Center. There is much computer-based data that is readily available; all that is required is to ask the right questions. A total student profile is available that includes GPA, persistence at the university, stop-out data, and whether the student enrolled in the coursework independently or following an advisor's recommendation. In addition to these student profiles, the director provides certain other information to the university administration—for example, the number of courses that were offered, the number of students initially enrolled, and the number returning the following semester. A demographic profile of the course takers that describes the racial and ethnic makeup of the students is also compiled.

Each instructor is evaluated by the students on a questionnaire developed by the program. It has both closed and open-ended questions regarding the course, the teacher, and the progress the student thinks he or she has made. The results are summarized by the program coordinator and shared with each instructor.

Physical Layout

The Academic Skills Program is located in a building used exclusively for all student support services and university administration. The facility includes a dedicated computer laboratory, a resource room (for audiovisual equipment, course-related syllabi, and the like), a separate area for student workers and graduate assistants, and a storage/kitchen area. All faculty and professional staff have private offices. In addition, there is a testing center with individual carrels as well as open space. Although there are four rooms appropriate for classes and seminars, the academic skills staff prefer to schedule their developmental classes throughout the campus. The physical space is large and modern; however, it is located off campus and can be inconvenient for students to access. They must go out of their way to find it.'

Oakton Community College: Instructional Support Services

"Once you help a student understand how to think about things and to understand how his or her own mind might work, it's just really amazing the differences that happen. We never look at a student as a fragmented piece. We try to see people who are whole. It's a gentle practice but of enormous significance" (Juele Blankenberg, manager, Instructional Support Services, Oakton Community College).

General Description of Institution

Oakton Community College is an open-admissions community college established in 1969. It is a member of the Illinois community college system and serves approximately eleven thousand postsecondary students who commute. Approximately two-thirds of its students identify themselves as transfer students. In addition, 16 percent of the students already have bachelor's degrees, and a substantial percentage beyond this have earned sixty or more college credits.

The student population is extremely diverse and changes significantly from one time of day to another. The daytime enrollment consists of a fairly traditional group of recent high school graduates. In the evening, however, the majority of students are returning adults, most of whom are working full-time. Many represent the first generation in their family to attend college, and 16 percent of the students are recent arrivals in the United States. In addition to the many language bases represented by the immigrant population, there are a substantial number of American ESL students who have experienced a bilingual secondary education or a second language spoken in the home.

Oakton is an open-admissions institution; however, students are encouraged to take assessment tests when they enter. On completion of twelve credit hours of coursework, they are required to take the tests if they have not already done so. The results of the tests determine placement in English, reading, and math courses, and restriction on registration may occur.

As a community college, Oakton's mission is determined by the Illinois Community College Act, which directs the college to "serve the post-secondary educational needs of the residents, employers and employees of organizations within District 535" (*Oakton Community College 1994/95 College Catalog*, 1994, p. 4). To meet this general mission, Oakton offers six educational services, two of which relate directly to the provision of learning assistance: (1) general or developmental studies for students requiring additional preparation before they can begin college-level education and (2) student services such as counseling, advisement, testing, and tutoring.

The official statement of Oakton's philosophy contains a definition of a "premier community college" that alludes to the instructional support services unit: "A premier community college . . . provides its community with academic programs and support services in a challenging, creative and caring environment . . . It sees the student as a whole person and prepares students to succeed by providing opportunities for learning, both formal and informal" (*Oakton Community College 1994/95 College Catalog*, 1994, p. 4).

Historically, support for learning assistance at Oakton has come from the president's office down. Indeed, in the handbook given to new tutors, a personal message from the president confirms Oakton's commitment by stating: "Oakton Community College is committed to the belief that each person should be provided the opportunity to develop his or her full potential. The College exists to provide that opportunity. Thus, we offer support services that enhance the chances for student success."

Evolution of the Instructional Support Services

The instructional support services unit came into being at Oakton in 1973 as a response to faculty concerns about the different levels of preparation students were bringing to the classroom. With the institution having an open-admissions policy and with course enrollment also being open, instructors felt that support services beyond the classroom were necessary in order for students to have the best opportunity to succeed. As a result of faculty efforts, a learning lab was established as a general content lab under the direction of the learning resources (library) director. Additional labs were established for reading, writing, and math, but these were managed by the English and math departments.

In 1977, there was a major reorganization of learning assistance services. A U.S. Department of Education basic skills grant permitted the merger of the individual labs and the tutoring program, resulting in a new instructional support services unit with its own director and staff. Though remaining in the learning resources center, the new entity became an independent unit within the curriculum and instruction division.

Since 1977, the program has grown, and most frequently, the expansion of services has been a response to needs identified within the institution. According to the manager of Instructional Support Services, when a need is articulated, the task is defined, a role description is written, and a staff member is hired to run the new service. One major component of the program that grew out of such a need is the Testing Center. In 1975, a faculty member, frustrated by his difficulty in monitoring student testing for a new program, requested help from Instructional Support Services. As other faculty members heard about the testing service he was receiving, they began to request it too. Today, the Testing Center has its own coordinator and two testing assistants and is responsible for all the academic testing done at Oakton outside of regular classes.

Throughout its development, Instructional Support Services has increasingly moved away from a discrete skills approach to one that is based on teaching students how to think. In 1988, Oakton became significantly involved in the critical thinking movement and, as an institution, sponsored five national conferences on the subject. As a result, critical thinking has been integrated across the curriculum at Oakton. Instructional Support Services emphasizes to students that it is more important to understand their own learning styles and processes for learning than it is to memorize sets of facts. This philosophy will increasingly influence its future programming.

Philosophy That Guides the Program

The philosophy that guides the tutoring program of Instructional Support Services is student-centered. The staff are trained to respect all students and to be nonjudgmental and caring when offering services. This extends from the director's office to the reception area, where students are personally welcomed with a standardized greeting designed to communicate warmth. There is even a prescribed telephone response to ensure that no student is transferred unnecessarily and that callers' needs are met from the very beginning. This service approach is guided by a statement of ethics, articulated by the staff, which focuses the entire program and appears at the beginning of the training manual along with the overall statement of purpose. It says:

> The purpose of the Oakton Community College tutoring program is to help students achieve their academic goals. The ethical principles that guide us in this work are fairness, honesty and equity. Therefore
> - All Oakton students are provided tutoring on a fair and equitable basis.
> - All tutors are expected to demonstrate respect for one another and the students they serve regardless of personal cultural differences.

- All tutors are expected to recognize the limitations
  of their duties, knowledge and experience and
  to make appropriate referrals when necessary
  [Blankenberg, 1994].

The ten goals that follow this statement further outline the program's commitment to provide assistance to all students in order to further their academic performance, their ability to advocate for themselves, and their development as "active independent learners." It is evident that the philosophy providing the foundation for the instructional support services unit is one that looks at the whole individual.

One of the guiding principles of the unit is that education is developmental, and that though all students move through similar stages, the time it takes to do so varies. This is reflective of Bloom's mastery learning theory, which asserts that most individuals are capable of achieving mastery in a given area, but that the rate at which it occurs cannot be predetermined (Bloom, 1982).

In addition to Bloom, the works of Perry, Belenky, and Baxter Magolda have been integrated into the overall philosophy of the unit (Blankenberg, 1994). Perry and Belenky have authored studies that describe the cognitive stages of development experienced by individual learners. Being familiar with this developmental process not only facilitates the delivery of learning assistance by tutors but also enables them to help students to become more independent. As students become more aware of their learning needs and styles, they can better monitor themselves and achieve increasing independence.

Knowing and Reasoning in College by Baxter Magolda (1992) has confirmed the framework for the learning profile that is done with students who schedule individual appointments. According to Juele Blankenberg, the learning profile is "the very first conversation most of them have had regarding how they learn, what they learn, and what they know about themselves." The retention studies of Pascarella and

Terenzini (1991) and Tinto (1987) also contribute to program development. And according to the Instructional Support Services manager, the work of Astin lends validity to the notion that learning assistance must be "intrusive and supportive" (Blankenberg, 1994).

Administrative Structure and Program Organization

Instructional Support Services is a component of the curriculum and instruction unit of Oakton Community College. This is the division in which all academic departments are housed at the institution. It is headed by a vice president who oversees three areas: educational services; all discipline-based departments; and institutional research, curriculum, and strategic planning. The instructional support services unit reports directly to the senior director of institutional research, curriculum, and strategic planning. The following chart summarizes this structure.

Vice President, Curriculum and Instruction

Educational Services	Academic Departments	Institutional Research, Curriculum, and Strategic Planning
		Instructional Support Services

Being a part of the academic division of the college allows staff of Instructional Support Services to serve on institutional committees. The unit has been represented on committees whose decisions have impact across the college in such areas as program review, student orientation, and English as a second language. This representation fosters communication with other units and heightens the program's ability to operate from the same set of standards and concepts as the rest of the college. The program manager feels this common framework is significant and that to try to work as a "peripheral" or "isolated" unit would negatively affect the students. She also adds: "It is important to interact as members of the college. We try to participate in absolutely everything. . . . We now do all school orientations and I don't think there's a member of our staff that doesn't sit on a school committee" (Blankenberg, 1994).

As well as participating on formal committees, the unit works informally to enhance contact across the college. Frequently, it holds "tea parties" for which written invitations are sent to faculty and staff. These receptions, enhanced by food and flowers, feature activities that will acquaint guests from outside the unit with some of its services. For example, selected interactive software might be available for everyone to experience. The staff of the unit take these receptions seriously, following up the written invitations with phone calls to ensure good participation.

The internal structure of Instructional Support Services includes a director who oversees the entire program and reports directly to the senior director of instructional research, curriculum, and strategic planning. In addition to being responsible for the unit, the director serves as the department chair for the one course that is offered through the program, "College Success Seminar," and participates regularly in the delivery of services to students. The program manager reports to the director and supervises the coordinators of the various services. She is generally in charge of personnel matters within the unit. The manager also participates in the delivery of services. Under the direction of these two administrators, there are sixteen full-time staff members.

Each component of Instructional Support Services is led by a coordinator. The components are tutoring, testing, non-native services, special needs services, academic skills lab, study skills instruction, and several grant programs. The special needs area has two additional coordinators who provide assistance to students in career orientation and in making the transition from school to work. The testing center, too, has additional assistants. The following chart shows this internal organization.

Director, Instructional Support Services

| STEPS Coordinator | Manager, Instructional Support Services | Secretary | Receptionist |

Program Coordinators

| Tutoring | ASSIST | Academic Skills Lab | Study Skills |

Tutors

| PACT | Testing Center | Non-Native |

Testing Assistants (4)

Although the primary responsibility of coordinators is to lead their component sections, they also serve as liaisons to various other academic departments. For instance, the study skills coordinator is the liaison to the allied health department. At the same time, the other departments may assign their faculty to act as liaisons to Instructional Support Services. Currently, the math department has a faculty member who is acting as liaison and is provided a stipend for this additional assignment. The liaison role is a significant one, as these individuals become actively involved in tutor training and setting up a direct dialogue between the departments and Instructional Support Services.

Tutors are assigned to the overall tutoring program as well as the Academic Skills Lab and the special needs area. There are approximately sixty tutors working each term throughout the unit. The tutors are peers, professionals, or faculty drawn from across the institution who have "alternate" time to provide this academic assistance. The tutoring program has been certified by the College Reading and Learning Association (CRLA), and tutors have the opportunity to earn level-three certification by tutoring a minimum of seventy-five hours, receiving positive student evaluations, gaining the recommendation of the coordinator, and either completing a special project or mentoring junior tutors.

One unique feature of the staff in the instructional support services unit is that everyone is "cross-trained" (Blankenberg, 1994). Most personnel, from the director on down, can carry out the various tasks of the unit. For example, the director participates as a mentor and tutor on a regular basis; the tutor coordinator has been trained to fill in at the reception desk; and the manager takes on the responsibility for the Academic Skills Lab at certain times.

Services Available to Students

Instructional Support Services offers help to students in a variety of formats—tutoring, workshops, labs, coursework, and individual appointments. The tutoring occurs in the Academic Assistance Center and is offered primarily in an open lab format: a tutor for a particular content area is available at a table, and students can drop in and receive the help they need. For example, if the tutor specializes in math, five students with different needs from a variety of math courses could receive help at one time. If it appears that any of these students needs additional, more personal assistance, the tutor recommends that an individual appointment be scheduled. Individual and small-group tutoring is available but is not used to the same extent as the open labs.

Workshops are offered regularly in the areas of study strategies, test review for the English and math assessment tests, and computer skills. Students, who must register in advance, pay a small fee for these workshops. In addition, there are open lab times in the computer center when students can access computer-assisted instruction in ESL, reading, writing, and math. The unit also offers one formal course. "College 101" is a seminar course in college success that carries three semester hours of credit and is designed "to enhance academic skills, interpersonal adjustment, cultural understanding and career awareness" (*Oakton Community College 1994/95 College Catalog*, 1994, p. 55).

Individual appointments are always available for students. They often begin with the development of a learning profile, where the facilitator and student discuss the student's style of learning and conclude with a plan for further assistance. The Testing Center is one of the most comprehensive components of the unit as it administers tests for the entire institution. It gives the math and English placement tests that are mandatory for all students registering for their thirteenth credit hour or wishing to register for a math or English course. It also administers make-up tests, constitution tests, media-based course tests, and College Level Examination Program (CLEP) tests.

Services for special populations are *coordinated* through Instructional Support Services, but the philosophy at Oakton is to mainstream all students, so special programs have not been designed. According to the manager, "You can't take a special program into the real world with you. You need to be prepared to learn your own strategies" (Blankenberg, 1994). The unit works with student affairs, which has counselors assigned to be available to students with special needs. Coordinators within Instructional Support Services ensure that help is available for non-native students in the areas of testing, tutoring, advising, study skills, and conversation groups, and also for the learning and physically disabled in the areas of tutoring, testing accommodation, assistive technology, evacuation safety procedures, and learning strategies.

Program Evaluation

In 1994, the instructional support services unit completed a self-assessment based on the National Association for Developmental Education *NADE Self-Evaluation Guides* (Thayer, 1995). The results were positive, with 81 percent compliance being the lowest on any of the scales. In reviewing the results of this assessment, however, the unit realized that it had never articulated a statement of ethics. As noted earlier, this statement has now been written and forms the framework for the program.

Once a year, in the spring, evaluation forms are completed by a sampling of students from each type of service offered. The sample consists of those students who, at the time they came for services, completed a card expressing their willingness to be surveyed later. The return rate for these evaluations is about 70 percent. Any faculty member who used the services of the unit during the year is also asked to complete an evaluation. Tutor evaluations are completed by students after three visits, and the results are compiled and returned to the tutors.

Student follow-up is difficult in a community college like Oakton. Because there is no lockstep program, Instructional Support Services has little opportunity to monitor achievement after students have received assistance. The manager feels that the best measure of the program's success is how well students perform in coursework following the assistance, but with the wide range of courses available and the frequent nonsequential enrollment patterns of the students, this data is difficult to collect. Rather than looking at subsequent achievement, then, the unit collects data on the overall use of services and student satisfaction. This information is detailed in an annual report distributed to the entire faculty.

Physical Layout

Oakton's main campus is contained within one large, two-story building that sprawls in several directions. The instructional support services unit is housed in part on the second level of the Learning Resource Center (the library) and is consequently easily located by both students and faculty.

There are five private offices on one hallway that has a reception area for students at one end. The Testing Center is also in this general area. Down the hall, separate from the program administrators, are the tutoring and computer centers. There are no classrooms within the program area; when space is needed for workshops or classes, it is found across the building, where all other classes at Oakton are held.

The institution is undergoing a major renovation project, and when it is complete, the instructional support services unit will occupy new space. According to the manager, staff are looking forward to more open space, which will foster more collaborative and incidental learning for both students and staff. The unit will also have its own classroom, as well as a larger testing center. There will be several private offices that will ensure confidentiality when needed, but for the most part, the unit wants fewer individual spaces and more openness. A major advantage will be that all the components of the program will be located in contiguous space.

DeVry Institute of Technology: Academic Support Center

"I was teaching a full load of classes and started to realize there was, more and more, a group of students that wasn't being helped, so I started an academic support center from my desk. I put up a sign that said, 'Come in if you need some help'" (Barb Eichler, Academic Support Center director, DeVry Institute of Technology).

General Description of Institution

DeVry Institute of Technology is a proprietary postsecondary institution with a uniquely focused baccalaureate program. It has eleven campuses across the United States and Canada, with a total of more than twenty-five thousand students. The school offers five programs, each with a distinctive technical focus: electronics technology, computer information systems, business operations, telecommunications management, and accounting. DeVry awards both bachelor's and associate's degrees.

A unique component of DeVry's programming is the general education core. This core curriculum and baccalaureate level of education distinguish DeVry from a traditional vocational school. All degree-seeking students take a minimum of three English classes, as well as other courses from the social sciences and humanities. There is little room for elective study; most of the general education core and the specialized coursework is prescribed. "It is efficient and lean; on the other hand, it promotes a general education as well as immediate application of skills. It is not trade; it is an educational approach toward the twenty-first century" (Eichler, 1994).

DeVry's mission statement further emphasizes the importance it places on a complete education: "The mission of DeVry Institute is to provide high quality career-oriented higher education programs in business and technology to a diverse student population. These programs incorporate general education to enhance graduates' personal development and career potential" (*DeVry Institute of Technology 1994 Academic Catalog*, 1994, p. 5). In addition to its overall mission, DeVry has enunciated six purposes that reflect its philosophy toward students. Two of the six purposes refer directly to the area of academic support: (1) to offer a variety of day and evening programs to accommodate the distinctive needs of both traditional and nontraditional students and (2) to assist students in realizing their potential by establishing basic skills assessment and developmental services.

Even though DeVry is highly accountable for showing a profit and for being responsible to its stockholders and the business community, it also places a significant emphasis on the overall development of its students. It acknowledges the existence of both traditional and nontraditional students and fosters achievement by assessing basic skills and providing the necessary support services.

The Academic Support Center reflects the institution's emphasis on developing a successful student. In conjunction with DeVry's mission statement, the school's purpose is "to provide academic support for students, teachers, and administrators, which will enable our students to become more efficient, self-confident, independent, and successful learners" (Eichler, 1994). The inclusion of all three communities—students, teachers, and administrators—is significant. It reflects a philosophy that commits the entire institution to students' development, and the Academic Support Center is a primary vehicle of that commitment. The center is defining itself as the academic unit that can bridge all others.

The students at DeVry are 80 percent male, with an average age of twenty-four. Many have been working or attending community colleges for several years, and most have a very directed focus when they enter the school. A basic math test is required for admission, and students must meet a minimum score set by the program for which they are applying.

The catalogue very clearly links initial test results to possible placement into developmental coursework. It states as general policy that basic skills assessments may be given during the first week of classes and that the students will be assigned to developmental coursework if that seems appropriate. In order to be perfectly clear, it adds, "Developmental coursework may increase the program length and cost." More specifically, the catalogue notes that if math scores are below a certain cutoff point for one program, the students will be required to complete an alternative plan of study (*DeVry Institute of Technology 1994 Academic Catalog*, 1994, p. 70). This alternative program was designed by the Academic Support Center and is described below as a service available to students.

Evolution of the Academic Support Center

The Academic Support Center is located at the Addison, Illinois, campus and was started informally in 1989, when a full-time faculty member offered learning assistance to students from her desk. Her initial realization that students needed more help was supported by other faculty members who were teaching the freshman orientation course. They had all observed the wide range of academic needs among entering students.

In 1990, the corporate administrators of DeVry appointed a task force to explore ways to increase student retention. They were concerned with their responsibility to deliver the necessary educational components for student success. The approach was similar to one routinely used in the business world: improve the quality of the process, and the product will improve. To this end, the task force designed a developmental program to improve the educational process, believing that increases in achievement and retention would ultimately result.

Following the recommendations of the task force, developmental programs and efforts to provide supportive help were initiated across the DeVry system. In Lombard, Illinois, a faculty member was hired on a half-time basis to direct a new learning assistance center. At first, the program operated from a small office. It soon expanded into two rooms and then finally into its present space of five hundred square feet. For two years, the program was operated entirely by one individual. By 1993, there were nine part-time staff members serving over 350 students in 1,400 learning assistance sessions per term.

The Academic Support Center on the Lombard campus, now located in Addison, regularly serves 20 percent of the daytime students. Its director sees continued growth in the number of students served through tutoring, but she also envisions expansion in other areas. She predicts that technology-based services will grow with the addition of CD-ROM capabilities and an expanded library of computer software. She also foresees computer networking through modem connections playing a larger part in the delivery of learning assistance. Another expected area of growth is video-assisted mini-sessions, where small student groups watch videotaped classes and work through them with the help of a tutor.

The Academic Support Center would also like to promote greater outreach to the faculty and administration to ensure an integrated plan of support for students. Another group that it hopes to reach is the evening student population. Currently, it serves only 2 percent of these students but looks forward to creating services that would meet their needs. Because this is a group with little extra time, the most effective medium might be a computer network offering learning assistance that could be accessed from any site at any hour. Academic services for students with disabilities are the exclusive responsibility of the center, and the director expects to expand those too.

Philosophy That Guides the Program

The Academic Support Center is seen as a liaison unit for the entire institution. Like the general education core, this unit bridges all components of the system—students, faculty, and administration. Because of its liaison function, the center must be known as a place not just for students but for everyone. It is a resource for faculty as they develop strategies for delivering instruction to students with varied learning styles. It also acts as a resource for administrators as they plan future policy. The center has already played a major role in redesigning curriculum in a specific program area to meet the needs of students who score low on initial assessment tests.

There are two guiding principles that provide the foundation for the Academic Support Center. The first relates directly to the administration's bottom line, and that is to increase student retention. The Academic Support Center is held highly accountable for making a difference in the attrition rate; therefore, it must design its programming with that in mind. The second principle is a more qualitative one and relates to student satisfaction. The center wants to be a place that students consider "their home, their resource, their retreat" (Eichler, 1994).

In describing itself as a "retreat," the center reaffirms its philosophy that the whole student must be supported. Students receive nurturing attention by the staff, and as the director states, "if the student only needs five or ten minutes, we want to be there for him" (Eichler, 1994). As its mission statement articulates, the center works to strengthen both the students' level of self-confidence and their learning strategies.

Administrative Structure and Program Organization

The Academic Support Center is a component of the academic affairs unit at DeVry. This unit is headed by a dean who reports to the president. The center is housed specifically in the general education division, which is administered by a dean who is responsible for the learning resource center (library) and all general education curriculum and faculty. The following chart summarizes the overall organization.

President
Dean of Academic Affairs
Dean of General Education
Learning Resource Center   General Education   Academic Support Center

The Academic Support Center is led by an individual who retained her faculty status when she was appointed coordinator and consequently does not have the more appropriate administrative title of director. In addition, she coordinates several other activities—for example, academic accommodations for disabled students and developmental services—but because of her faculty position, there is no formal title.

She feels strongly that faculty status for the support unit's manager brings greater credibility and support to the center. Also, at DeVry, it allows academic changes to be initiated by that individual. For instance, if she wanted to recommend a freshman orientation program, she could, as a faculty member, initiate an exploratory task force; a nonacademic administrator would need to go through a bureaucratic process in addition to building faculty support, from the position of an "outsider," to accomplish the same result.

The coordinator is the only full-time staff member of the unit; there are nine part-timers—eight tutors and one assistant from the faculty ranks of another department. The internal organization looks like this:

Center Coordinator

Faculty Assistants (8)   *Professional Assistant (1)*
(part-time peer tutors)   (released faculty:
                                 10 hours weekly)

The professional assistant is a faculty member from the general education department who has been given released time from her regular load to work for the Academic Support Center. In this role, she teaches reading courses, leads mini-sessions, and provides individual learning assistance to students.

The peer tutors come from a general pool of students who have qualified to be faculty assistants at DeVry. These assistants provide a unique support system across the institution: they are assigned to all classes to provide whatever assistance the instructor and students need. From this overall pool of qualified students, tutors for the Academic Support Center are selected. They must have a 3.5 overall GPA and demonstrate through an interview process that they are caring, versatile, and capable of mentoring fellow students.

Training for the tutors as well as for the entire group of faculty assistants is conducted by the Academic Support Center once a term. A three-hour session is scheduled that includes an overview of the holistic approach to learning and an administration and discussion of the Kolb Learning Styles Inventory. Tutors complete assigned outside reading prior to this session. In addition, they receive ongoing formal and informal training on a weekly basis.

The costs of the Academic Support Center, aside from the coordinator's salary, are diffused across various units. Staff are funded through the office of faculty assistants as well as from college work study funds. The general education department assumes many of the indirect costs of functions such as photocopying. There is a budget to cover computer software and certain other materials, but that is the only specific budget line for the support center.

Services Available to Students

The primary service provided by the Academic Support Center is tutoring of walk-in students. Appointment times are available, but walk-ins are more common. Each hour, two to three tutors are available who have expertise in different program areas in addition to math and English. Depending on the activity at any given time, these tutors rotate among the various roles of receptionist, administrative assistant, and computer expert as well as tutor. It is always someone's role to watch the door and welcome any new student and provide appropriate follow-through.

Computer-assisted instruction is another very popular service. Students come in to complete assignments on the computers or to brush up on basic skills, and they frequently need tutorial assistance. According to the coordinator, "Computer-assisted instruction is something the students just love as long as it's backed up with tutor interaction and help. If it's just neutral and simply sitting there, it's not going to be as effective" (Eichler, 1994).

The center administers assessment tests for DeVry, as well as individual diagnostic tests when students request them. Staff score and provide feedback on any tests that are taken.

Mini-sessions for small groups of students are held frequently by the tutors. During these sessions, regular classes are processed by faculty assistants who are very familiar with the particular class, its teacher, and its focus. The tutor keeps in communication with the teacher and may attend the classes. Also offered is developmental coursework that includes classes in reading, writing, and math. For each course, there is a software tutorial program available as a laboratory component that can be completed in the center.

The most recent addition to the services provided by the center is the "alternative plan of study for the electronic technology program." This curriculum has been designed for students who score below a minimum cutoff on the initial math assessment and is required of them before they are allowed to enroll in the core program. It includes developmental coursework that integrates the basic skills of reading, writing, and math with content-specific materials for the electronic technology program. Institutional credit is awarded for these courses, and grades are given, but they do not count toward the student's overall GPA.

Program Evaluation

The Academic Support Center is evaluated with the help of a detailed computer database that allows the institution to review all programs from a quantitative perspective. Numbers are available for all student activities, including course enrollment, attendance, grades, and persistence. There is a strong sense of accountability across the institution that pervades all program evaluation.

In addition to the institutional database, the center has developed its own software program for student log-in; this allows it to collect more program-specific information each term. For instance, it can generate reports detailing how many times a student came for assistance, what type of assistance was provided, and in which program most of the students were enrolled. A future goal for this log-in program is to add a qualitative component so that student satisfaction can be monitored.

Physical Layout

The Academic Support Center is located on the second floor of the library. This space is directly up the stairs from the general reception area and is in a central position relative to all classrooms. The space is long and narrow, and with its glass interior walls is easily visible and inviting to students as they study in the adjacent library or walk to classes. The center frequently shares its space with faculty assistants who are not part of the center but are providing help to students.

At each end of the space is an open area, one housing computers and the other containing the coordinator's office. There is much space in the middle that is too narrow to be used. Also, there is no privacy, as the glass walls look out onto both the library and hallways leading to classrooms. Even though the square footage is three times what it was previously, the center has outgrown it and often must look across campus for additional space.

Summary

This chapter has provided an extensive description of four very different learning assistance programs, reviewing their evolution as well as their overall structure, services, methods of evaluation, and physical layout. The intention has been to demonstrate how programs must be designed to fit their individual institutional frameworks. Within those frameworks, however, there are certain guiding principles that must be considered when designing or reviewing a program.

The following worksheet (Exhibit 6.1) has been designed to lead practitioners through a set of questions that will reveal much about their institutions. By reflecting on their responses, they will gain a sharper focus on how to apply the general principles of learning assistance within their own institutional environments.

After completing this focused review and deciding how best to apply the principles that have been discussed throughout Part Two, the reader may turn to Chapter Seven, which presents a new model for effective practice. This model provides a framework that will help practitioners to connect the various components necessary for maximizing student potential.

Exhibit 6.1. Worksheet to Facilitate Reflection on Practice.

Before a new program is introduced or an existing one revised, consideration of the following questions will provide a reference point for critical reflection. You may not find all the answers, but by asking the right questions you will establish a framework for planning.

1. What does my institution look like?
   - What is there in the mission statement that relates to learning assistance for students?
   - What types of students enroll, and what are their primary needs with respect to academic success?
   - What support systems are already in place across the institution? How will they interface with this new program?
   - Does this program present a conflict with any other support service being offered?

- How is this program integrated across the institution? Is the staff viewed as a resource with respect to campuswide issues such as retention and testing?
- How is the faculty involved in this program?

2. Why am I looking at the need for a learning assistance program?
   - Who has charged me with developing/reviewing a program?
   - What is the purpose of this program, explicit and implicit?
   - How does the faculty view learning assistance?
   - How does the administration view learning assistance?
   - How do the students view learning assistance?
   - Is there long-term support, financial and philosophical?

3. What is the organizational and administrative structure?
   - Which institutional unit houses the program—student affairs or academic affairs?
   - How does the institutional unit affect the philosophy guiding the program?
   - Is the program's philosophical framework mandated by the larger unit?
   - What other programs are housed in the same unit, and how do they affect learning assistance?
   - To whom is the program's director directly responsible?
   - Is there an institutional budget line for learning assistance?
   - What is the process for requesting funds?

4. What is the internal program structure?
   - What staff positions are needed?
   - What are the job descriptions and minimum qualifications for each staff position?
   - What institutional title do staff members have—for example, faculty, professional staff? Is this equitable with other units?
   - What is the hiring process? Is it controlled externally or internally?
   - Who decides the ratio of full-time to part-time staff?
   - Is there the necessary support staff? Is it shared with another unit?
   - Is there a mission statement and set of goals for the program?
   - Does the mission statement relate to the institution's overall mission?
   - Is there a statement of ethics to guide the program?
   - Does the program need to be organized into components—for example, learning center, academic department, testing center?

5. What types of services should be offered?
   - What will best meet the needs of the students and faculty?

- Is the program designed to serve all students or only designated populations?
- If tutoring is offered, should it be by appointment or on a walk-in basis?
- Does the institution support developmental coursework? Can the coursework carry credit? Is it graded or pass/fail? Is it listed in the catalogue?
- How does computer-assisted instruction fit into this program?
- If there is institutional placement testing, how does it relate to this program?
- Are there any services—for example, coursework or tutoring—that the institution requires of students?
- How is the faculty supported by the program?
- What schedule does the program need to follow? Is there a need for evening and weekend hours? Is there a need for programming during academic breaks?
- Do other units need support services for their students that this program can provide—for example, workshops, diagnostic testing?

6. How can program evaluation be built in from the beginning?
- What is available in the institutional database?
- What in this program is important to the institution?
- How can the program best demonstrate that its mission and goals are being met?
- How does the program maintain an effective balance between quantitative and qualitative data?
- How is the data disseminated through the institution?

7. What kind of physical space does the program need?
- Is the space centrally located within the institution?
- Is the space accessible to all populations?
- Can the space accommodate classes, private tutoring/testing/counseling, computer-assisted instruction, storage, offices?
- Is the space secured?
- Is the space shared with another unit?
- Can the space be rearranged easily with room dividers, shelving, cubicles?

7

Constructing a New Model
for Effective Practice

We have taken a look at different program models and explored the role of tutor training. We have examined the importance of assessing individual student needs and seen how to organize and manage a successful program. Now we are ready to look at the construction of a new model for effective practice in our field.

Much of what we do is already founded in theory and research, but we are not always consciously aware of how this occurs. When we are developing and managing programs, assessing students, and training tutors, we function as professionals who must have a heightened awareness of why we do what we do. It is not enough to say that we know something works because we tried it before or because we saw someone else do it. We need to have a full understanding of our professional behavior, to be able to predict outcomes on the basis of sound principles and know why some actions are more successful than others. We need a framework to guide practice in our field.

The development of a professional understanding of our work is a dynamic process, forever changing and evolving. New information continues to present itself, requiring that we change or modify our methods and approaches. But this does not happen automatically, without form or order. This chapter presents one way to better understand how change occurs in our profession. A new model,

Figure 7.1. TRPP Model.

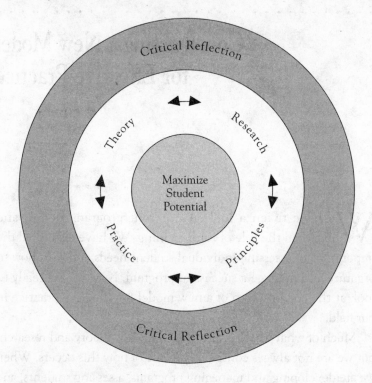

named TRPP (see Figure 7.1), is offered to guide our effective practice and to direct us in the pursuit of excellence.

TRPP stands for *theory, research, principles,* and *practice.* These four components interact to help us understand why we do what we do, and why one approach may be more effective than another. A process of *critical reflection* that focuses on the four components and leads to the goal of maximizing student potential is essential to TRPP. (Several different terms—*framework, system,* and *model*—are used interchangeably to refer to TRPP. These terms have very specific meanings in other contexts, but for the purposes of this chapter, they all refer to ordering things for increased understanding.)

TRPP is a new way of integrating different theoretical perspectives so that we may better understand what we do, why we do it, and how it ultimately leads to desired outcomes. This model does not construct a new theory. It takes the best of some existing theories and organizes it under two headings: *Who is the learner?* and *What is the teaching/learning process?* In addressing these questions, TRPP does not simply list theoretical ideas, relating them to the research, and producing principles to guide our practice. TRPP is a model of connections. In the presentation of the model, the discrete nature of a particular theory may be obscured; however, this is not the intention. It is important that individual theories be recognized and stand on their own for future interpretation, application, and research. The authors mention this to assure the reader that they are aware of the risk of oversimplification in their attempt to integrate several theories.

Critical reflection is essential in examining the connections between theory, research, principles, and practice. What does critical reflection mean? To reflect critically is to look at something with an eye toward analysis, to search for meaning, to discover inconsistencies, and to question the basis for one particular approach or outcome. In critical reflection, we explore a phenomenon in depth in order to understand interaction effects and ultimately to use the insights gained to improve practice.

As we reflect, it is helpful to recognize that using theory in a framework of connections is important for four main reasons: (1) to organize information and data into a meaningful whole, (2) to better explain to others what we do, (3) to make decisions in our daily work, and (4) to dream about the future (Delworth, Hansen, and Associates, 1980).

In the following consideration of the two questions Who is the learner? and What is the teaching/learning process? all four components of TRPP are included. The presentation begins by stating a principle and then discussing how that principle is connected to theory. A few selected research results follow in support, and finally, examples of practice are offered. However, this sequence is not necessarily the one in which TRPP is most effective. TRPP is a cyclical model. The cycle can begin at any point with any one of the components and continue in any direction.

For example, another way to apply TRPP would be to start by looking at the research. One might choose to begin by reviewing studies about learning assistance or developmental education and considering how these results relate to theory, principles, and practice. Kulik and Kulik (1991) worked in just this way. They conducted a meta-analysis of research studies in the area of developmental instruction and produced a summary of the results. These results can be viewed through the TRPP model to reflect on effective practice.

To begin the TRPP cycle with theory, one might choose favorite theorists and study their basic ideas. This could then lead to reviewing or conducting research that either supports or refutes the theory. A revision of principles and practice might then follow. Belenky, Clinchy, Goldberger, and Tarule (1986) began work in this way by examining Perry's theory and conducting research with women that led to new ways of looking at how principles and practice need to be adapted for different sexes.

Starting the TRPP cycle with practice is also valid. The practitioner may want to focus on a specific activity, such as lecture note taking, and reflect critically on why a particular method seems more effective than another. Perhaps the practice includes activities like consolidation, recitation, and regular and consistent review. Why would these factors be keys to the success of the approach? Critical reflection through TRPP that started with practice would lead one to discover the theories, research, and principles that support the practice and give insights into how it might be improved.

This chapter begins the TRPP cycle discussion with principles because the authors' critical reflections led them there first. Although the focus is on both the experienced professional and those new to the field, the discussion is particularly conscious of those who are new. When the new professional enters developmental education, the overriding need is for a set of principles on which decisions about daily activities can be based. Principles provide a good start for those just beginning. However, the experienced professional can benefit, too—by reflecting on the principles that are most obvious and revisiting those that may have been overlooked.

The following discussion provides a concrete example of how TRPP can be used to help maximize student potential. The principles, theories, research, and practice examples are illustrative of how connections can be made to increase our understanding. However, in no way are the illustrations intended to reflect all possible examples of principles, theories, research, and practice. They are simply representative of the best in our field. (The principles discussed are summarized in Table 7.1 and Table 7.2.)

Table 7.1. Who Is the Learner? An Overview.

Principles	*Research/Theory*
1. The learner moves back and forth through a series of well-defined hierarchical stages.	Erikson; Piaget; Perry
2. The learner behaves in ways that are related to self-concept and self-efficacy beliefs.	Rogers; Flippo and Caverly; Kulik and Kulik; Bandura; O'Brien, Brown, and Lent
3. The successful learner interacts with the environment in a unique way that is characterized by a natural tendency toward growth and development and the desire to meet basic needs.	Lewin; Maslow; Kulik and Kulik; Bloom
4. The learner is concerned about establishing or reinforcing a sense of identity in the college learning experience.	Chickering; Branch-Simpson
5. The learner has specific needs and ways of learning as an adult that are distinct from those of younger students.	Knowles
6. The learner approaches learning tasks in ways that are often characterized by differences specific to gender status.	Belenky, Clinchy, Goldberger, Tarule; Baxter Magolda

Who Is the Learner?

Principle One: *The learner moves back and forth through a series of well-defined, hierarchical stages.*

Several theorists espouse the idea that the learner progresses through stages on a continuum from the simple to the more complex. Erikson, Piaget, and Perry are representative of this theoretical stance. According to Erikson (1968), the learner faces conflicts that must be resolved in order to progress. Conflict resolution is at the core of development, and it occurs repeatedly during one's lifetime. For instance, learners in a developmental math class may feel "inferior" in their capacity to succeed and be conflicted about the value of putting forth effort or "industry" into the tasks they are assigned. In Erikson's language, they are faced with the conflict of "inferiority versus industry" and must resolve it in order to accomplish the tasks at hand. However, a single resolution of a conflict does not mean that the conflict is permanently eliminated. Over time, learners will revisit old conflicts in new and different circumstances, and new resolutions must be achieved for further learning to take place.

Like Erikson, Piaget (1966) describes the learner as "stage bound." At first, learners interpret new experiences in terms of existing mental structures. Eventually, however, they alter those structures in order to explain new experiences, and this results in higher-level thinking. The impetus to develop and use new structures usually results from maturation and experience. Piaget, whose work was done with young children, did not say much about individual differences and how they affect learning. Even so, the idea that learners progress through a series of set stages, each more complex than the one before, is an important contribution to our understanding of the learner.

Perry views the learner as someone who develops through encounters with the world that raise "cognitive dissonance." As a stage theorist, he describes the learner as moving through a series of worldviews beginning with a simple, dualistic view characterized by well-defined notions of what is right and wrong and moving up through stages to a relativistic view. Here, knowledge is disconnected from a rigid concept of truth and instead is viewed in a complex, analytical way that identifies assumptions, draws implications, and evaluates different points of view. Even though Perry's work focused exclusively on men, it is a valuable contribution to our view of the learner.

According to cognitive stage theorists, the learner moves through a continuous series of steps, from simple to complex, often moving back and forth among stages depending on circumstances. A level of understanding reached in one learning task may need to be completely reworked in another. Exactly how this progression occurs and why it varies so among different individuals has not been fully explained.

Studies have found that problem solving takes place in five discrete stages (D'Zurilla and Goldfried, 1971). These problem-solving stages are hierarchical, each one being dependent on the successful completion of the one preceding it. The stages of problem solving begin with the acceptance of the fact that problems are normal features of reality. The second stage is problem identification and verification, and the third is generation of alternative solutions. In the fourth stage, a selection is made from that set of alternatives, and in the fifth and final stage, the selection is verified and evaluated. This research based on stage theory is helpful in daily practice. No matter what content area is being studied, it is important to recognize the learner's need to proceed methodically through a set of well-defined stages leading to a satisfactory solution.

Principle Two: *The learner behaves in ways that are related to self-concept and self-efficacy beliefs.*

Self-concept, or beliefs about one's own nature and unique qualities, is integral to an understanding of the learner. Ideas about self-concept and its importance in learning are present in the person-centered theory of Carl Rogers (1961). Self-concept can affect the learner in a variety of ways, not the least of which is as a self-fulfilling prophecy. For example, one person may view the self as hardworking and behave in ways that support that view. Another individual may view the self as easygoing, and as a result of this belief, lack initiative or drive to succeed in challenging situations.

If one views oneself as "intelligent" but receives poor grades, a gap exists between the self-concept and reality—a phenomenon referred to as "incongruence." Everyone experiences some incongruence, but the crucial issue is how much. Too much incongruence can undermine one's psychological well-being and create significant barriers to learning.

There are numerous studies investigating the relationship between overall academic achievement and self-concept. Whereas some of these studies have found positive relationships, others have not found any significant relationship. Although inconsistent findings may be confusing to the practitioner, patterns of research findings can give some guidance. For example, a summary of findings on the effect of rewards on learning shows that extrinsic rewards can enhance academic performance, and this is especially true when the rewards are combined with other forms of reinforcement (Flippo and Caverly, 1991). Other studies related to self-concept have shown that individual counseling of students on academic probation resulted in improved grade point averages (Kulik and Kulik, 1991).

Research findings like this can demonstrate to the practitioner the importance of integrating counseling sessions into academic intervention programs and of maintaining a carefully designed system of reinforcements.

Self-efficacy, or the belief in one's ability to complete a particular task, is not the same as self-concept, but it is closely related to it. Research has shown that academic performance is related to self-efficacy beliefs. For example, Bandura (1986) suggests that unrealistically high self-efficacy beliefs may have a detrimental effect on performance because such beliefs may encourage individuals to try activities with a high probability of failure. Of course, gross underestimates of academic ability may also have a negative impact on performance. When a student grossly underestimates ability, the result may be avoidance of potentially rewarding experiences—for example, certain courses in college.

One study of the effect of self-efficacy beliefs on academic performance (O'Brien, Brown, and Lent, 1989) found that self-efficacy beliefs that approximate the ability of the student are facilitative of academic performance and that for underprepared students, overestimating one's ability may be detrimental to academic performance.

In practice, it is helpful to know how the overestimation or underestimation of one's ability may affect academic performance. For example, if academic performance is facilitated by self-efficacy beliefs that closely approximate ability, intervention strategies to promote realistic ability appraisals may be the first step toward success.

Principle Three: *The successful learner interacts with the environment in a unique way that results in a natural tendency toward growth and development and the desire to meet basic needs.*

Behavior is the result of an interaction effect between the person and the environment. Each individual interacts differently with each unique environment, which makes generalized predictions about behavior tentative at best. Some forty years ago, Lewin (1951) contributed this idea to our understanding of individual differences. We now accept the notion that the learner is someone with highly specific and individualized needs and behaviors. In any one setting, two different learners may respond in very dissimilar ways.

For example, the environment of a noninteractive, highly structured straight lecture class may be experienced quite differently by two students. The student who is comfortable with the auditory presentation of material and does not desire opportunities for group discussion is likely to be satisfied in this setting. However, the student who needs the opportunity for collaborative learning and discussion and desires a variety of presentation modes is likely to be frustrated. The uniqueness of each learner and the interaction effect between setting and learner can yield highly diverse results. To understand the learner, we must describe both the individual characteristics of the person and the important features of the specific environment of interaction.

One way to explain these differences is through Maslow's theory of motivation. According to Maslow (1970), all individuals are motivated to behave so that basic needs are fulfilled, and needs are arranged hierarchically according to priority. For example, physiological and safety needs have priority over love and esteem needs. In the educational context, the learner who has significant unmet safety needs will be focused primarily on getting those met, often at the expense of other goals such as performing well academically. However, even when the learner is distracted by the priority of a more basic need, behavior always has a natural tendency toward growth and satisfaction. Maslow's conception of the learner is positive. Individuals are viewed as striving toward excellence through behaviors aimed at satisfying basic needs.

The uniqueness of individual responses to learning environments has been well established in research. Kulik and Kulik (1991) cite studies that point to the importance of adjusting instruction to individual learner characteristics, including learning rate, motivation, and personality. One instructional example is found in Bloom's "mastery learning" approach (1982). The recognition that individuals have different rates of learning is a central component of Bloom's research and principles of practice. Another example of unique responses to environment is found in the research related to individual learning styles. Research in this area has shown that learners differ not only in rate of learning but in the way they learn. These differing styles take many forms and are presented as preferences—for example, a preference for learning analytically rather than globally, or for acquiring information visually rather than auditorily. The practitioner can put research on learning rate and style to good use by tailoring instruction to individual differences.

Principle Four: *The learner is concerned about establishing or reinforcing a sense of identity in the college learning experience.*

The primary theorist dealing with identity development in the college student is Chickering (1969). At the core of his theory are seven vectors of identity development in young adulthood, among them developing competence, managing emotions, developing autonomy, and clarifying purpose. If we are to understand the learner, we must know what is involved in each of these vectors. For example, how does one become competent in a task? What goes on in the process of becoming autonomous? How does a learner manage emotions and clarify purpose in the learning environment?

Like Lewin, Chickering emphasizes the importance of the learner interacting with the environment. The college environment is seen as a source of potential supports and challenges. Its characteristics include the clarity and consistency of the college's objectives, the size of the institution, the type of curriculum and teaching, the atmosphere in the residence halls or commuter lounge, the nature of the faculty and administration, and the type of student culture on campus. As the student strives to complete the task of identity development and interacts with major elements in the college environment, specific behaviors result that either promote or impede learning. Sometimes student learning outcomes are attributed to a factor called "institutional fit," predicated on the idea that student success depends on the "match" between student and institutional characteristics. The better the match, the more likely the student is to succeed in the learning environment.

Some interesting research in the area of identity formation is found in the work of Branch-Simpson (1984), who studied the way developmental tasks are achieved by African-American students. Whereas Chickering found identity formation to be characterized by achievement orientation for men and relationship orientation for women, Branch-Simpson found that with African-American students, identity formation in both sexes is achieved in relationships with extended family. Knowing the influence of family on African-American students, and particularly the influence on the formation of identity, is of paramount importance in the design and delivery of instruction. Is course content challenging long-standing values and mores of particular African-American cultures? If so, how is this going to affect the academic performance of African-American

students? These are important questions for all educators and particularly for developmental educators who are working to improve
access and quality for previously underrepresented groups.

Principle Five: *The learner has specific needs and ways of learning
as an adult that are distinct from those of younger students.*

One of the best-known "theories" of adult learning is andragogy.
However, the idea of andragogy as a theory has been challenged
because it has not been tested and validated. Many prefer to call it
a philosophical stance concerning adult education. We will not
debate this issue here. Andragogy may actually be seen as a set of
principles effective with adults. Promoted by Knowles (1990), the
main elements of andragogy are the adult learner's needs to be
involved in the planning of instruction, to formulate personal learning objectives, and to be intimately involved in evaluating learning. The effective learning climate for adult learners is characterized
by collaboration, trust, and mutual respect. Overall, the adult
learner requires freedom from authority and control.

The concept of self-directed learning is also relevant for the
adult learner—indeed, the concept is considered central by some
specialists. In self-directed learning, students assume primary responsibility for their own education. For example, students may prepare
learning contracts in which they commit themselves to specific
activities that will advance them toward their course goals. Instead
of working on teacher-developed tasks, they develop their own. In
order for adult learners to be self-directed, they must have a well-
developed sense of autonomy and be able to work relatively free of
direction from others. Self-directed learning is seen as both a characteristic of adult learners and a goal to be attained.

Research in the area of adult learning is relatively new. There is
much that still needs to be discovered about the way adults in general and individually approach learning. For example, are adults by
nature autonomous and self-directed in their learning, or are their
responses more situational? Can adults be taught to be more self-
directed, or is this characteristic relatively fixed? Answers to these

questions will be important research contributions and will help define and direct programming and instruction for adults as they enter educational institutions in ever-increasing numbers.

Principle Six: *The learner approaches tasks in ways that are often characterized by differences specific to gender.*

Although this principle focuses on differences between men and women, not everything about the sexes is characterized by difference. We know, for example, that both men and women move through identifiable stages in their development. However, it is how they progress and the patterns of behavior through these progressions that distinguish them from each other.

Belenky, Clinchy, Goldberger, and Tarule (1986) use Perry's stages to compare and contrast the differences between men and women. Although it is recognized that both sexes move through stages, what occurs within the stages is quite different for each sex. For example, it has been found that women do not relate to authority figures in the way men do. Women tend to be hesitant to challenge authority, whereas men are open to criticizing it. For women, learning occurs through discussion and sharing, whereas for men it is achieved through argumentation. In the reasoning process, men tend to base their thinking on logic and objectivity. Women's reasoning is most often based on feelings and relationships.

It is important to be mindful that all generalizations have exceptions. Even though the above findings hold true for *groups* of women and men, there will always be individuals whose attributes differ from those ascribed to the group. However, understanding that women learners as a group have characteristics that are different from those of men is crucial to the design and delivery of instruction.

Research on women's cognitive development is exemplified in the work of Baxter Magolda (1989), who asked whether women and men differ in their views of knowledge and their approaches to learning and whether women and men exhibit differences within cognitive structures and learning styles. Her research showed that women rely greatly on concrete experiences in their learning and use intuition more frequently than men. In addition, the role of relationship to others was found to be a significant factor in women's personal and educational decision making. These examples from research point to the importance of including concrete, personal experiences in the learning environment and for providing opportunities for intuitive responses in the classroom.

What Is the Teaching/Learning Process?

Principle One: *An effective process assesses and values the learner's talents and experiences and proceeds from that point to maximize potential.*

Bloom, in his writings about a theory of learning, states that "modern societies no longer can content themselves with the selection of talent; they must find the means for developing talent" (1982, p. 298). This is an important instructional framework for educators, who too frequently believe that the student arrives with little talent and few valuable experiences. Instruction often proceeds with the goal of fixing deficiencies and trying to minimize the effects of the past. Bloom disagrees with this notion. He believes that the learner's history is at the core of the learning process. The instructor must understand the individual's past and utilize it to construct new learning.

Hull and Rose have conducted considerable classroom research that validates the importance of getting under the surface of a student's written or oral presentation to promote new connections. They assert that teachers "transcend deficit attitudes when teaching serves to invite rather than deny." Their study describes a strategy of engaging in a dialogue with a student whose response to a poem is initially incomprehensible to the instructor (Hull and Rose, 1990). The method proves effective, as it clarifies for the instructor the thinking process of the student and how he truly has connected his prior experiences to the poem. This dialogue leads to constructive teaching rather than a disregard for the student's culturally determined response.

Table 7.2. What Is the Teaching/Learning Process? An Overview.

Principles	Research/Theory
1. An effective process assesses and values the learner's talents and experiences and proceeds from that point to maximize potential.	Bloom; Rose; Bruner; Belenky, Clinchy, Goldberger, Tarule; Cross; Vygotsky; Knox
2. An effective process assumes that almost every learner has the potential for growth.	Bloom; Carroll; Sternberg; Kulik and Kulik
3. An effective process facilitates transfer to new learning situations.	Freire; Lochhead; Rose; Anderson and Armbruster; Wittrock; Weinstein and Mayer; Dole, Duffy, Roehler, Pearson; Paris; Stahl; Brown, Campione, Day; Brown, Armbruster, Baker; Dansereau; Schallert, Lemonnier, Alexander and Goetz; Burmeister
4. An effective process increases cognitive self-awareness and encourages the learner to gradually assume responsibility for learning.	Fischer and Mandl; Wang; Caverly and Orlando; Weinstein and Mayer; Simpson and Nist; Pearson; Winograd and Hare; Hermann; Paris; McCombs; Dansereau; Dole, Duffy, Roehler, Pearson; Davey; Casazza
5. An effective process recognizes that learning goes beyond cognitive development and includes risk taking and personal transformation.	Brookfield; McClusky; Daloz; Mezirow

Another theorist who asserted the importance of starting where the learner is was Bruner (1960). He suggested, through his spiral curriculum, that new learning could be facilitated by using the individual's established modes of thinking and either activating or reconfiguring them. Bruner saw learning as a problem-solving experience and suggested that instructors find a way to link new problems to some aspect of the learner's thinking that was already in place. Not only did Bruner acknowledge the significance of the learner's current abilities, but he used them to facilitate further development. This parallels Hull and Rose's strategy for providing assistance to basic writers.

Belenky, Clinchy, Goldberger, and Tarule (1986) theorized about the way women learn. They suggested that knowledge is often latently present in the learner, and that the role of the instructor is similar to that of a midwife. The primary responsibility is to draw from the learner the knowledge that exists but has just not yet been articulated. They advocated that through acceptance and collaboration, the instructor guide learners to develop their own voice. This perspective also implies that a value is being attached to learners' talents and experiences that have simply not yet been discovered.

The pluralistic model for instruction suggested by Cross (1983) also assumes that talents exist in students that have not been valued by the educational system. Cross felt that the talents of "new students" were not being acknowledged. She proposed an instructional system based on the three general areas of data, people, and things. According to Cross, these areas cover the basic competencies needed for employment. She suggested developing one of these areas—selected on the basis of the students' entering strengths—to a point of excellence; the other two would be developed to a level of adequacy. Cross believed that too often in the traditional curriculum, students' weaknesses are highlighted as they are forced into study that does not build on their talents. She surmised that many "new students" had unacknowledged talent in the area of working with people.

These theorists have emphasized the importance of recognizing the existing talents of the learner and using them as building blocks for new learning. Others, having acknowledged the same point, have gone on to emphasize the maximizing of student potential. Vygotsky (1965), for example, urged that instruction begin with a determination of what a learner can do independently (the lowest threshold) and continue with guidance across the "zone of proximal development"—the area in which the learner cannot operate without assistance—to the point of independence at a more advanced level (the upper threshold).

Knox (1986) also emphasized the significance of maximizing performance. His "proficiency theory" looked at setting optimal standards for the learner, similar to Vygotsky's upper threshold, and providing opportunities for reaching those proficiencies. He asserted that learning would best be facilitated by determining the discrepancy between the incoming proficiency level and the desired level. The instructor, according to Knox, acts as a change agent who can facilitate achievement of the higher level. Both Vygotsky and Knox viewed the learning process as an opportunity for a person to develop to the highest possible standard. This perspective, in addition to valuing the learner's existing talents, places a very positive framework around the instructional process.

Principle Two: *An effective process assumes that almost every learner has the potential for growth.*

Although the learning theory of Bloom (1982) evolved from a behaviorist foundation more than did the theories of Vygotsky and Knox, Bloom promoted the very positive construct that almost everyone can learn given the right conditions and enough time. Instruction, for Bloom, too, begins with determining where the student is, but then it proceeds on a prescribed linear path that is based on the individual's rate of learning. Bloom emphasizes the importance of external reinforcement and sets minimal standards of competence, usually at 70 percent mastery; Knox and Vygotsky would focus on a higher threshold of achievement.

Bloom was influenced by Carroll's "model of school learning" (1967), which argued that given a normal distribution of students, the majority would achieve mastery if the kind and quality of instruction as well as the amount of time allocated for learning were made "appropriate to the characteristics and needs of each learner" (p. 724). A significant feature of both Bloom's and Carroll's theories is that rather than assuming that a performance problem arises from the learner, they put the responsibility for achievement on the instructional process.

With the regular reinforcement that is built into these instructional models, students clearly see that they are capable of succeeding and receive immediate feedback when they make an error. The negative aspect to this approach is that if it is used without additional instruction to explain how an error was made, students are dependent on external reinforcement; they do not need to become active learners or monitors of their own development.

A very different perspective on the potential for growth has been suggested by Sternberg (1988). His triarchic theory of intelligence assumes that intelligence can be taught and that it is a much broader construct than traditionally defined. He emphasizes the significance of practical intelligence in addition to the abilities to analyze and to synthesize. Sternberg argues that in adulthood, tacit knowledge, or the ability to get along in one's environment, contributes to success more than the traditional IQ measure. Traditional testing depends too much on speed, which is not necessarily significant in the real world. One of the strengths of Sternberg's work is that he has developed instructional materials to facilitate its practical application. His problem-solving exercises could easily be integrated across the curriculum as critical thinking components.

Both the behavioral influence of Bloom's theory and the cognitive perspective of Sternberg's are significant to the field of developmental education. Sternberg questions the traditional notion that simply because students' standardized test scores are low, they are incapable of advanced learning. He also places a value on the social component of intelligence, the ability to "manipulate" one's environment. This is frequently a strength of returning older students and needs to be seen as an achievement.

Although Bloom's theory assigns learners a more limited role by placing much of the control in the hands of the instructor, his work has a valid place in learning assistance. For developmental students who have often experienced failure in the educational setting, Bloom's mastery learning provides an opportunity to immediately experience success. By breaking the learning task into small units and providing reinforcement at each step, this system builds confidence and a foundation for further learning. Indeed Bloom thought the affective component as important as the skill-building element.

In a comprehensive analysis, Kulik and Kulik (1991) found that mastery learning had a positive effect in college and high school classes. When it was used, scores on criterion exams generally increased for college learners from the 50th to the 75th percentile, low-aptitude students gained more on test scores with a mastery learning approach than without, and students developed positive attitudes toward the subject matter. Kulik and Kulik (1987) also reviewed forty-nine studies to examine what effect, if any, specific components of mastery learning had. They found the following elements contributed to increased achievement: frequent formative testing with or without required mastery and a requirement that low scorers on formative tests do make-up work. It seems that ongoing assessment with feedback and additional instruction when necessary should be built into any curriculum, developmental or core.

Principle Three: *An effective process facilitates transfer to new learning situations*.

Even though mastery learning shows positive effects in terms of test scores and attitude, in order to facilitate transfer, the instructional process must encourage the active participation of the learner and emphasize critical thinking. One of the foremost advocates of this approach is Freire (1970), a Brazilian educator. He popularized the active approach to learning by distinguishing between a "banking" instructional system and one that is problem-centered.

When instruction is based on a banking approach, learners are viewed as empty vessels into which knowledge must be deposited. This implies that learners are passive and promotes what Lochhead (1985) has called the "copy theory of learning." Frequently, learners are most comfortable with this authoritative approach, as it minimizes their fear of public failure and represents a teaching method with which they may be most familiar. A problem-posing approach, on the other hand, views the teacher as a partner in the learning process and as one who is responsible for helping the learner to think critically and to see learning through a problem-solving lens. Freire emphasizes the importance of developing the learner's "critical consciousness" and ability to reflect, two assets that can be transferred to all learning situations.

Lochhead also emphasizes the importance of students being active as problem solvers, even when they are simply listening to a lecture. As they listen, they should be questioning, organizing, and reorganizing as they reflect on the information that is being shared. Lochhead suggests that often, students are poor thinkers and less active because they do not believe there is anything they can do other than come up with right or wrong answers to questions. This perspective is reinforced in classrooms where discussion follows the IRE sequence. Hull, Rose, Fraser, and Castellano (1991) frequently observed in their classroom study that instructors *initiate* the class activity; look for a correct *response* to a question; and then *evaluate* the response on the basis of how well it matches their expectation. Students in such learning situations are not really active participants; rather, they are merely trying to guess what the instructor wants.

In contrast, Lochhead teaches students how to think actively, through his training in pair problem solving. He has students articulate their processing strategies to a peer as they work through problems. In addition, he shows them how to become active listeners when it is their partner's turn to verbalize. Through this model, the instructor becomes somewhat like a coach, using a Socratic method to promote thinking. This strategy has been used effectively in a reading class where students work in pairs to comprehend text. One student talks through the processing of information while a partner listens and then asks questions. When they can come to a consensus on the meaning of a particular section, the listening partner becomes the speaker (Casazza, 1993).

The concept of *transfer appropriate processing* also emphasizes the active nature of learning. It refers to the learner's goals when incoming information is being processed. According to the research of Anderson and Armbruster (1984), learners' understanding and expectations of what they will do with new information influence how they will process it. For example, if learners believe they will not need the information in the future, they may process it on a more superficial level than they would if they considered it more applicable. This has direct implications for the instructor. When presenting information, the instructor must explain its relevance and suggest connections with either prior knowledge or future applications.

If practitioners are to optimally facilitate learning, they should be aware of the information processing model of cognition, which has four basic stages: acquisition of new knowledge; encoding of the information in short-term memory and transfer to long-term memory; integration of the information in long-term memory; and retrieval of information when it is needed in the future.

This processing is closely linked to schema theory, which explains how retrieval of stored information is facilitated when it has been organized in an orderly way. The operation is much like that of a filing system, where items are placed in folders that are labeled so that new items can be filed appropriately and old items found when necessary. This filing system does not happen automatically; someone has to develop labels that describe the folders' contents and distinguish one from another. Likewise, the processing of new knowledge and its organization for future reference do not happen automatically; these activities must be learned.

What is the developmental educator's role in facilitating this process? When new information is being presented, instructors need to relate it to prior knowledge and to suggest where it might be filed and why. This implies that instructors understand the prior knowledge students are likely to have stored and how it might have been organized. For instance, if the new information is related to re-seeing reading as an active, constructive process, instructors might refer to what students may have stored in memory about reading being a process of decoding words. As they teach the new perspective, they can contrast it with the older one and then provide a model by talking through both processes as they attempt to "comprehend" a sample text aloud for the students.

Using this cognitive view of learning as a basis, Weinstein and Mayer (1986) have proposed a framework for the teaching-learning process that asserts that the learning outcome depends "jointly on what information is presented and on how the learner processes that information" (p. 316). The strategies of the learner are at least as significant as those of the teacher, a concept ignored in earlier, behaviorist models of teaching. Cognitivists assume that the learner is actively involved in the process and needs to have a set of strategies to apply when taking in new information. Bloom's model of mastery learning ignores this cognitive processing component and probably does not greatly enhance transfer as a result.

Weinstein and Mayer (1986) argue that learning strategies can be taught, and that they do indeed lead to more effective learning. Their research (conducted in 1982) indicates that students have shown gains in academic performance, reading comprehension, and stress reduction in core coursework following participation in an undergraduate learning strategies course. They have constructed eight categories of learning strategies, ranging from rehearsal to elaboration to organization for both simple and complex learning tasks.

Their categories are based on an information processing model of learning. A range of strategies is offered that allows students to be more aware of their general processing methods, and this in turn promotes transfer to a variety of learning tasks. For example, a rehearsal strategy for a complex task could be underlining significant ideas in a text. An organizational strategy for a complex task could include outlining. These strategies each relate to a different stage of the information processing model and consequently affect overall ability to learn effectively.

Wittrock (1986) confirms this view with his model of learning strategies that identifies three cognitive processes: attention, motivation, and comprehension. He contends that learners must focus carefully on the instruction but must attribute subsequent outcomes to their own efforts. They must also relate the task at hand and the available materials to their own knowledge and from that interaction construct a meaningful learning experience.

Dole, Duffy, Roehler, and Pearson (1991) have drawn a distinction between skills and strategies that seems important when we consider the factors that facilitate transfer. They define *skills* as representing lower levels of thinking that are simply automatic routines. Skills, in this definition, are fairly rigid and are used with little conscious intent on the part of the learner. *Strategies*, in contrast, involve reasoning and reflection and are applied intentionally, with an awareness of the underlying rationale. Because of this, strategies are more adaptable than skills. Paris, Lipson, and Wixson (1983) have referred to them as "skills under consideration."

A study technique called SQ3R (survey, question, read, recite, and review) can illustrate how a method could develop as either a skill or a strategy, depending on how it is taught. If students are simply told to apply SQ3R to reading a short practice passage, they probably will never use the technique again outside of their "Reading 095" class. It will seem time-consuming, rigid, and often not suited to their purpose for reading. In contrast, if a rationale is discussed for each step, and if each component is modeled by the instructor, students will understand why it is often an effective strategy and how it can be adapted for a variety of reading purposes.

Brown, Campione, and Day (1981) have conducted research that compares blind training techniques—where students are simply told that a particular method is effective—to cognitive skills training. They concluded that when students are not given a rationale for a technique, there is no transfer; the students do not understand how to adapt techniques like SQ3R to new situations. In related studies, Brown, Armbruster, and Baker (1986) found that when training in cognitive skills includes an awareness component related to why the techniques are effective, students begin to recognize how to adapt to the "task at hand, the nature of the material, and their personal preferences and abilities" (p. 67). This produces a greater level of control and an ability to solve problems that transfers across settings and tasks.

Other studies have shown that transfer is most likely to occur when the strategy is directly related to the learning task at hand. On the basis of these findings, Dansereau (1985) suggested that either of two approaches may be effective: teach strategies that fall in a middle range between general and specific or teach from a hierarchical perspective, starting with the most general and moving to the more specific. For example, a general skill could be note taking by the Cornell method (Pauk, 1974). If a hierarchical approach is used, instruction could begin with an explanation of the overall format, following which students could be asked to apply it as they listen to a simulated lecture. Greater specificity could then be added by providing information on how to proceed from the overall format to utilization of the notes for purposes such as objective tests, essays, or oral presentations. Even narrower specificity could be addressed by looking at organizational patterns within specific disciplines—for example, math problems and solutions and historical chronologies. By adding a metacognitive component, an explanation of why a particular strategy is being applied, the instructor would make it very clear when a certain application would be appropriate or inappropriate.

In related research, Schallert, Lemonnier, Alexander, and Goetz (1988) recommended integrating strategy training into the instructional system to promote optimal transfer. They asserted that students need strategies that they will immediately apply to their core content work. Indeed, Stahl, Simpson, and Hayes (1992) have included "high utility strategies for immediate acceptance" as one of their ten principles for teaching high-risk college students (p. 6). Such a model has been used in supplemental instruction, where an adjunct instructor attends a given content class with students and then, in supplemental sessions, discusses strategies that would best facilitate their learning. Results indicate that students who attend the extra sessions persist longer and achieve appreciably higher grades than those who do not (Burmeister, 1994).

Weinstein and Mayer (1986) have stressed the effect of direct instruction on transfer. Their research shows that to facilitate transfer from a college reading class to regular classes, direct instruction is most effective. Paris, Lipson, and Wixson (1983) have suggested a successful model for strategy training based on research that highlights five components. First, the training must be functional and meaningful: the model stresses finding a match between the task, the context, and the strategy. Second, it should address the rationale behind the strategy, including a consideration of when application of the strategy would be most appropriate. Third, the learner must be convinced that the strategy is worth the time and practice necessary to apply it effectively. Fourth, the training should instill confidence and increased feelings of self-efficacy in the learner. Finally, control must be transferred from the instructor to the learner. This important step leads to the next principle, which includes the gradual release of responsibility to the student.

Principle Four: *An effective process increases cognitive self-awareness and encourages the learner to gradually assume responsibility for learning.*

Closely related to successful transfer and active involvement in the learning process is the learner's level of cognitive self-awareness, or metacognition—that is, an awareness of how information is processed. A more specific component of this self-awareness is cognitive monitoring, which includes the ability to evaluate one's understanding of incoming information and also to control it by applying the most appropriate learning strategies. This implies two things: first, that the learner knows when a breakdown in understanding occurs and, second, that he or she has a repertoire of strategies to apply in order to "fix it."

Fischer and Mandl (1989) interviewed college students about their metacognitive awareness and the study strategies they applied during text processing. They found that those classified as good readers were more aware of the nature of the task and their own problems during processing and were more flexible in adapting to the task than those students who were considered to be poor readers. These weaker students expressed a more emotional response, as they concluded that any problems they encountered were simply a confirmation of the failure that they expected. In related research, Wang (1983) found that self-monitoring by learners increased the acquisition, generalization, and transfer of knowledge and skills.

Caverly and Orlando (1991) used a tetrahedral model to review the literature on the use of study strategies. They explain the necessity of teaching students that in an effective study strategy, all four vertices on this model must interact: students' own abilities and knowledge; the text structure, including length and content; the orienting task or assignment; and the criterion task, the final outcome. Too often, instruction prescribes one type of strategy for one type of task, which leads the student to believe that there is little decision making involved. The tetrahedral model indicates that if students are truly to have control over the learning process, they must consider all four vertices.

One of the strategies that Caverly and Orlando suggest for increasing students' awareness of how these variables interact is to present them with a "demand model" for choosing study strategies. This model places strategies on a continuum ranging from effective (heavy teacher/material demands) to efficient (light teacher/material demands). The students are taught to decide which strategy to consider on the basis of the continuum's two criteria: teacher demands and material demands. When the teacher's demands are heavy, for instance, students may want to outline the material in a textbook; when the teacher's demands are light, they may simply choose to reread the text. Likewise, when the material demands are heavy, students may need to outline; when they are light, rereading may be sufficient. The significant element here is that the students are making a conscious decision based on several variables.

These perspectives imply that effective learning strategies depend on active learners who are aware of their own repertoires of strategies and can utilize them flexibly and appropriately. In Weinstein and Mayer's theoretical scheme of learning strategies (1985), they have also included the "management" strategy of comprehension monitoring, which they assert "requires the student to establish learning goals for an instructional unit or activity, to assess the degree to which these goals are being met, and, if necessary, to modify the strategies being used to meet these goals" (p. 323). According to Weinstein and Mayer, poor comprehenders generally lack these strategies.

One successful method for operationalizing the metacognitive process has been outlined by Simpson and Nist (1984). Their model, PLAE, takes students through four stages as they learn how to evaluate and take control of their learning through study strategies. For a given task, they first *preplan* by defining what they must do and setting goals. Next, they *list* appropriate strategies and make a specific study plan. Third, they *activate* the plan and monitor its effectiveness. Finally, they *evaluate* their plan following completion of the task. Research has shown PLAE to increase the metacognition and test performance of high-risk college students across the curriculum (Nist and Simpson, 1989).

Weinstein and Mayer (1986) cite several approaches for teaching self-monitoring. Most of them include the modeling of cognitive strategies and the use of self-statements that help learners guide their processing and evaluate its effectiveness. For instance, learners may start with "What is it I have to do?" and finish with "That worked well because . . ." These statements guide learners toward accepting more responsibility for learning as they become more conscious of their own strategies.

A more comprehensive approach to releasing this responsibility to the student is Pearson's model of *explicit instruction* (1984). In his design, the responsibility for "task completion" begins with teacher modeling and then proceeds through guided practice, where the responsibility is shared jointly between teacher and learner, to the final stage, where the student is fully responsible. This model emphasizes the importance of a gradual release that can be implemented through various instructional methods. One example is reciprocal teaching (Hermann, 1988), where instructors first verbalize their own processing of a task and then relinquish the modeling to a student, who in turn passes it on to others.

Most models for direct instruction that are designed to release the responsibility for learning include both a teacher explanation and a modeling component. Winograd and Hare (1988) conducted research that showed the explanation portion of instruction to be critical. In their review of models for teaching learning strategies, they found that the explanation needed to be "metacognitive, not mechanistic. They (the teachers) make students aware of the purpose of the skill and how successful readers use it to activate, monitor, regulate and make sense out of text" (p. 125).

Winograd and Hare suggest that a good teacher explanation consists of five parts. In the first part, the strategy is described. In the second, the teacher explains why learning it is necessary. This begins to lead the student from teacher dependence to self-control. Third, the teacher explains how to use the strategy, breaking it down into segments. Garner's research (1987) on independent strategy usage found that students often master part of a strategy and proceed to apply only that part. She suggested that strategies not be taught as a unitary whole but rather broken into logical segments, with instruction proceeding from one to another so that mastery of each can be assured.

The fourth part of a good explanation, according to Winograd and Hare, deals with when and where the strategy can be applied. At this point, the teacher may suggest both appropriate and inappropriate applications. Finally, the student must learn how to evaluate the effectiveness of the strategy. These final two steps are crucial if the student is to assume responsibility for learning. Considered to be conditional knowledge (that is, an understanding of the conditions in which a strategy will be most effective) by Paris, Lipson, and Wixson (1983), these two steps are the least frequently found during instruction but are probably the most significant in releasing control to the student. They are the steps that go beyond a mechanistic approach and address the importance of adaptability and metacognitive awareness of when a strategy works or does not work.

McCombs (1986) suggests that perceived personal control is central to any model of strategy training designed to increase the student's metacognitive awareness. She emphasizes the importance of directly addressing motivational aspects of learning and not assuming that they will automatically feature in strategy training. Her motivational strategies include teaching students how to maintain positive self-evaluations and how to manage and maintain control of perceived learning problems. Her research indicates that establishing this metacognitive self-awareness is integral to an intrinsic motivation to learn and leads to student perceptions of control and self-direction. She suggests that once this is developed, students are more apt to utilize other learning strategies. In other words, students must learn to change negative attitudes before they will use self-management skills and learning strategies.

Teacher modeling is a key component in releasing responsibility to the student. Dansereau (1985) found it to be a most significant instructional method. Dole, Duffy, Roehler, and Pearson (1991) have likened instructional modeling to scaffolding that exists solely to permit a process of construction to take place. This scaffolding is gradually pulled away or restructured, depending on the needs of the student. For modeling to be most effective, it must be explicit and flexible and must include a rationale. Dansereau concluded that students' intrinsic motivation is maximized when a substantial rationale is provided with any instruction.

Modeling can include a variety of methods. Certainly, a verbal articulation of one's thoughts is effective. Davey (1983) developed a strategy of "think-alouds," where the instructor verbalized what went through her mind as she read portions of a text. This practice can then be released to the students as they engage in paired reading (Casazza, 1993) and think aloud to each other. Such interactive peer modeling has been shown to facilitate subsequent application in individual situations. Another type of modeling can be done with written examples—for example, the instructor can complete a task and provide written annotations for the students that explain how it was accomplished.

Assuming responsibility for learning and attributing success or failure to oneself constitute a major risk and imply that the learner is engaging in more than cognitive development.

Principle Five: *An effective process recognizes that learning goes beyond cognitive development and includes risk taking and personal transformation.*

We regularly encounter students for whom returning to school represents a major life change. Often, they do not have an extensive support system; in fact, the return to school may permanently cut them off from their culture, their established belief systems, and their friends and family. Brookfield (1990) has referred to this as "cultural suicide." Learners may experience resentment from former friends as schoolwork places increased demands on their time and they begin to reprioritize their activities. Peers may misinterpret this as elitist. The potential loss of their support network may cause students to stop out and ultimately drop out.

McClusky (1970) discusses the significance of having a support system in his theory of *margin*, where he explains that adult learners are continually looking for the energy that will provide a balance between their level of power and their load. Margin equals power level minus load. For instance, one's power might include strong family support, dependable employment, and financial resources, and one's load might include care of an elderly parent, enrollment as a full-time student, and a fifty-hour-a-week job.

McClusky contends that when individuals can find a reserve of power, they are more willing to take risks and are also better able to learn. When the load is greater than the power, it becomes a barrier to learning. An effective teaching process must take this into account by helping the student to find additional sources of power. This may mean that the instructor refers the learner to the counseling center or assumes a mentoring role or provides academic assistance. Another approach might be to invite to a class outside speakers who can serve as employment resources or role models. The underlying implication is that an effective instructor must know more about his or her students than how they perform in class.

An additional perspective on personal transformation resulting from the learning process comes from Daloz (1986). He asserts that personal growth is risky because much of what the individual is comfortable with is left behind in the process; therefore, it is the instructor's responsibility to act as a mentor. In this mentor role, it is imperative to foster personal growth along with cognitive development. The theories of both McClusky and Daloz suggest the importance of attending to the whole individual within the teaching/learning process. If a load is greater than a learner's power to handle it or if learners perceive that education is cutting them off too much from their former, comfortable environment, their learning will be affected. Indeed, without a "relationship of care" as Daloz describes it, they may decide to stop out or quit altogether.

Mezirow (Mezirow and Associates, 1990) has developed the concept of *perspective transformation* to help explain adult development. He contends that the learning process does more than add new knowledge; rather, it has the potential to transform the individual's ways of thinking. He describes the learner as someone who lives within a "meaning system"—a set of beliefs and assumptions through which life's experiences are filtered. When these basic assumptions are challenged and subsequently revised, the individual's view of the world is transformed. According to Mezirow, this occurs when learners have the opportunity to reflect critically and become aware of their own beliefs. Other theorists refer to a "change of consciousness" and place it at the center of adult growth and development.

Let us consider a change of consciousness that the nontraditional student may experience and how the teaching process can productively facilitate it. Suppose a student returns to school after serving in the military in a war zone. Several of his close friends have been killed there, and he has formed a very definite set of beliefs about U.S. involvement in the war. He not only believes that his country was right to become involved, but he has extended this belief to include a noncritical perspective toward everything the government does. The student is not particularly conscious of how unwilling to criticize the government he has become, but in his history class, he experiences problems when he is unable to objectively listen to or discuss current foreign policy issues. In fact, the instructor may find the student to be disruptive when the subject is raised.

In a case such as this, the instructor needs to be sensitive to the student's background and should confer with him privately. In addition, during class discussions, the instructor might verbalize his or own personal struggles to maintain objectivity on certain topics and the strategies that can be applied to overcome any biases. If cooperative learning or a group project is assigned, the instructor should ensure a grouping for the student that will challenge his beliefs through respectful discourse. One activity that would assist all the students to reflect critically on their attitudes and assumptions would be the writing of a weekly journal; this could form the foundation of a written dialogue between teacher and students. Over the course of the term, the student will likely become more conscious of his own beliefs, and he may also begin to see things from a different perspective as he listens, reflects, and discusses in small groups or works individually with the teacher or a tutor.

Summary

We have shown here how the TRPP model can be used to guide us so that principles of practice are connected to theory and research. Using TRPP to direct our activities and incorporating critical reflection in all that we do, we are fulfilling our role as professionals. Professionals share a general body of knowledge and can adapt knowledge and practice to novel situations. As new situations arise, we can address them using the TRPP framework, which advances us toward our goal of maximizing student potential.

Part III

. . . .

Shaping the Future

This final part challenges practitioners to take an active role in shaping their professional future, and this challenge takes three forms. Chapter Eight guides the reader through a thought process that can be applied to practitioner-based research. As stated throughout the text, our field of practice needs a firm conceptual base that integrates theory and practice with research. We must also take a scientific approach to demonstrate the value of our efforts to those who do not understand what we do.

The second challenge is issued in Chapter Nine, which describes the common ground that we all share. Here, the practitioner is asked to set aside differences and examine the professional and philosophical framework that directs us toward the common goal of maximizing student potential.

The third and final challenge is presented in Chapter Ten. This chapter lists six areas in which we must continue to be assertive and proactive. As we head into the next century, and as the educational system is directed to serve a more and more diverse population of students, our practice will become increasingly significant. No one is in a better position than we are to provide the services and resources that will be needed by those students. But it is crucial that we be prepared.

8

Conducting Research
to Advance Practice

As we reflect on our current practices and articulate the principles and theories that guide them, it becomes clear that we need to strengthen the research component of our field. Our experiences are significant, and in order to ensure that they become part of the growing body of literature dedicated to learning assistance and developmental education, we need to validate them formally. One way to do so is by applying the process of scientific investigation more regularly to our practice. This will help make our accomplishments today a resource for tomorrow's practitioner.

The field of learning assistance has evolved to its current stature mainly through the efforts of extremely earnest, dedicated practitioners. Its practical foundation is a strong one, in part because of the multidisciplinary backgrounds of its professionals. As stated often in this text, a learning assistance program is rarely based on one perspective; rather, it emanates from an integrated base combining ideas from many disciplines.

Although the multifaceted backgrounds of practitioners have a valuable contribution to the integrated approach found in the delivery of developmental education, they may have slowed down the attainment of a more coherent theoretical foundation. Learning assistance professionals have respected each other's perspectives and have accommodated each other as they have worked toward effective practice. This inclusive approach has generated a wealth of good practice but has ignored the importance of applying a scientific method that would give practice a unifying conceptual base.

The Exxon study (Boylan and others, 1992) confirmed that much of the practice being conducted in the field is effective, even though it is often based on intuition and experience rather than hard data. It made clear *within* the field that we know what we are doing. At the same time, it forced us to think about validating our efforts for those outside the area of learning assistance. The first National Conference on Research in Developmental Education, held in 1992, extended an invitation to practitioners to participate in additional scientific investigation. In addition to presenting a significant body of information related to developmental education, the conference challenged practitioners to continue the research enterprise and add to the knowledge base. Gathering input from those in attendance, Boylan and others (1993) compiled fifty ideas for future research. This chapter, looking at the process through the lens of a practitioner, discusses how such research might be conducted. Drawing on Boylan's suggested research topics, it identifies a likely area for inquiry and outlines a realistic process for conducting a scientific investigation.

The major purpose of this chapter is to guide the reader through a thought process that can be applied to most practitioner-related research. By "thinking aloud," the authors model a scientific approach to investigating a problem in the field of learning assistance. The chapter begins by articulating a research question and then proceeds to discuss the importance of framing any research within a set of ethical guidelines. Following this, a research framework is suggested that includes both qualitative and quantitative methods. Less attention is given to statistical measures than to general methodology. It is the *scientific thought process*, which determines the direction and ultimate significance of the research, that is emphasized.

Constructing the Framework

Frequently, in a staff meeting, someone will raise a question concerning the effectiveness of practice within the program. This is often followed by an informal discussion in which individuals share various perspectives based on their own experiences. If notes are taken, a written set of recommendations may result that provides a framework for future practice, and the program is likely to improve as a consequence. But how many other programs could also improve if such discussions led to formal investigations, the results of which were widely disseminated?

For the accumulated wisdom of practice to have more permanent, far-reaching effects, we as practitioners need to apply a scientific thought process to our activities. Suppose that when we raised an issue related to our programming, we constructed a formal research question and developed an inquiry process designed to find an answer to it. By following such a methodical process of investigation, we would validate our wisdom for a wider audience and contribute to the knowledge base of the field in general.

Focusing the Research Question

The issue of student persistence comes up regularly in discussions among learning assistance professionals. It was ranked high as an area for potential research at the 1992 national conference; consequently, it seems like a good subject to use in constructing a model for a scientific inquiry process.

How do we take the subject of persistence and the questions it raises and move them from the level of informal discussion to that of scientific study? The first step could be to brainstorm all the questions that are generated by the topic. The resulting list might look like this:

- How do we define persistence?

- Do developmental students who persist have character-istics that distinguish them from those who do not persist?

- Do persisters initially set goals for themselves that are different from those set by nonpersisters?

- Do persisters become more involved in institutional activities than do nonpersisters?

- Do developmental students who receive learning assistance persist longer than those who need it but reject it?

Although these questions stimulate a great deal of lively discussion, they provide little basis for a scientific inquiry. The second step of the process involves finding a focus for further study. This might involve narrowing the inquiry to one question and precisely defining the terms within that question. For the sake of setting up a model for inquiry, let us consider the last question from the brainstorming list: *Do developmental students who receive learning assistance persist longer than those who need it but reject it?* An investigation of this issue could have practical implications for mandatory assessment and placement as well as student advising and counseling. In other words, a formal inquiry could effect change at both the programmatic and institutional levels.

Defining the Terms

One thing we must do at the outset is to define the terminology we are using. What do we mean in this investigation by *persistence*? Are we referring to the number of consecutive academic terms for which a student enrolls? If this is the case, how many terms do we want to study—one, two, or more? What about the student who stops out for one term but returns? Do we include such a student in our study?

Another term that needs a more focused definition is *learning assistance*. Could this include one hour of tutoring, or must it be enrollment in a developmental course? Suppose a student needs three developmental courses but only registers for one; is that student included in the study? Do we want to limit our student sample to those who choose to use formal learning assistance, or do we include students who spend extra time outside of class with study groups or with the instructor?

We also need to define what we mean by *developmental student*. Is it the older student who is returning to school after many years out? Or is it the provisionally admitted student whose transcripts reflect grades and/or test scores that do not meet the institution's academic requirements? Perhaps it is the student who took placement tests on admission and received scores indicating the need for academic assistance? Should we consider only full-time students? If so, how do we define *full-time*?

Another way to bring a focus to this scientific inquiry would be to conduct a review of current literature. Reading professional articles related to learning assistance and student persistence may help us to define our terms and also to develop a hypothesis or simply a more refined question for our study. One way to organize information from such a review is to construct a chart using the relevant variables as headings. For instance, in this case, we might consider the following headings: population, type of institution, method of inquiry, focus, finding. We could then enter any significant information in columns under those headings.

Let us suppose that the literature review leads us to construct the following two-part research question about student persisters: (1) Do developmental students who seek learning assistance persist longer than those who need it but reject it? (2) Are there personal characteristics that distinguish those students who seek assistance from those who reject it? The very nature of this question implies that we must design an inquiry that includes all of the following: collection of student statistics, a quantitative approach, and the interpretation of more personalized input—a qualitative approach.

Now that we have a focused question to guide our inquiry, the terms can be defined and the goals of our research articulated. For the purpose of this study, we will define our terms as follows:

Developmental students: those students enrolling full-time whose placement test scores indicate that they need academic assistance in at least one area.

Learning assistance: enrollment in at least one developmental course and/or scheduling of at least two tutoring sessions during one academic term.

Persistence: full-time enrollment for at least three consecutive academic terms.

Full-time enrollment: registration for the minimum number of credit hours required to qualify for financial assistance.

Articulating the Goals of the Inquiry

In addition to the focused question and the well-defined terminology, we need to articulate the reasons we are conducting the study. As we consider our own rationale for the study, we must determine who will have access to the findings and who could be affected by them.

Although we may assume that scientific study is positive when it is conducted with the intention of improving programming and of better understanding students, it carries a certain risk. We may discover that a component of the learning assistance program is turning students away or that an institutional policy is contributing to students' reluctance to seek assistance. These components may be sensitive ones within the institution and may have implications for change outside the learning assistance program. For instance, the research may find that students who choose not to enroll in developmental coursework have been encouraged to bypass these courses by faculty advisers in their major areas of study in order to increase enrollments in their specialized areas. This could raise questions about the advising process, the credibility of the learning assistance program, admissions criteria, and mandatory placement into developmental coursework. Although such possibilities should not stop our research, they must be taken into consideration at the start.

Once we have considered the possible effects of the findings on institutional units, it is wise to specifically write down our goals and the intended audience for the final report. It also makes sense at this point to communicate these to the appropriate administrator(s) and to obtain any institutional permissions that might be necessary.

For this study, the following primary goals could be articulated:

1. To determine the percentage of students who seek learning assistance because their entering test scores indicate a need and who then enroll in the institution for at least three consecutive terms

2. To determine the percentage of students who choose not to receive learning assistance even though their entering test scores indicate a need and who do not enroll in the institution for at least three consecutive terms

3. To establish a control group by examining the percentage of students whose entering test scores do not indicate a need for learning assistance and who enroll for at least three consecutive terms

4. To determine if there are personal characteristics that distinguish the first two groups of students

5. To share the results of the study with all appropriate units across the institution, including department chairs, office of admissions, office of student affairs, office of academic affairs, and naturally, the learning assistance staff

6. To initiate an institutionwide discussion of the findings that will foster collaboration and further study to enhance student persistence

Two points about these goals should be noted. First, as written, they reflect only a descriptive study with no assumption of causation. Second, by stating at the beginning that the results will be shared across the institution and not limited to selected units, they lay a foundation for further, collaborative efforts.

Considering the Ethics

It is good practice to consider the ethical implications of a study at the start, as they may impact the overall research design. The researcher should be aware of relevant institutional policies as well as any guidelines that have been established by the profession. Institutional policies usually relate to the treatment of human subjects and are often found in faculty handbooks that may be available from the office of academic affairs.

The National Association for Developmental Education has included criteria related to ethics in the various components of its self-evaluation guides (Thayer, 1995). Adhering to such an accepted set of ethical standards within a profession reinforces a collegial bond as practitioners recognize a shared set of values. When these standards are regularly applied, the discipline itself becomes more formalized, and its scientific foundation is more easily validated. Thus, it is important for practitioners to reflect on and subsequently acknowledge those guidelines established by the profession that affect their particular project.

Basically, researchers should take into account the groups to whom they are responsible. The primary group is the student participants, but there are other significant groups, including colleagues and the institution as a whole.

The following guidelines are suggested as prompts for reflection. They are based on the NADE guides as well as elements generally found in institutional policies.

Related to Student Participants

- The study respects the confidentiality of records regarding individual students.

- The study respects the confidentiality of information obtained from student or faculty interviews.

- The researcher engages in no deception regarding the purpose of the study or the use of any information that is shared by students.

- The researcher engages in no activity that will harm the students' self-esteem or achievement.

- The researcher does not deny necessary services to students for the sake of scientific inquiry.

- The researcher is sensitive to any cultural or ethnic factors that may relate to the study.

- The researcher behaves in an objective, nonjudgmental manner when interacting with students.

- The researcher does not use unfair pressure to obtain participation.

Related to Colleagues

- The researcher acknowledges collaborative efforts appropriately.

- Limitations of the study are clearly articulated.

- Raw data remain available for purposes of validation and replication.

- The researcher engages in no activity that will intentionally limit the operations or the credibility of colleagues.

- The researcher informs colleagues of the study if it may have implications across institutional units.

Related to the Institution

- The research does not compromise the overall mission, goals, or standards of the institution.

- Funding related to the research is handled with established, responsible accounting procedures.

- Released time granted to the researcher is used responsibly.

- Procedures for gaining appropriate permission are identified and followed.

- Institutional data that are obtained for the study are used responsibly.

- The scope of the study is clearly articulated before the research begins.

- The audience for the final dissemination of findings is identified before the research begins.

Designing the Research Process

To strengthen the findings of a study, it is good practice to use multiple methods and sources for gathering information. This process is called *triangulation*, and it enhances the validity of the final data. For the purposes of the inquiry that we are thinking through in this chapter, four methods of collecting and analyzing data that reflect good practice are described: case study, participant-observation, survey, and a statistical test of significance. These procedures could theoretically be used alone or in a variety of combinations. They represent both quantitative and qualitative methodology, and again, if these two approaches are used together, the validity of the results is enhanced.

Once the methods for collecting data have been determined, there are several initial steps that will facilitate the inquiry process, no matter what the nature of the study. The first step is to identify the *resources* that will be needed. The following questions can assist with this component:

Materials. Are there specialized instruments such as tests or surveys that must be obtained? What quantities are needed, and how long will it take to receive them once they are ordered? Is there computer software that would facilitate data collection and analysis? Is the necessary hardware in place to accommodate the software that will be used? Are stationery supplies needed—for example, institutional letterhead, envelopes?

Staff. Are qualified staff available to provide assistance with clerical functions such as computer input and data collection? Do the primary investigators need released time?

Data access. What relevant data are already available through the institution? Is there a charge for accessing these data?

Postage. Does the institution have postal indicia that can be accessed for mailing? Will there be a charge for this?

Nonstaff personnel. Are there faculty and staff outside the unit whose expertise (for example, in data analysis or materials development) or relationships with students would be helpful to the study?

A second important step is outlining a *budget* for the project based on anticipated needs. Assuming that the study is being funded by the institution and not an outside agency, this would be done in collaboration with the appropriate supervisor. Items to consider include materials, released time, postage, copying, clerical needs, computer time, telephone use, and staff training.

A third step is to establish a *timeline* for the inquiry. It is important to be realistic and to specify each task along with the individual responsible for its completion. The academic calendar should be consulted to ensure student and staff availability and also to ensure that during times when regular institutional obligations are high—for example, during exams and grading—there are fewer responsibilities in the inquiry project. Also, if data are needed from the institution, it is advisable to ask the appropriate office if they have any time constraints. The timeline should function as a general framework that is regularly reviewed and adjusted as reality dictates.

Answering the Questions

It was stated earlier that the nature of the question we are preparing to investigate implies that both quantitative and qualitative methodology will be employed. The quantitative portion of the study will give us the straightforward numerical information we need regarding the students who do or do not persist. It will provide the data to answer the first part of the question, Do developmental students who receive learning assistance persist longer than those who need it but reject it? The qualitative portion will provide us with the data we need to look for patterns of student characteristics and to apply an inductive approach to answer the second part of the question, Are there personal characteristics that distinguish those students who seek assistance from those who reject it?

The Quantitative Component

As the first part of the research question is the more clear-cut of the two, let us begin by outlining a process for collecting that data. The quantitative portion of the inquiry helps us to see the extent of the relationship between several variables: seeking learning assistance, rejecting learning assistance, and persistence at the institution. Our goal in this study is not to establish cause and effect; rather, we are describing the current situation and setting a foundation for further investigation.

Since we have already articulated a specific inquiry and limited the scope of our study, the next step is to identify precisely the target population to be examined. We know that we are interested in patterns of enrollment over three consecutive terms. Then, let us determine from which terms we will collect data for our study; this may be affected by how long the appropriate records have been kept and what access we have. For the sake of this study, we will collect data for each of three terms within one academic year. Consequently, we will need a list of placement test scores for students who first entered the institution during the fall, winter, and spring terms of a given academic year. To facilitate this process, it makes sense to begin with the fall term two years prior to our study, as that ensures that three terms have elapsed since the last start date.

Once we have this information, we must separate the students into two groups: those who needed learning assistance and those who did not. Next, because of our definition of persistence, we need to eliminate those students classified as part-time. We then have the target population that we must categorize according to our established variables.

To facilitate this process of organizing the data and of later applying a test of statistical significance, we could now construct a chart that clarifies the population under study as well as the variables. Such a chart might look like this:

Students Who Need Learning Assistance

	Use Learning Assistance	Do Not Use Learning Assistance	Total
Persist 3+ terms	x percent	x percent	x percent
Do not persist 3+ terms	x percent	x percent	x percent
Total	x percent	x percent	x percent

A second chart on which to record data from the control group (those who did not need assistance and persisted for at least three terms) should also be constructed to ensure careful organization of information.

At this point, following a simple numerical tabulation, percentages for each category can be calculated and recorded. It is important to preserve all the raw data, including the paperwork with the initial calculations, in case any clarifications need to be made later on. For some purposes, the percentages might suffice, but let us assume that we want to enhance the validity of the results. To do this, we should apply a test of statistical significance; in this case, the chi-square test would be appropriate.

The test of chi-square allows us to compare observed persistence rates with rates that would occur simply by chance. The chart that was just used for percentages can now be used for the raw numbers, to which we apply the formula for chi-square. The value thus derived can then be compared with a given value in a table of chi-square (found in the appendix of most statistics texts), to determine whether our observed value is statistically significant. The novice researcher may choose to seek assistance from someone with statistical expertise.

The Qualitative Component

The qualitative portion of the research will supply a richness and depth that enhance the inquiry's overall validity as well as its readability. This part of the study stands in stark contrast to the quantitative work, where the final significance of the data was determined through a simple arithmetic calculation and application of a concise formula; once a numerical value was computed, we had only to locate it in a table and record the finding.

When the researcher engages in qualitative work, the results are not formulaic, and they are subject to broader interpretation. Furthermore, in this particular study, a large amount of data has to be collected and sifted because we do not know in advance what student characteristics will emerge. The part of the question that we are attempting to answer is, Are there personal characteristics that distinguish those students who seek assistance from those who reject it? The answer must come from the data themselves and not from our own biases and expectations.

It is most important during this stage of the investigation that the staff members who will assist in either the collection or the interpretation of data be carefully trained; consistency is of the utmost importance. The development of materials must also be effectively managed. It makes good sense to pilot any internally designed instruments with a small group of representative students to verify clarity of directions, accurate interpretation of questions or statements, and the time frame needed for completion.

In the following sections, three qualitative methods for collecting data that seem appropriate are described: conducting a mail survey, engaging in a participant-observer activity, and developing a case study. Any of these methods could be used alone; alternatively, all three could be integrated into a multifaceted qualitative approach that is combined in the final report with the quantitative results.

Conducting a Mail Survey

Although there are several methods for collecting data through surveys, a mailed questionnaire process has been described here, rather than a face-to-face interview or a telephone survey, primarily for two reasons. First, mailing a survey is considerably less costly than making telephone calls or paying travel expenses and stipends for the interviewer and/or interviewee. Second, this method reduces the possible sample bias that could occur if we assumed that a representative sample of our target population had telephone service or the ability to travel to campus for an interview. Even though a mailed questionnaire may also produce a biased sample because respondents may have different characteristics from nonrespondents, given our target audience, it is the most efficient way to proceed.

It is important to articulate these considerations at the outset of any data collection and to weigh the advantages and disadvantages of each method within the overall context of the inquiry project. For instance, if cost is not a factor and if personal contact with the sample is considered very important, face-to-face interviews might be considered. They certainly allow the interviewer to clarify confusions, which is not possible with a mailed questionnaire, and also to obtain additional information about the interviewee through body language, appearance, and informal remarks.

Once the decision has been made regarding the type of survey to be used, its limitations should be acknowledged and noted. With a mailed questionnaire, for example, there are several hazards that must be kept in mind when generalizing from the data collected. As already noted, those who respond to a mailed survey may not represent the target population. If the responding sample is nonrepresentative, bias error will result, and any generalizations made in the final analysis may be limited. To reduce this possibility, the sampling procedure should be well-constructed, and there should be planned follow-up with nonrespondents.

Another limitation of the mailed survey is its inability to guarantee consistent understanding and interpretation of the written questions. One way to reduce this problem is to run a pilot survey. By administering such a pilot and requesting feedback on issues such as clarity of both instructions and survey questions, the investigator can somewhat control this variable.

It is apparent that when the limitations of any method are understood and discussed at the beginning of a study, the investigators can at least partially compensate for them by building some safeguards into the overall process. This will not eliminate them or the need to articulate them in the final report, but it will greatly enhance the ability to generalize from the ultimate findings.

Determining the Sample. We have already described explicitly the population that we want to study in our inquiry project. This target population consists of those students who needed learning assistance and accepted it and those who needed learning assistance and rejected it during a specific calendar period covering three academic terms. To use the jargon of researchers, this population has "explicit boundaries"; they allow us to proceed to the next step, which is to determine an appropriate sampling frame or representative group of students from whom we can gather data.

The most significant aspect of a sample is not necessarily its size but how well it represents the target population. The more representative the sample is, the more generalizations we can draw from the data in the final analysis. Of course, if your institution is fairly small and the target population totals only a few hundred students, you may choose to survey all of them. Since a predictable return rate for a mailed survey is about 40 percent, such a survey would provide a manageable amount of data to organize. If, however, your target population numbers in the thousands, then it is unreasonable to survey the entire group, and a sample must be selected.

There are several ways to determine representative sample groups. The first, and easiest, is *simple random sampling*. Applying this method, each student in the target population has the same chance of being selected, and no one selection is contingent on another. To generate such a sample, simply assign numbers to the population, and then use a table of random numbers (the Rand Corporation prepared such a table in 1955) to determine which numbered students will be selected for the survey.

Another method for obtaining samples is the *stratified sampling procedure*. The difference between this and simple random sampling is that the target population is first subdivided into categories and then a table of random numbers is applied within each category. The advantage of this method is that all identified subgroups of interest are represented in the sample. For example, if the researcher were interested in gender differences, the target population could first be divided into males and females, with names then randomly selected within each group. The number of names selected from each subgroup should represent the proportion of that group in the total population.

A third method for determining a sample is called *systematic sampling*. This can be achieved by simply starting with one name from the total population and then selecting every *n*th name after that. For instance, the researcher randomly begins with a name on the list and then selects every fifth name thereafter. A disadvantage of this very simple technique is that it is not totally random because each name selected is dependent on its place on the overall list.

One final possibility for sampling is the *cluster approach*. Using this procedure, the researcher identifies particular groups that are known to contain the necessary representatives and then gathers data from all members of an identified group. For our purposes, one logical group would be a developmental reading class. We may be certain that the instructor will cooperate and allow us the time we need to distribute a survey, and that follow-up is assured because of this cooperation and also the accessibility of the students. The sample could conceivably represent that segment of our target population who needed assistance and took advantage of it. We would then need to identify another group who needed assistance and rejected it.

In choosing this method, we are assuming that the selected groups are representative of the entire population. A limitation here is that group membership itself is selective, and that the data collected may not be as generalizable as we would like. For instance, the time of day of the reading class is a variable that limits this sample; daytime classes may not include working students, and we do not necessarily want to eliminate them from our sample.

After considering the four options for determining samples, the authors recommend the second one, the stratified sampling method, for this inquiry. It would allow the researchers to divide the target population into whatever identifiable categories of students they may want to study further. In this case, they would subdivide the target population into those students who have accessed learning assistance and those who have not. This ensures that the sample will not be skewed by chance in the direction of either the users or the nonusers.

Designing the Questionnaire. The development of the survey instrument itself needs to be viewed as a process that will take time and a great deal of collaboration. Each component should be reviewed and revised in the context of the whole project, and nothing should be included that does not relate directly to the focus of the inquiry. For these reasons, the research question should be at the center of all discussions related to design of the instrument.

In fact, a natural starting point for the development of the survey would be a brainstorming session for the purpose of identifying as many variables as possible that might bear on the question. One important consideration here is that, because we are engaged in an inductive approach, we are careful not to set expectations that might bias the interpretation of the data in the final analysis.

Let us look again at the research question, Are there personal characteristics that distinguish those students who seek assistance from those who reject it? One brainstorming session could establish general categories for personal characteristics; from these general categories, more specific variables might be articulated. After we frame these variables as questions, the results might look like this:

1. Does employment affect the student's use of learning assistance?
   a. Is the student employed full-time?
   b. Is the student able to afford tuition without working?
   c. Is the employer paying for coursework?
2. Do family commitments affect the student's use of learning assistance?
   a. Is the student a single parent?
   b. Does the student use day care regularly?
3. Does the student who has specific goals seek learning assistance more often than those without such goals?
   a. Is the student pursuing a specific profession?
   b. Does the student have a specific timeline for course completion?

In an actual brainstorming session, the list of questions would be more fully developed, but this example gives an idea of how to establish a framework that can help focus much of the question-naire. It is important to keep in mind that respondents are more likely to complete a survey that is concise and to the point. By checking questions against this type of outline, extraneous ones will be eliminated.

A further strategy for anticipating alternative responses and designing an inclusive set of questions would be to ask "representa-tive" students to respond to the open-ended general questions listed above. For instance, sample responses to the question "How do fam-ily commitments affect your participation at school?" could lead to additional relevant survey questions that might not be apparent to the researchers.

There are several elements to consider when constructing a sur-vey questionnaire:

- The questionnaire should be limited to two pages.

- Only essential questions should be asked.

- Each question should be clear and unambiguous.

- Sentence structure should be simple and direct.

- Language should not include jargon or emotional words.

- Two questions should not be asked in one.

- "Other" should always be included as an option.

- Because a response should not be forced, a "do not know" option should always be provided.

- In multiple-choices questions, responses should be listed vertically rather than horizontally to increase readability.

A key component of any survey is the first section. This is where the researcher must arouse the interest of the potential respondent.

The directions must be clear and easy to follow. It may help to include closed questions (those with options given for responses) at the beginning because they are usually easier and take less time to complete. Once the respondents have started with these, they are more likely to answer open-ended questions (those the respondent answers in his or her own words) later.

A cover letter written on appropriate letterhead stationery is another essential ingredient of a good survey. The origin of the survey should be evident, and a purpose stated that seems relevant and directly linked to the respondents. In addition, the letter should guarantee the confidentiality of the responses and affirm the importance of the respondents' participation. The letter could also include a willingness to share the survey's results. A deadline for responding should be given that provides for a fairly quick turnaround: two weeks from the date of receipt is more than enough time.

Distributing the Questionnaire. While distribution may seem fairly simple, designing an efficient process will increase the rate of return for the survey. Timing is an important consideration when surveying students. It is probably best to avoid mailing the survey during major exam periods. A week or two into the term, when enthusiasm is still high and commitments not yet too overwhelming, would be a good time. A further advantage of such a choice is that the institution may have a fairly accurate record of current addresses.

A member of the inquiry team should be specifically responsible for maintaining a record of those to whom the survey is sent and those from whom a response is received. By enclosing a self-addressed return envelope with the mailed survey, you can ensure a higher return rate. On the enclosed envelope, you can write the addressee's identification number, and as responses are received, these numbers should be checked off against the master list. This gives you the option of following up on nonrespondents as the deadline nears. Do not wait until after the deadline to follow up, as the survey may have been lost by then. The return envelopes should be kept with the surveys in case verification is needed later.

Analyzing the Data. A process for analyzing the data should be in place before the responses are returned. In fact, tables and charts should be designed at the time the survey is developed to ensure a compatible format that will ease the transference of data.

At the time of receipt, questionnaires should be routinely checked for completeness and general logic. For instance, if someone reports his or her age as 100, the questionnaire should be further checked for overall usefulness to the inquiry. Rules specifying the types of returned questionnaires that should be discarded can be established ahead of time. For example, questionnaires that are only half completed might be eliminated from consideration, as might those that seem to ridicule the questions or that avoid all the open-ended ones. Whatever the rules, they should be clearly agreed on before the analysis process begins, and they should be applied consistently. In some cases, it may be clear that the respondent was confused by a question but had made an honest attempt to answer it. Should the respondent be called in order to clear up the confusion? Will this follow-up contaminate the results? Should the staff member making the phone call follow an agreed script in order to ensure unbiased results? Decisions are required on all such issues.

Once the questionnaires have been screened for completeness and usable data, responses to the closed questions can easily be transferred to the format that has been designed earlier. For this particular inquiry, a chart like the one shown here would be a useful vehicle for recording the information:

	Employed Full-Time	Family Commitments	Stated Goals	Total
Users	x percent	x percent	x percent	
Nonusers	x percent	x percent	x percent	
Total	x percent	x percent	x percent	

This chart would be based on the questions that resulted from the brainstorming session that helped to develop the survey originally. Assuming this chart was constructed at that point, it is now a straightforward matter of transferring the data into the appropriate cells.

Before the responses to the open-ended questions can be transferred to a concise format, they must be coded. Although the actual transferring of data may be done by a trained staff member, the codes must be developed by the main researchers. The coded categories must not overlap, but they must be comprehensive so that all responses will fit somewhere exclusively. It will probably be necessary to have a miscellaneous category.

Let us look at a code that might be constructed for responses to an open-ended question in the survey. Suppose the question was, How does caring for your children affect your participation at school? After scanning the questionnaires for a range of responses, the research team might determine that the following categories exhaust all possibilities:

Unavailability of day care

Unwillingness to use day care

Cannot afford day care

Cannot manage time effectively enough to complete assignments

Unsure of priorities between school and home

Miscellaneous

Once the labels have been agreed on, a number can be assigned to them to facilitate the transfer of data. For example, using the categories listed above, a "1" could be assigned to "unavailability of day care," and all responses that fell under that label would be recorded as a "1." Again, a chart must be constructed, this time using the codes for all possibilities. At this point, a training session could be held for all staff members involved in the transfer of data; samples of questions would be categorized by individuals, following which the choices and rationales would be discussed by the group. Once the team has established consistency, the remaining data can be coded and transferred to an appropriate chart.

Now that the data have been recorded and transferred to a workable format, the final analysis takes place. All of the raw data should be carefully stored for later verification in case that becomes necessary.

The two additional qualitative methods, discussed below, can be used to add a unique depth and interest level to the final research report, which will include the results of all three methods. (We take a look at how to best structure such an integrated report at the conclusion of this chapter.)

Engaging in a Participant-Observer Activity

There are several levels of activity possible when collecting data by a participant-observer method. At the highest level, investigators may be actively involved with the students they wish to observe. For instance, individuals teaching a class are very directly involved with students. The interaction is regular and continuous, and the individuals know the subjects well and understand the overall context. A limitation to this method is that the individuals are so involved in teaching that they are not able to devote enough time to being investigators and conducting the observation. In addition, they may be so familiar with the students and the environment that it becomes difficult to record complete and unbiased data.

At the second level of activity, the investigator is granted a special observer status. This can be achieved if the investigator is engaged, for example, as an instructional aide. In this more limited role, there can be regular observations with additional time for recording events. The arrangement also facilitates a more comprehensive record with perhaps less bias. As the assistant is less familiar with the overall environment, fewer behaviors are taken for granted, and consequently more will be recorded. A limitation to this method is the amount of time required for the investigator to become unobtrusive enough not to influence the students' behavior.

A third level of activity is that of the limited observer, where the investigator is granted access to the students only at certain times and then as an outsider clearly conducting a study. In this situation, the necessary level of trust may never be established with the students. Furthermore, the observations may not represent the entire environment or subject pool and may be recorded without the advantage of understanding the whole context.

To add to the qualitative portion of our study, we have chosen to describe a participant-observer method that fits into the second level of activity. The following section outlines a process for collecting data from the perspective of an investigator who has obtained the special status of an assistant in the academic advising process. Some guidelines are offered for recording the observations and also for analyzing the resulting data.

Outlining the Process. Let us assume that our investigator has obtained whatever special permission is needed to become an advising assistant. Now, a systematic process for participation needs to be identified.

First, the investigator meets with the adviser. Together, they decide how much of a role the investigator will be able to assume while making observations during an advising session. Perhaps they agree that the investigator will be introduced to the student and will then simply listen for the first portion of the session while placement test results are shared and the adviser recommends coursework or other forms of learning assistance. As the investigator listens, he or she may take notes on any relevant student reactions, including both verbal and physical responses to recommendations of learning assistance.

During the second portion of the advising session, they decide, the investigator will lead the student into a discussion of academic goals and of concerns the student may have that are related to success at the institution. The informal conversation will give the investigator an opportunity to expand on any topics that seem relevant to the inquiry. Although the conversation will be basically unstructured, the investigator will be actively listening for topics that were covered in the earlier survey as well as any unanticipated issues.

Recording the Observations. Before the advising sessions begin, the investigator must decide how to record the observations—whether to openly take notes while the student is present or to wait for the student to leave. Whichever method is chosen, it would be helpful to first design an observation sheet that will facilitate efficient note taking. The sheet could include preprinted sections that identify the advisee and any institutional information relevant to the study—for example, current student status or prior enrollment in developmental coursework.

The investigator could also include headings such as physical and verbal responses to suggestions of learning assistance, student quotes, and topics of conversation. Within each category, separate spaces could be set aside for an objective description of the behavior together with an interpretation. Perhaps the description could be completed while the student is present and the interpretation recorded as soon as possible afterward.

Once the conversation with the student is completed, the investigator may disclose that a study of the advising process is being conducted and ask for permission to use any information that may have been shared.

Analyzing the Data. Before the data can be analyzed, they must be reviewed for readability and transcribed into a format that will allow them to be preserved for future validation and interpreted by someone other than the primary investigator. It is wise to either type the observations or to enter them into a computer database as soon as possible after they have been made.

To begin the analysis of data, the investigator must sort the observations by relevant categories. The student categories of interest to this study are learning assistance users and nonusers. To make this initial sort, the investigator needs to verify with the registrar and the learning assistance center which students actually enrolled in the developmental courses or signed up for tutoring sessions. Of course, there must also be a control group category of students for whom learning assistance was not recommended.

Once the observation sheets have been sorted according to these three categories, the investigator begins to reread the notes in depth, looking for patterns. Key topics may be repeated frequently within groups of students. Once these key topics are identified, examples can be recorded on separate charts designed to illustrate the topic for each category of student. For example, if having academic goals seems to be a significant topic, a three-column chart could be constructed in the following format:

Academic Goals

Users	Nonusers	Control
Plans accounting major to upgrade current job status	Family wants student to get degree; unsure of major	Always wanted to be teacher

Once the raw data have been transcribed into a workable format, the original notes should be carefully stored for future reference.

Developing a Case Study

A natural complement to the participant-observer activity would be the development of a case study. The investigator could select a student from among those who were advised and design a systematic method for studying this student in greater depth. A personal connection would already have been made through the advising conversation, and this might facilitate further cooperation.

The greatest advantage of the case study method is that it allows for an in-depth look at complex systems in their natural setting. These systems can be individuals or groups of individuals. For instance, in our inquiry, we could choose to study a classroom of developmental students (a social system) or one student (an individual system). The important thing is that the system be well defined and include boundaries that facilitate data collection. If we were studying a developmental class, for example, we could set the boundaries of the study as follows: in-class behavior of students in "Strategies of Effective Reading," fall term, Monday section.

Although establishing boundaries enables us to study a system in depth, it naturally limits the breadth of our inquiry and also the extent of generalization. Case studies help us to identify complexities within systems and to raise speculations regarding cause or how complex behaviors might be connected. This process often leads to additional possibilities for inquiry; rather than providing definitive answers, case studies frequently lead to further questions.

The case study, then, may not be representative of our entire subject population, but it does allow us to identify issues that we may not have predicted. It also lets us study patterns of behavior that may add support to other components of the inquiry project or may lead us to a new area of investigation.

It is important when using a case study method to incorporate a variety of techniques into the overall design. This triangulation enhances the validity of the results. Typical methods employed in case studies include interviews, observations, and written logs.

For our inquiry, we describe how the case study method could be applied to an individual student identified through the earlier participant-observer component. We also discuss several techniques, including interviews and observations.

Outlining the Process. For our case study, we have chosen an individual who was advised to register for developmental coursework but did not do so. It will be highly informative to study such a student, particularly if we can identify personal characteristics that might help us design early intervention strategies for future advising or orientation sessions.

First, investigators need to articulate the conceptual framework for this part of the study. They must decide what they are looking for and how to proceed within a naturalistic setting. Let us say that they decide to observe the student over a full academic term as the student engages in daily activities at school. The activities will include both class participation and between-class behavior for at least two days out of five each week. The investigator will attend classes and record the student's level of activity both in the formal and informal interactions that occur. Between classes, the investigator will observe the student while she remains at school. These observations will include any involvement with other students, faculty, and staff.

In addition to observing the student, the investigator will interview her every other week, seeking *her* perspective on her studies—satisfaction level, academic development, and any events outside of school that may be affecting her.

Guiding the design of this procedural framework are some assumptions that should direct the study but not limit it. For instance, the investigator will observe between-class activity to record the student's level of involvement at the institution. Given that this student rejected learning assistance, one assumption could be that, in general, her level of involvement will be low. (Studies have shown that interpersonal involvement is positively related to educational persistence and attainment, Pascarella and Terenzini, 1991.) Consequently, the investigator will look carefully for behavior that indicates involvement, including conversations, attendance at student association meetings, and contact with faculty and staff.

These assumptions regarding student involvement can help to determine when and where to conduct observations. They must not, however, blind the investigator to behaviors outside of the anticipated range. One of the benefits of qualitative methodology is discovering unanticipated variables during the course of the study. In this study, for instance, the investigator may observe the student attempting to make an appointment with a faculty member but experiencing frustration because she is unable to locate his office. This should be recorded and the incident brought up at a subsequent interview.

Once a student has been identified for the case study, the investigator needs to obtain several permissions before proceeding. First, the student should be contacted and asked if she is willing to be involved in a study related to the advising process. Unless the student insists on more details, this description, along with an outline of the procedure to be followed, should be enough. To describe the purposes in greater depth could bias the results by influencing the student's behavior. The case study procedure is not violating any of the ethical guidelines stated earlier, and since it could lead to more effective programming, it is appropriate to be vague at this point. The investigator should assure the student of complete anonymity and offer to share the results of the study.

In addition to the student's consent, the investigator must obtain permission from the instructors whose classes will be attended. Again, it is wise to be somewhat vague with the instructors. They certainly should not know which student is being observed. Not only is the student entitled to such privacy, but this knowledge may affect the instructor's interactions with the student. The instructors can be assured, however, that their teaching is not the focus and that all observations will be recorded without identifying their class.

Recording the Observations. To facilitate classroom observations, the investigator could construct a chart with labels for expected types of behavior—for example, initiation of questions, discussion participation, responses to questions, informal peer conversation, participation in small-group activities. Using these headings, check marks could simply be entered when appropriate, or a number code could be devised to indicate the level of interaction, from a low of

"1" to a high of "5." As the term proceeds, categories might be changed, deleted, or added, depending on the observations.

In addition to the categories, there should be a space to record a narrative of the observation. For instance, specific behaviors could be described, or comments could be written that connect one observed situation with another. This space could also include any insights that might occur to the investigator during the observation.

When conducting the interview portion of the study, the investigator might use a tape recorder if it is not too intrusive and if the student does not object. If a tape recorder is used, the interviews should be transcribed as soon as possible. Transcribing a session soon after it has been recorded improves the chances that the investigator will remember any nonverbal behavior that may have occurred, such as a facial expression of anxiety or a shifting of the student's sitting position.

The interviews can combine structured and unstructured components. If the investigator has observed an activity during the week that needs to be pursued further, a series of questions can be carefully constructed beforehand. Also, if there is interest in the student's activities outside of school—for example, family relationships, past or present—it may be more effective to structure questions about these ahead of time; this will ensure appropriate sequencing and comprehensiveness. A portion of the interview, however, should be reserved for more informal, open-ended dialogue. A question as simple as, How are things going at work? could lead to a student response filled with unanticipated variables that might have a direct impact on the student's activities at school.

Analyzing the Data. Analyzing the data from a case study is similar to the analysis of the participant-observer activity. The investigator rereads all notes, looking for patterns of behavior and general categories that may have been repeated frequently. A chart is an efficient method for finding patterns. In this case, two charts could be constructed, reflecting the behavior observed in class and outside of class. As the two sets of data are compared, themes are likely to emerge—for example, failure to make eye contact with others, tendency to sit alone, or a habit of leaving school as soon as classes are over. These behaviors may lead to the tentative conclusion that the student is not comfortable in the school environment.

Following the comparison of data obtained from the observations, the investigator reviews the transcripts from the interviews. These data can perhaps suggest causes for the observed behaviors. Let us assume, for instance, that the investigator has indeed reached the tentative conclusion just described. When the interview data are reviewed, it becomes clear that the student has frequently said that she feels out of place and is fearful of being discovered. This fits with the behavioral pattern that was observed and suggests a likely cause.

The investigator has now established a pattern of behavior and a likely cause. It is not yet clear how representative this case is, but there is evidence for a tentative speculation and a focus for further inquiry.

Preparing the Final Report. There are three basic elements to keep in mind when preparing the final report: simplicity, significance, and sensitivity. If the inquiry team applies these criteria during the editing process, it will enhance the report's overall effectiveness.

Keeping it simple. Administrators receive more written material than they can possibly read. If a report is to stand out, it must be neatly formatted, professional-looking, and succinct. The major highlights should be summarized on the first page in a manner that attracts attention. This page should include the research question and the general purpose of the study, particularly as it relates to the institution's overall mission. It should also state which unit or units participated in the study. Simple, clear graphics can then condense most of the findings into an easily readable format. If no one on the inquiry team is proficient at producing such graphic illustrations, it is worthwhile to find someone who is; doing so could mean the difference between a report that is read and one that is discarded.

The second page can show the team's conclusions and also any recommendations for further action. A bulleted list is more apt to gain attention than a narrative format.

The report should have an appendix, with its own table of contents for easy reference. The appendix can contain the study's timeline, the overall design (including the method for determining the student sample), the instruments that were developed, and more detailed data. It will have a more select audience; most administrators will not take the time to read it very carefully. However, it will demonstrate to them the professionalism and thoroughness with which the study was conducted.

Highlighting its significance. The significance of the study must be stated clearly on the first page. It is most strategic to present it within the context of the institution's overall mission and purpose. Using language from the mission statement, institutional planning documents, or accreditation reviews will enhance its value in the eyes of the administration. Also, even if economic implications were not the focus of the study, it is wise to show what the findings mean in terms of financial return to the institution. In our example, for instance, we could graphically show how much tuition revenue is being lost from students who do not persist. Then, if we found that learning assistance increases student persistence, we could present figures that demonstrate the dollar value of such assistance to the institution.

Maintaining sensitivity. Even though we may be enthusiastic about the findings of the study and believe that the outcomes clearly point to the need for change, there is a process to be followed if any long-term reform is to occur. For this reason, it is important to articulate any limitations of the study. It is also imperative not to overgeneralize from the results. Far more effective than asserting causation is raising tentative hypotheses and suggesting directions for further study. When causes are definitively stated, particularly in a written report, other units may become resentful if their programming is involved.

A practical course is to identify any units that could be affected by the findings of the study. The report should be reviewed with the head of such units *before* being forwarded to the administration. Such a joint review may lead to further collaborative efforts. A plan for such future efforts could then be included in the final report section that makes recommendations. The inclusion of other units in this section increases the probability that the administration will pay attention and that change will occur.

Summary

The following list succinctly outlines the process outlined in this chapter:

Checklist of Researcher Responsibilities

1. I have established a clear focus for my research.

2. I have clearly defined all the terms in my research question.

3. I have identified the resources needed.

4. I have obtained all necessary institutional permissions.

5. I will respect all ethical guidelines related to the students, the institution, and my colleagues throughout the study.

6. I have established a realistic timeline for the study.

7. I have integrated both quantitative and qualitative methods.

8. I have designed a process that will highlight collaboration rather than competition across the institution.

9. I understand the audience for my final report.

10. I will present my findings within the overall context of the institution and make recommendations that are sensitive to all units within the institution.

As we apply the scientific thought process to our work, we undergird the effectiveness of our practice and strengthen the body of knowledge that will increasingly define our field. By engaging in this process, we help to create the unifying framework that will be essential to our establishing a coherent professional identity. The next chapter looks at some of the criteria underlying this professionalism.

9

Creating a Guiding Philosophy and a Professional Identity

Professional dialogue in the field of education too often focuses on differences. Indeed, in developmental education, we continuously engage in debate over terminology (*remedial* versus *developmental* or *learning assistance* versus *developmental education*) and organizational structure (academic affairs versus student affairs or individual departments versus an integrated curriculum). Debate is healthy and should be encouraged in any discipline; however, we need to construct a professional and philosophical framework that connects us. We need to critically reflect on the beliefs we share that give direction to our work and define our discipline. As we discover what we have in common, a philosophy will emerge enabling us to define ourselves *to* ourselves and also to others who continue to ask, "What is it you do, anyway?"

This chapter will look at who we are, first by examining the various roles we have assumed in the field of education. Second, it will discuss what it means to be a professional and how developmental educators meet the criteria. Finally, the chapter will look at commonly shared beliefs about our various professional roles. These beliefs, which have been derived primarily from practice, will then be merged into a statement of philosophy that will help us to advance our field of practice by strengthening our own self-concept.

Who Are We?

Frequently, roles in developmental education have emerged from a need to solve particular problems. The problem may be related to an institution's loss of revenue when too many students do not re-enroll or not enough students enroll in the first place. A problem may arise when an accrediting agency asks whether sufficient support is being provided for the range of students accepted by the institution. There may also be a problem if the support mandated by law for special populations is not being provided.

All such problems represent a single dilemma: how to better meet the needs of students. Often, our positions—indeed our entire units—have been created to help provide solutions to this dilemma. Learning assistance centers and departments of developmental education have been organized around us as institutions look for ways to better serve students. Developmental educators are seen as problem solvers and are routinely consulted by others across the institution on complex issues associated with such areas as student retention and services for special populations.

Although the overall goal of helping the institution meet the needs of its students is implicit in most developmental educators' job descriptions, specific titles and responsibilities vary widely. We are housed in various types of units, ranging from departments of developmental education to learning centers to traditional academic departments to counseling centers. Within these units, our positions range from faculty to professional staff to administrator. Faculty members may hold adjunct or full-time tenure-track positions. In their roles, they often assume some combination of the following responsibilities:

Direct instruction of developmental coursework and/or traditional core coursework

Curriculum design

One-on-one instruction

Student counseling and advising

Faculty/staff development

Student assessment

Consulting or advocacy work for special populations

Materials development

Core faculty members have the advantage of serving on institutionwide committees and consequently creating visibility and credibility for the developmental education unit. They may also affect policy decisions, as they are voting members of the faculty.

Within the category of professional staff, responsibilities vary widely, from management to direct instruction. Professional staff members direct individual programs and entire learning centers. They may assume the role of tutor or classroom instructor. Frequently, they function as counselors or advocates for students. In many institutions, they are very likely to serve as consultants when issues such as student assessment and retention arise.

Because of their ability to solve problems that affect the entire institution, developmental educators are not infrequently promoted to institutionwide administrative positions. It is not uncommon to see them elevated to the office of dean or vice president. Often, this is accompanied by a job description that focuses their responsibility in such specific areas as student retention, freshman year programs, and the recruitment and enrollment of special populations. Such job descriptions indicate that a wide range of abilities is called for. Successful practitioners must be capable of managing people, developing programs, designing curricula, communicating clearly, fulfilling many roles simultaneously, relating to students, and delivering instruction.

With these diverse responsibilities, what exactly is it that connects us? How can we define this profession? What makes developmental educators professional?

First, let us consider what constitutes a profession in general. The following criteria provide a starting point. Individuals within a profession share

- A common body of knowledge and skills

- A way to transmit and store knowledge

- Professional associations

- A set of ethical guidelines

- Standards for practice

- An accepted terminology

- An ability to adapt knowledge and practice to novel situations

Let us now apply these criteria to the field of developmental education and learning assistance to determine the level of professionalism that currently exists. First, do developmental educators share a common body of knowledge and skills? Developmental education has evolved from an interdisciplinary perspective. Practitioners have applied to their work formal training from various fields, including education, psychology, sociology, and counseling. As they evaluate the results of their practice and disseminate this information, a body of knowledge and skills emerges for the profession. However, there are only a few graduate programs that have developed curricula to formalize this emergent body of knowledge, and this may be one of the weaknesses of the field.

One such graduate program is offered by National-Louis University in Chicago. Its master's degree program in developmental studies is offered through the department of adult education; it thus formalizes the connection between developmental education and adult learning theory. The curriculum organizes a body of knowledge into eight core courses and twelve specialized offerings that represent the areas of reading, writing, and math. The coursework emphasizes the application of theory to practice and stresses an interdisciplinary approach to the field by integrating psychology, counseling, research methodology, and adult development. Through an independent inquiry component, the program stresses the importance of applying coursework to individual areas of interest.

Second, what means are used to transmit and store knowledge? The field of developmental education has relied primarily on methods other than traditional degree programs for transmitting ideas. One significant contribution to the transmission and storage of knowledge in the field comes from the National Center for Developmental Education at Appalachian State University. The center sponsors two regular publications, a journal and a research newsletter, through which practitioners can become familiar with both theory and practice. In addition, major research projects that have advanced the state of knowledge in developmental education have been generated by the center, and their results have been widely disseminated. The largest data collection on developmental education programs was assembled at the center in 1992 and provides a foundation for ongoing research. The center is also engaged in a project to compile an annotated bibliography for the field.

Another means of transmitting knowledge is short-term, residential institutes for professional development, where experienced mentors assist practitioners in applying theory and research to practice. Such institutes are held regularly at a number of sites. The National Center for Developmental Education provided the initial model through its Kellogg Institute. The newest vehicle for the transmission of knowledge in the field is the Internet, particularly its electronic mail facilities. Several listserves (electronic networks of professionals in specialized areas of interest) have been initiated especially for professionals in developmental education and learning assistance, and information is shared daily with colleagues around the world.

Third, does the field have its own professional associations? There are several professional associations dedicated solely to developmental education and learning assistance, including the National Association for Developmental Education (NADE), the Midwest College Learning Center Association (MCLCA), the New York State College Learning Skills Association (NYSCLA) and the College Reading and Learning Association (CRLA). They host annual conferences where practitioners from around the world share their ideas through presentations and networking. These associations publish journals, position papers, and newsletters.

The fourth criterion is the existence of a set of ethical guidelines. Earlier in this book, guidelines for the conduct of research were suggested, but the field does not have an accepted set of ethical standards that can be applied to practice. Individual programs frequently have developed their own. In fact, this is one of the standards suggested in the *NADE Self-Evaluation Guides* (Thayer, 1995). The profession would be strengthened if it had a set of fundamental ethical principles that were generally accepted and applied to practice. The following principles could serve as a core:

- All students are treated fairly and equitably.

- All interactions with students are confidential unless there is reason to believe that withholding information might cause harm to the student or to others.

- All students are treated with dignity and respect.

- Honesty with sensitivity underscores all communication with students.

- A realistic understanding of his or her professional limitations guides the practitioner in decisions whether to

deliver assistance directly or to refer the student
to another resource.

- Meeting the needs of students efficiently and
effectively is the major criterion in setting policy
and making decisions.

Most institutions have their own ethical guidelines. Practitioners should be familiar with them and should appropriately apply
principles such as those listed here within those larger frameworks.

A fifth area to review is whether or not the field has developed
standards. Developmental education and learning assistance have
had written standards for practice since 1986, when the first guidelines were produced by the Council for the Advancement of Standards (CAS) for Student Services/Developmental Programs. These
were contained in a larger document written primarily to guide
practice in the area of student services. Outlining general components for learning assistance programs, they were compiled by professionals across the United States who were mainly involved in
student personnel work. The purpose was to guide practice, not to
impose mandates, and the emphasis was on assisting professionals
to develop programs.

In 1995, a new set of guidelines was published by the standards
and evaluation committee of the National Association for Developmental Education (Thayer, 1995). This document contains four
self-evaluation guides—for tutoring programs, adjunct instructional
programs, developmental coursework programs, and the teaching/
learning process. The guides were developed over six years by a
national team of practitioners that included members of the earlier
CAS committee. The primary reason for developing this new set of
guidelines was to provide a more academic focus than that found in
the earlier ones. The 1995 guidelines encourage practitioners to use
the standards for self-evaluation in order to facilitate decision making, identify strengths and weaknesses, develop long-range planning,

make budget decisions, and guide new programming and proposal writing. Like the CAS guidelines, the standards are for self-assessment and are voluntary; no professional accrediting agency exists to mandate implementation.

The sixth criterion for reviewing professionalism focuses on terminology. The *NADE Self-Evaluation Guides* (Thayer, 1995) includes a glossary of professional terminology. The core of this glossary was taken from a set of definitions developed by a task force of the College Reading and Learning Association (Rubin, 1991). Again, a national team of practitioners followed a process of drafting, gathering input, and revising over a period of four years to develop a listing of terminology that includes definitions from a variety of perspectives. A valuable by-product of this effort to define terms has been increased communication among the many practitioners involved in the process. Also, rather than affirming one meaning for terms such as *developmental education*, the listing offers several definitions representing different viewpoints. Currently, however, there is much discussion, both on the electronic mail system and at professional gatherings, about developing a more standard set of definitions. There is heated debate about the merits of adopting a uniform language, particularly where this might affect the use of the general labels *developmental education* and *learning assistance*.

The last criterion for defining a professional is the ability to adapt knowledge and practice to novel situations. To assess this, we can review the graduate program at National-Louis University that was described earlier and the additional means the field has developed for transmitting information—for example, short-term institutes and professional association meetings. A major emphasis in each of these delivery systems is the application of theory to practice. Theory is not taught in isolation; rather, the practitioner is encouraged to explore how it relates to practice. This encourages continual application and consequently fosters an ability to individualize and contextualize principles and concepts.

Furthermore, in developmental education, it is the practitioner who is advancing the state of knowledge. There is no elite group of researchers operating apart from practice; the practitioner *is* the researcher. Everyday practice is regularly examined by the practitioner for its effectiveness in novel situations. This was confirmed at the 1995 annual conference of the National Association for Developmental Education, which was entitled, "Transforming Practice Through Research and Innovation." More than two hundred professionals presented their ideas at this gathering.

It is the practitioner, again, who has developed the standards of practice and defined the terminology of the field. The standards and terminology reflect input from many perspectives and situations and are purposely inclusive and adaptable. These criteria, inclusiveness and adaptability, are essential when input is sought from a broad range of practice and when the goal is to create material that can be used by everyone. If practice is to remain inclusive and flexible, three things must be maintained: application of theory to practice, the practitioner's role as researcher, and practitioner-based standards and terminology. What is also vital is that the practitioner remain engaged in dialogue and in a process of critical reflection.

What Beliefs Do We Share?

It may be easiest to examine our common beliefs by considering them in three general areas, the first related to the practitioner, the second to the learner, and the third to the overall learning process. Because these areas form the heart of our profession, they are a logical starting point for constructing a philosophy of developmental education and learning assistance.

Regarding practitioners, we believe that they

- Facilitate and encourage learning and development

- Provide direct instruction when appropriate

- Consider the affective needs of learners

- Assess strengths and weaknesses and communicate them to the learner

- Respect learner diversity

- Gradually release responsibility for learning and self-assessment to the learner

- Recognize and respect individual rates of development

- Provide a range of instructional delivery methods and materials

- Communicate clearly and directly

- Assess individual development

- Enhance learner motivation

Regarding learners, we believe that they

- Must assume responsibility for learning

- Must respect the diversity of other learners, faculty, and staff in the learning environment

- Embody individual learning styles

- Must learn to monitor their own development

- Must learn to assess their own learning

- Must internalize a motivation for learning

- Display varied learning rates

- Must be active partners in the instructional/learning process

- Must be willing to take risks in order to succeed

Regarding the learning process, we believe that it

- Reflects a talent development model rather than a deficit model

- Begins with the learner's current state of development

- Assumes all learners have the potential for growth

- Fosters critical thinking abilities

- Recognizes individual differences

- Provides for individual styles and rates of learning

- Assigns responsibility for learning to all members of the learning community—instructor, learner, and cohorts of learners

- Incorporates collaborative and cooperative learning principles

- Ensures active learning

- Facilitates the transfer of skills and strategies to new learning situations

- Focuses on relevancy

- Utilizes materials that are sensitive to all learners

- Includes continuous learner assessment

- Is continuously reviewed and revised to produce the most desirable learner outcomes

- Is based on an appropriate theoretical foundation

- Is clearly communicated to the learner

What Is Our Philosophy?

If we look back at the belief system that many practitioners of developmental education and learning assistance share, we find that one major theme emerges: placing the learner at the center of our practice. Closely aligned with this learner-centered approach is the understanding of the word *developmental*. The word denotes an educational process that begins with a determination of where learners are, what they want to achieve, and how to help them realize their greatest potential as they work toward their goals.

The notion of maximizing individual potential injects a positive energy into our practice. It is consistent with a talent development model rather than a deficit model, where student weaknesses are identified and then remediated, often outside any meaningful context. In an approach based on talent development, the learner is looked at holistically. Both strengths and weaknesses are assessed, and development is facilitated by applying the strengths to the task of modifying the weaknesses. The process includes not only cognitive development but, when appropriate, emotional and social development, too.

Another important element of the developmental approach is the active involvement of the learner. The responsibility for success needs to be shared at first between practitioner and learner but must be gradually released to the learner. The student needs to learn how to monitor and measure progress on a regular basis. By emphasizing such a positive, general approach to providing learning assistance to students, the practice of developmental education becomes very inclusive. Rather than focusing solely on students who need help with basic skills—a focus that has traditionally fought a negative connotation—this approach offers assistance to all students, from the underprepared to graduate students.

Can we summarize our basic beliefs and philosophy in one statement? Perhaps the following will serve as a starting point for further reflection:

The philosophy that underlies both developmental education and learning assistance programs is based on a belief system that focuses on maximizing the potential of all learners so that they may meet their goals. The philosophy assumes that to maximize learner potential, responsibility and commitment must be shared by the learner and the practitioner. It also assumes that the learning process takes place in a meaningful context and is sensitive to the cognitive, emotional, and social needs of the learner.

Summary

By focusing on our shared beliefs and engaging in collaboration through research and dialogue, we affirm our identity as professionals. Not only is this identity important to us as practitioners, but it also has significance to those outside our field who do not always recognize that we represent a formal field of study. Our field becomes stronger as we articulate a common philosophical foundation. This philosophy enhances our collegiality, and it also helps others to understand exactly who we are and what we do.

We have many challenges ahead of us, and we will be most prepared to face them and to assume a leadership role in the field of education if we have a strong sense of who we are and can articulate it to others. In Chapter Ten, we take a look at the challenges to come.

10

. . . .

Preparing for New Challenges

We have looked at the challenges of conducting research and developing a professional identity and seen that we must examine our work and ourselves if we are to be successful. Evolving bodies of research and developed standards of professional competence and ethical behavior demonstrate our profession's vitality. The final charge is to be prepared for new challenges, to be ready to address problems that have not emerged before, to find new solutions to problems that continue to occur, and to share our expertise with each other.

After years of growth and development, the field of learning assistance and developmental education has entered an era of excellence. Despite the rumblings of some elitists who wish it would disappear, its presence in higher education has become increasingly accepted. As the focus of concern moves from access to retention, efforts to assist students academically through tutoring and other types of learning assistance and developmental programming take on even greater importance.

Higher education is facing significant demands, both nationally and internationally. Costs are rising significantly, competition for students is keen, resources are often limited, and demands for quality are resounding. It is not enough to recruit and admit. Students must be retained and their learning advanced so that they become fully educated and competitive in society. To achieve this goal, we face at least six main challenges: (1) developing and maintaining professional standards, (2) meeting diverse student needs, (3) increasing accountability, (4) managing resources effectively, (5) making the best use of technology, and (6) promoting leadership and advocacy worldwide.

Developing and Maintaining Professional Standards

Chapter Nine addressed the importance of crystallizing a philosophy and a professional identity. This process requires, in part, that we adopt standards and guidelines like those developed by the National Association for Developmental Education (NADE) and apply them in all settings.

When hiring staff, it is important that we identify minimum qualifications and adhere to them. Professional organizations like NADE, the College Reading and Learning Association (CRLA), and the Midwest College Learning Center Association (MCLCA) could help by initiating an accreditation process for developmental education programs. Such a process could, for example, be based on NADE standards and guidelines. Individual educators could apply for credentialing through one of these professional organizations and complete a set of requirements designed to assure competence in the field. CRLA currently has a certification process for tutors. Something similar is needed for professionals in the field. Many organizations have developed standards and guidelines. We suggest that these different groups work together toward a common base for practice.

Ethical standards for practice are also integral to maintaining professionalism. A universally accepted standard of ethics needs to be developed, and this standard could be built into the professional accreditation process. Ethical standards concerning confidentiality, minimal levels of staff competence, and appropriate professional behavior with students must be established.

Meeting Diverse Student Needs

The range of student diversity is increasing. Access initiatives and legislation have made college and university education available to an ever expanding group of students. Students with physical and learning disabilities and students who speak English as a second language are two groups experiencing greater inclusion in postsecondary education.

Mandates to provide education to these students are often not funded, which places new demands on already limited resources. Such mandates may also require types of expertise that are not readily available. Developmental educators and learning assistance professionals are frequently called on to assist students with special needs. In this role, professionals must be knowledgeable about legislation. They must know what kinds of accommodations are required and must be ready to act as both advocates for students and protectors of the institution against demands that have no grounding in law. In addition, those assisting students with special needs are often called on to educate the wider institutional community about students with disabilities and to help faculty make accommodations.

Increased student diversity, though an educational challenge, enriches and strengthens the institution as a whole. The learning assistance professional and developmental educator can help bring out the benefits of diversity in higher education, but they must be educated and prepared to do so.

Increasing Accountability

Every successful program must be able to show the results of its work. Chapter Four discussed the importance of regular and systematic program evaluation. Regular reports outlining program activities and summarizing student usage and progress are essential.

It is recommended that progress reports be generated annually, and more often if necessary.

The program director is ultimately responsible for accountability. However, all staff members must contribute to the effort. Clearly defined expectations with respect to accountability activities must be communicated to staff, including deadlines for the collection of information. Developmental educators are often so busy delivering service and instruction that summary and evaluation functions are never performed. This is one of the biggest challenges in the profession. If we do not record what we do, analyze how it was done, and use the results to improve our work, we are missing one of the most important elements of professionalism.

Program evaluation and accountability must be top priorities in every learning assistance or developmental program. Without them, the program may at best be plodding along in a cloud of uncertainty. Are the goals of the program being met? Which ones need refinement or redefinition? In some cases, the continued existence of a program is dependent on evidence that it is working. Such evidence must be systematically collected and organized and then communicated to those who will decide whether the program is to survive.

Managing Resources Effectively

Another major challenge involves the use and management of resources. In an era of belt tightening and directives to maintain and even expand offerings within strict resource limitations, this is a challenge of immense proportion. Developmental education and learning assistance programs are most vulnerable in this respect because in most instances, the programs are not revenue producing. Unless tuition is generated by enrollment in developmental courses or fees are collected for service, programs are dependent on institutional funds or grant money.

Even if evaluation reports show that programs help increase student retention, the quest for additional resources may be futile

in a time of budget and staff reductions. In such a situation, inge-
nuity is called for. Sometimes, reductions result in an increase in
part-time staff. Though this may address the problem in the short
run, the long-term effect may be one of decreased staff commitment
to the program, lack of program continuity, and an overall decline
in morale and enthusiasm. A viable professional program needs to
be staffed with a core of full-time committed individuals who
strongly identify with the program goals and dedicate themselves to
achieving them. This does not mean that part-time staff members
are unimportant. It means that they must not become the core of a
department, and even when they are not regularly employed, they
need to be included in all staff development initiatives so that they
become more involved and committed.

The competent administrator discloses resource allocations and
limitations to others in the department. When information is
shared, problems can be resolved collaboratively. Often, resource
reductions lead to new and creative ways of accomplishing tasks,
and the combined effort of a team of individuals can result in a
renewed commitment to support the program and its objectives.
This is not to suggest that resource reductions be meekly accepted.
Sometimes, it is important to make a case for more during a period
of less, and such an argument, if well made, may result in renewed
or increased assets. However, reductions are the more common
occurrence, and the well-managed program must be prepared to deal
with them.

Making the Best Use of Technology

Increased use of technology may be seen as a challenge, but it is
more aptly viewed as an advance that can make our work more
exciting, meaningful, and effective. Technology poses a challenge
only in that it requires new knowledge and expertise, and in that
its use must be made to conform with the goals of a program. There
are also resource implications: new technology costs money, and

with budget cuts, departments may be unable to purchase the tools they need.

New technology is evident in computer-assisted instruction, distance learning through E-mail, interactive learning experiences with specialized software, and writing networks in which students and faculty share their compositions via the electronic highway.

In addition, technological advances assist students with disabilities, who are major clients of developmental and learning assistance programs. Computers are able to scan a written text and read it aloud in simulated voice for students unable to see. A student with a hearing impairment may be assisted by a relay device worn by a teacher that amplifies sound directly to the student.

Information technology departments are important resources for developmental education and learning assistance programs. Using the knowledge of experts in these departments and tailoring the use of technology to the specific goals of a program are essential for success. Even when resources are reduced and equipment purchases limited, technology must be treated as a priority.

Promoting Leadership and Advocacy Worldwide

Finally, we must be prepared to meet the challenges of leadership and advocacy in our field. As leaders, we must promote ourselves as professionals by evaluating our work and publishing our findings. Vehicles for publication already exist in the form of the *Journal of Developmental Education*, *Research in Developmental Education*, and a newcomer, the *Learning Assistance Review*. However, we need not limit ourselves only to those publications. The *Journal of College Reading and Learning*, the *Journal of College Personnel*, the *Journal of Higher Education*, and many others are also available for the dissemination of our work.

Because so many of us are already overburdened by our current responsibilities, the first challenge we face if we want to write and publish is finding the time. Working with others on collaborative writing projects is one way to solve this difficulty. Whether in the same institution or elsewhere, it is possible to find others with similar interests and to share our work with them. Initially, this sharing may be done by E-mail on the Internet. The discussion groups available through the MCLCA and the Learning Assistance Network are excellent places to find collaborators.

Once collaboration begins through discussion, it can lead to more formalized interactions that result in joint writing ventures. Ultimately, articles may be submitted for publication. This book is an example of how collaboration can facilitate the process of getting ideas into print. Each of the authors had long desired to write such a book, but neither alone had brought this dream to fruition. It was only when we began discussing our ideas and sharing our goals that we saw the possibility of collaborating. We highly recommend collaboration as a way to promote and communicate ideas and to advance leadership in the field.

It is not enough for all of us as professionals to collaborate with our professional peers. We must reach into all educational arenas and form partnerships. To help advance access to higher education, four-year institutions must communicate with two-year colleges and develop patterns of articulation. Learning assistance and developmental educators, with their expertise in academic readiness and success in the classroom, can play an important role in this process.

Both two- and four-year institutions need to develop alliances with high schools and community-based agencies so that learners are encouraged to aspire toward higher education and are taught how to move into it. Some college learning assistance programs, for example, offer tutoring services in high schools. College and high school students thereby get to meet each other and develop bonds. This can be a powerful influence in encouraging nontraditional students to attend college. As developmental educators, we need to reach beyond our colleges and universities and interact with institutions whose students might not otherwise enter our world.

Collaboration and publication are only two parts of the leadership and advocacy picture. As professionals, we must become legislatively aware as well. Much of what shapes our daily work is decided in the halls of our state and federal legislatures. For example, funding for support programs and mandates to provide services to students with special needs come directly from government. The elected officials who vote on these issues listen to their constituents, among whom we constitute a well-defined professional group with distinct interests. We must make these interests known. We must communicate both individually and collectively with those in office so that they will be well informed when they vote on issues that affect our students and the programs that serve them. Only with a concerted effort to have the voices of developmental educators and learning assistance professionals heard in government will we position ourselves to receive the support we need for our work.

Lastly, we must meet the challenge of leadership and advocacy by connecting with our counterparts around the world. Developmental education and learning assistance programs are not unique to the United States. Providing access to higher education and assuring quality in the programs offered are worldwide objectives. For example, the European Access Network was created so that educational experts from many European countries could work together to open higher education to underrepresented groups. At a 1994 meeting of the network, the vice president of the Technical University of Berlin stated that within the next few years, Berlin universities would lose about fifteen thousand student places as a result of financial cutbacks. The effect of this reduction on access to higher education will be enormous (Lee, Mendick, and Woodrow, 1994).

In the Netherlands, a primary concern is that the percentage of ethnic minorities in the population is not reflected in higher education (Lee, Mendick, and Woodrow, 1994). It is suggested that to encourage more participation, more and better information about higher education must be disseminated, and successful students of diverse ethnic backgrounds must act as role models.

These examples of access concerns in two different European countries underscore similar issues in the United States, where traditionally underrepresented groups in higher education continue to be poorly represented even after access initiatives have been implemented. In less well-developed countries outside Europe, the issue of higher education access is even more acute. Very large segments of the world's population remain illiterate, and individuals who do become educated face many barriers to enrollment in institutions of higher learning, where space is limited and access is often restricted.

Developmental education and learning assistance are about the broadening of access and the enhancement of quality in higher education—concerns shared by countries around the world. The International Access Network is a group of educators from Australia, Asia, the Middle East, South America, Europe, and the United States. Their common bond is the objective of making higher education available to those previously unable to obtain it. The group's focus embraces the very same issues central to the meetings of NADE, CRLA, and MCLCA in the United States: How can we improve access to higher education for traditionally underrepresented students? Once they gain access, how can we ensure that the programs designed to serve them will be of high quality and will assist them in remaining enrolled and graduating?

We have much to learn from each other across the oceans and the borders of our countries. As in the world of business and economics, we are in a global arena—a worldwide village of common educational concerns, and we cannot afford to live in isolation.

Summary

Six main challenges are significant now and will continue to be in the future. They are (1) developing and maintaining professional standards, (2) meeting diverse student needs, (3) increasing accountability, (4) managing resources effectively, (5) making the best use of technology, and (6) promoting leadership and advocacy worldwide. As professionals, we must work together to meet these challenges by sharing research and resources and by advancing practice on the basis of sound principles that support the goal of maximizing student potential.

References

Anderson, T. H., and Armbruster, B. B. "Reader and Text-Studying Strategies." In N. Otto and S. White (eds.), *Reading Expository Material*. Madison, Wis.: Board of Regents of the University of Wisconsin System, 1984.

Arkin, M., and Shollar, B. *The Tutor Book*. White Plains, N.Y.: Longman, 1982.

Austin, M. J. *Supervisory Management for the Human Services*. Englewood Cliffs, N.J.: Prentice Hall, 1981.

Bales, R. F. "Systematic Multiples Field Level Theory." In R. F. Bales, S. C. Cohen, and S. A. Williamson (eds.), *SYMLOG: A System for the Multiples Level Observation of Groups*. New York: Free Press, 1979.

Bandura, A. *Social Foundations of Thought and Action: A Social Cognitive Theory*. Englewood Cliffs, N.J.: Prentice Hall, 1986.

Barbe, W. "Reading-Improvement Services in Colleges and Universities." *School and Society*, 1951, 74(1907), 6–7.

Baxter Magolda, M. B. "Gender Differences in Cognitive Development: An Analysis of Cognitive Complexity and Learning Styles." *Journal of College Student Development*, 1989, 30, 213–220.

Baxter Magolda, M. B. *Knowing and Reasoning in College: Gender-Related Patterns in Students' Intellectual Development*. San Francisco: Jossey-Bass, 1992.

Belenky, M. F., Clinchy, B. M., Goldberger, N. R., and Tarule, J. M. *Women's Ways of Knowing: The Development of Self, Voice, and Mind*. New York: Basic Books, 1986.

Bentley, R., Quinn, K., and Piokowski, G. K. *Center for Academic Potential Proposal*. Unpublished document, University of Illinois at Chicago, Mar. 16, 1993.

Blankenberg, J. Interview conducted by M. E. Casazza at Oakton Community College, June 23, 1994.

Bloom, B. *Human Characteristics and School Learning*. New York: McGraw-Hill, 1982.

Book, W. F. "Educational Research and Statistics: How Well College Students Can Read." *School and Society*, 1927, 26(660), 242–248.

Boylan, H. R., Bonham, B. S., and Bliss, L. B. "Summary Report of the National Study of Developmental Education: Students, Programs, and Institutions of Higher Education." Paper presented at the First National Conference on Research in Developmental Education, Charlotte, N.C., Nov. 1992.

Boylan, H. R., and others. *Exxon National Study of Developmental Education*. Boone, N.C.: National Center for Developmental Education, 1992.

Boylan, H. R., and others. "A Research Agenda for Developmental Education: 50 Ideas for Future Research." *Research in Developmental Education*, 1993, 10(3), 1–4.

Branch-Simpson, G. "A Study of the Patterns in the Development of Black Students at the Ohio State University." *Dissertation Abstracts International*, 1984, 45, 2422A.

Brier, E. "Bridging the Academic Preparation Gap: An Historical View." *Journal of Developmental Education*, 1984, 8, 2–5.

Brookfield, S. D. *Understanding and Facilitating Adult Learning: A Comprehensive Analysis of Principles and Effective Practices*. San Francisco: Jossey-Bass, 1986.

Brookfield, S. D. *Developing Critical Thinkers: Challenging Adults to Explore Alternative Ways of Thinking and Acting*. San Francisco: Jossey-Bass, 1987.

Brookfield, S. D. *The Skillful Teacher: On Technique, Trust, and Responsiveness in the Classroom*. San Francisco: Jossey-Bass, 1990.

Brown, A. L., Armbruster, B. B., and Baker, L. "The Role of Metacognition in Reading and Studying." In J. Orasanu (ed.), *Reading Comprehension: From Research to Practice*. Hillsdale, N.J.: Erlbaum, 1986.

Brown, A. L., Campione, J. C., and Day, J. "Learning to Learn: On Training Students to Learn from Texts." *Educational Researcher*, 1981, 10, 14–24.

Brubacher, J. S., and Rudy, W. *Higher Educational Transition: A History of American Colleges and Universities 1636–1976*. (3rd ed.) New York: Harper-Collins, 1976.

Bruner, J. S. *The Process of Education*. Cambridge, Mass.: Harvard University Press, 1960.

Burmeister, S. "The Challenge of Supplemental Instruction (SI): Improving Student Grades and Attention in High Risk Courses." In M. Maxwell (ed.), *From Access to Success*. Clearwater, Fla: H&H Publishing, 1994.

Butts, R. F., and Cremin, L. A. *A History of Education in American Culture*. Troy, Mo.: Holt, Rinehart & Winston, 1953.

Cameron, S. "The Perry Scheme: A New Perspective on Adult Learners." Washington, D.C.: U.S. Department of Education, Educational Resources Information Center, 1984. (ED 244698)

Canfield, A. *Canfield Learning Styles Inventory.* Los Angeles: Western Psychological Services, 1988.

Carnegie Foundation for the Advancement of Teaching. *Priorities for Action: Final Report of the Carnegie Commission on Higher Education.* New York: McGraw-Hill, 1973.

Carriuolo, N. "Why Developmental Education Is Such a Hot Potato." *Chronicle of Higher Education,* Apr. 13, 1994, pp. B1–B3.

Carroll, J. "A Model of School Learning." *Teaching College Record,* 1967, *64,* 723–733.

Casazza, M. E. "Using a Model of Direct Instruction to Teach Summary Writing in a College Reading Class." *Journal of Reading,* 1993, *37*(3), 202–208.

Caverly, D., and Orlando, V. P. "Textbook Study Strategies." In R. F. Flippo and D. Caverly (eds.), *Teaching Reading and Study Skills at the College Level.* Newark, Del.: International Reading Association, 1991.

Chickering, A. W. *Education and Identity.* San Francisco: Jossey-Bass, 1969.

Clowes, D. A. "More Than a Definitional Problem: Remedial, Compensatory, and Developmental Education." *Journal of Developmental and Remedial Education,* 1980, *4*(1), 8–10.

Clowes, D. A. "Remediation in American Higher Education." *Higher Education Handbook of Theory and Research,* 1992, *8,* 460–493.

Cohen, A. M., and Brawer, F. B. *The American Community College.* San Francisco: Jossey-Bass, 1982.

College Entrance Examination Board. *Descriptive Tests of Language Skills.* New York: College Entrance Examination Board, 1989a.

College Entrance Examination Board. *Descriptive Tests of Math Skills.* New York: College Entrance Examination Board, 1989b.

Cook, T. D., and Reichardt, C. S. *Qualitative and Quantitative Methods in Evaluation Research.* Newbury Park, Calif.: Sage, 1979.

Costa, A. L. "Medicating the Metacognitive." *Educational Leadership,* 1984, *42,* 57–62.

Council for the Advancement of Standards for Student Services/Developmental Programs. *CAS Standards and Guidelines for Student Services/Developmental Program.* College Park, Md.: Consortium of Student Affairs Professional Organizations, 1986.

Cremin, L. A. *American Education: The Colonial Experience 1607–1783.* New York: Harper Torchbooks, 1970.

Cross, K. P. *Beyond the Open Door: New Students to Higher Education*. San Francisco: Jossey-Bass, 1971.

Cross, K. P. *Adults as Learners: Increasing Participation and Facilitating Learning*. San Francisco: Jossey-Bass, 1981.

Cross, K. P. (ed). *Underprepared Learners*. Washington, D.C.: U.S. Department of Education, Educational Resources Information Center, 1983. (ED 233636)

Daloz, L. A. *Effective Teaching and Mentoring: Realizing the Transformational Power of Adult Learning Experiences*. San Francisco: Jossey-Bass, 1986.

Dansereau, D. F. "Learning Strategy Research." In J. W. Segal, S. F. Chapman, and R. Glaser (eds.), *Thinking and Learning Skills*. Vol. 1: *Relating Instruction to Research*. Hillsdale, N.J.: Erlbaum, 1985, 209–239.

Davey, B. "Think-Aloud—Modeling the Cognitive Processes of Reading Comprehension." *Journal of Reading*, 1983, *27*, 44–47.

Delworth, U., Hanson, G. R., and Associates. *Student Services: A Handbook for the Profession*. San Francisco: Jossey-Bass, 1980.

DeVry Institute of Technology 1994 Academic Catalog. Oakbrook Terrace, Ill.: DeVry Institute of Technology, National Office of Admission, 1994

Dole, J., Duffy, G., Roehler, L., and Pearson, P. D. "Moving from the Old to the New: Research on Reading Comprehension Instruction." *Review of Educational Research*, 1991, *61*(2), 239–264.

D'Zurilla, T. J., and Goldfried, M. R. "Problem-Solving and Behavior Modification." *Journal of Abnormal Psychology*, 1971, *78*, 107–126.

Eckert, R. E., and Jones, E. S. "Educational Research and Statistics: Long-Term Effects of Training College Students How to Study." *School and Society*, 1935, *42*(1094), 685–688.

Eichler, B. Interview conducted by M. E. Casazza at DeVry Institute of Technology, July 12, 1994.

Eliot, C. W. *American Education: Its Men, Ideas and Institutions*. New York: Arno Press and New York Times, 1969.

Erikson, E. H. *Identity, Youth, and Crisis*. New York: W.W. Norton, 1968.

Fischer, P. M., and Mandl, H. "Learner Text Variables and the Control of Text Comprehension and Recall." In H. Mandl, N. L. Stein, and T. Trabasso (eds.), *Learning and Comprehension of Text*. Hillsdale, N.J.: Erlbaum, 1989.

Flippo, R. F., and Caverly, D. *Teaching Reading and Study Strategies at the College Level*. Newark, Del.: International Reading Association, 1991.

Freire, P. *Pedagogy of the Oppressed*. New York: Continuum, 1970.

Gardner, E. "Five Common Misuses of Tests." ERIC Digest No. 108. Washington, D.C.: American Institutes for Research/ERIC Clearinghouse on Tests, Measurements, and Evaluation, 1989.

Garner, R. "Strategies for Reading and Studying Expository Text." *Education Psychologist*, 1987, *22*, 313–332.

Gleazer, E. J., Jr. "The Community College Issue of the 1970s." *Educational Record*, Winter 1970, 47–52.

Hall, J. C. "A History of Baccalaureate Programs for Adults 1945–1970." National Institute of Education Research Report. Washington, D.C.: National Institute of Education, 1974. (ED 101607)

Hardin, C. J. "Access to Higher Education: Who Belongs?" *Journal of Developmental Education*, 1988, *12*(1), 2–4, 6, 19.

Harper, S. C. "Adding Purpose to Performance Reviews." *Training and Developmental Journal*, 1986, *40*(9), 53–56.

Hergnhahn, B. R. *An Introduction to Theories of Learning.* (3rd ed.) Englewood Cliffs, N.J.: Prentice Hall, 1988.

Hermann, B. A. "Two Approaches for Helping Poor Readers Become More Strategic." *Reading Teacher*, 1988, *42*(1), 24–28.

Hersey, P., and Blanchard, K. H. *Management of Organizational Behavior: Utilizing Human Resources.* (4th ed.) Englewood Cliffs, N.J.: Prentice Hall, 1982.

House, R. J., and Mitchell, R. T. "Path-Goal Theory of Leadership." In P. Hersey and J. Stinson (eds.), *Perspectives in Leader Effectiveness.* Columbus: Center for Leadership Studies, Ohio State University, 1980.

Hull, G., and Rose, M. "This Wooden Shack Place: The Logic of an Unconventional Reading." *College Composition and Communication*, 1990, *41*(3), 287–298.

Hull, G., Rose, M., Fraser, K., and Castellano, M. "Remediation as Social Construct: Perspectives from an Analysis of Classroom Discourse." *College Composition and Communication.* 1991, *42*(3), 299–329.

Ivey, A., Gluckstern, N., and Ivey, M. *Basic Attending Skills.* North Amherst, Mass.: Microtraining Associates, 1982.

Keimig, R. T. *Raising Academic Standards: A Guide to Learning Improvement.* ASHE-ERIC Higher Education Research Report No. 4. Washington, D.C.: Association for the Study of Higher Education/Educational Resources Information Center, 1983. (ED 233559)

Kerr, L. Interview conducted by M. E. Casazza at Loyola University Chicago, June 15, 1994.

King, R. C. "The Changing Student." *National Forum*, 1985, *65*, 22–27.

Knowles, M. S. *The Adult Learner: A Neglected Species.* (4th ed.) Houston: Gulf, 1990.

Knox, A. B. *Helping Adults Learn: A Guide to Planning, Implementing, and Conducting Programs.* San Francisco: Jossey-Bass, 1986.

Kohlberg, L. *The Meaning and Measurement of Moral Development*. Worcester, Mass.: Clark University Press, 1981.

Kramer, S. *Talk, Understand, Tutor, Organize, Reflect*. Chicago: Loyola University Chicago Learning Assistance Center, 1993.

Kulik, J., and Kulik, C. "Mastery Testing and Student Learning: A Meta-Analysis." *Journal of Educational Technology Systems*, 1987, *15*, 325–345.

Kulik, J., and Kulik, C. *Developmental Instruction: An Analysis of the Research*. Boone, N.C.: National Center for Developmental Education, 1991.

Lee, M. F., Mendick, H., and Woodrow, M. *Crossing the Frontiers: Access to Higher Education in Eastern and Western Europe*. Proceedings of the European Access Network East-West Convention, Berlin, 1994. London: University of North London, 1994.

Lewin, K. *Field Theory in Social Science*. New York: HarperCollins, 1951.

Lewis, J. A., and Lewis, M. D. *Management of Human Service Programs*. Pacific Grove, Calif.: Brooks/Cole, 1983.

Lindemann, E. *The Meaning of Adult Education*. Norman, Okla.: Oklahoma Research Center for Continuing Professional and Higher Education, 1961.

Lochhead, J. "Teaching Analytic Reasoning Skills Through Pair Problem Solving." In J. W. Segal, S. F. Chipman, and R. Glaser (eds.), *Thinking and Learning Skills*. Vol. 1: *Relating Instruction to Research*. Hillsdale, N.J.: Erlbaum, 1985.

Loftus, E. R., and Loftus, G. R. "On the Performance of Stored Information in the Human Brain." *American Psychologist*, 1980, *35*, 409–420.

Loyola University Chicago. *Loyola University Chicago Undergraduate Studies Catalog, 1993–95*. Chicago: Loyola University Chicago, 1993.

Loyola University Chicago. *Loyola University Chicago Learning Assistance Center Policies and Procedures Manual, 1995*. Chicago: Loyola University, 1995.

Lucas, A. F. "Using Psychological Models to Understand Student Motivation." New Directions for Teaching and Learning, no. 12. San Francisco: Jossey-Bass, 1990.

McCabe, R. H. "Miami-Dade Results Justify Program." *Community and Junior College Journal*, 1983, 54(1), 26–29.

McClusky, H. Y. "An Approach to a Differential Psychology of the Adult Potential." In S. M. Grabowski (ed.), *Adult Learning and Instruction*. Syracuse, N.Y.: Educational Resources Information Center Clearinghouse on Adult Education, 1970.

McCombs, B. "The Role of the Self System in Self-Regulated Training." *Contemporary Educational Psychology*, 1986, *11*, 314–332.

MacDonald, R. "An Analysis of Verbal Interaction in College Tutorials." *Journal of Developmental Education*, Fall 1991a, *15*, 2–12.

MacDonald, R. *California Tutoring Project*. Walnut Creek, Calif.: Ross MacDonald, 1991b.

MacDonald, R. "Group Tutoring Techniques: From Research to Practice." *Journal of Developmental Education*, Winter 1993, *17*, 12–18.

McGrath, E. J. *The Predominantly Negro Colleges and Universities in Transition*. Washington, D.C.: U.S. Bureau of Publications, 1965.

McGregor, D. *Leadership and Motivation*. Cambridge, Mass.: MIT Press, 1983.

Maslow, A. H. *Motivation and Personality*. New York: HarperCollins, 1970.

Maxwell, M. *Improving Student Learning Skills*. San Francisco: Jossey-Bass, 1979.

Maxwell, M. *Evaluating Academic Support Systems: A Sourcebook*. Kensington, Md.: M. M. Associates, 1991.

Merriam, S. B. (ed.). *An Update on Adult Learning Theory*. New Directions for Adult and Continuing Education, no. 57. San Francisco: Jossey-Bass, 1993.

Mezirow, J., and Associates. *Fostering Critical Reflection in Adulthood: A Guide to Transformative and Emancipatory Learning*. San Francisco: Jossey-Bass, 1990.

Mooney, R. L. *Mooney Problem Checklist*. New York: Psychological Corporation, 1950.

National Education Association of the United States. Committee of Ten on Secondary School Studies. *Report of the Committee on Secondary School Studies*. New York: Arno Press, 1969. (Originally published 1893.)

Nist, S. L., and Simpson, M. L. "PLAE: A Validated Study Strategy." *Journal of Reading*, 1989, *33*(3), 182–186.

Norman, D. A. *Learning and Memory*. San Francisco: Freeman, 1982.

Oakton Community College 1994/95 College Catalog. Des Plaines, Ill.: Oakton Community College, 1994.

O'Brien, K., Brown, S. D., and Lent, R. W. *Relation of Self-Efficacy Beliefs to Academic Achievement and Career Development in At-Risk College Students*. Paper presented at the 97th annual convention of the American Psychological Association, New Orleans, Aug. 1989.

Paris, S. G., Lipson, M. Y., and Wixson, K. "Becoming a Strategic Reader." *Contemporary Educational Psychology*, 1983, 8, 293–316.

Parr, F. W. "The Extent of Remedial Reading Work in State Universities in the United States." *School and Society*, 1930, *31*(799), 547–548.

Pascarella, E. T., and Terenzini, P. T. *How College Affects Students: Findings and Insights from Twenty Years of Research*. San Francisco: Jossey-Bass, 1991.

Patton, M. Q. *Qualitative Evaluation Methods*. Newbury Park, Calif.: Sage, 1980.

Pauk, W. *How to Study in College*. Boston: Houghton Mifflin, 1974.

Pearson, P. D. "Direct Explicit Teaching of Reading Comprehension." In G. G. Duffy, L. R. Roehler, and J. Mason (eds.), *Comprehension Instruction: Perspectives and Suggestions*. New York: Longman, 1984.

Perry, W. G., Jr. *Forms of Intellectual and Ethical Development in the College Years*. Troy, Mo.: Holt, Rinehart & Winston, 1970.

Piaget, J. *Psychology of Intelligence*. Totowa, N.J.: Littlefield, Adams, 1966.

Quinn, K. Interview conducted by M. E. Casazza at University of Illinois at Chicago, July 9, 1994.

Rand Corporation. *A Million Random Digits with 100,000 Normal Deviates*. New York: Free Press, 1955.

Reynolds, C. R., and Brown, R. T. *Perspectives on Bias in Mental Testing*. New York: Plenum, 1984.

Rogers, C. R. *On Becoming a Person: A Therapist's View of Psychotherapy*. Boston: Houghton Mifflin, 1961.

Rose, M. *Lives on the Boundary*. New York: Penguin Books, 1989.

Roueche, J. E. "Let's Get Serious About the High Risk Student." *Community and Junior College Journal*, 1978, 49(1), 32–35.

Roueche, J. E., and Baker, G. A. *Access and Excellence: The Open Door College*. Alexandria, Va.: Community College Press, 1987.

Rubin, M. "A Glossary of Developmental Education Terms Compiled by the CRLA Task Force on Professional Language for College Reading and Learning." *Journal of College Reading and Learning*, 1991, 23(1) 1–13.

Rumelhart, D. E., and Norman, D. A. "Accretion, Tuning, and Restructuring: Three Modes of Learning." In J. W. Cotton and R. L. Klatzky (eds.), *Semantic Factors in Cognition*. Hillsdale, N.J.: Erlbaum, 1978.

Schallert, D., Lemonnier, A., Alexander, P. A., and Goetz, E. T. "Implicit Instruction of Strategies for Learning from Text." In C. E. Weinstein, E. T. Goetz, and P. A. Alexander (eds.), *Learning and Study Strategies*. San Diego, Calif.: Academic Press, 1988.

Silverman, S. "A Developmental Interpretation of Help Rejection." *Journal of Developmental Education*, 1993, 17(2), 24–26, 28, 30–31.

Simpson, M. L., and Nist, S. L. "PLAE: A Model for Planning Successful Independent Learning." *Journal of Reading*, 1984, 28(3), 218–223.

Skinner, B. F. *About Behaviorism*. New York: Knopf, 1974.

Stahl, N. A., Simpson, M. C., and Hayes, C. G. "Ten Recommendations from Research for Teaching High-Risk College Students." *Journal of Developmental Education*, 1992, 16(1), 2–10.

Sternberg, R. J. *The Triarchic Mind: A New Theory of Human Intelligence*. New York: Viking Penguin, 1988.

Thayer, S. (ed.). *NADE Self-Evaluation Guides*. Clearwater, Fla.: H&H Publishing, 1995.

Thorndike, E. L. *Educational Psychology*. New York: Teachers College Press, 1913.

Tinto, V. *Leaving College*. Chicago: University of Chicago Press, 1987.

Tomlinson, L. M. *Postsecondary Developmental Programs*. Report No. 3. Washington, D.C.: School of Education and Human Development, George Washington University, 1989.

U.S. Department of Education. "College-Level Remedial Education in the Fall of 1989: Contractor Report." U.S. Department of Education, National Center for Education Statistics, 1991.

U.S. Department of Education. "Number of Disabled Students Taking Special SATs Rises." *Education Daily*, 1994, *27*(170), 5.

Vygotsky, L. S. *Thought and Language*. New York: Wiley, 1965.

Wang, M. C. "Development and Consequences of Students' Sense of Personal Control." In J. M. Levine and M. C. Wang (eds.), *Teacher and Student Perceptions: Implications for Learning*. Hillsdale, N.J.: Erlbaum, 1983.

Wechsler, D. *Wechsler's Measurement and Appraisal of Adult Intelligence*. (5th ed.) Baltimore, Md.: William and Wilkins, 1972.

Weidner, H. Z. *Back to the Future*. Paper presented at the annual meeting of the Conference on College Composition and Communication, Chicago, Ill., Mar. 1990. (ED 319045)

Weinstein, C. E. *Learning and Study Strategies Inventory*. Clearwater, Fla.: H&H Publishing, 1987.

Weinstein, C. E., and Mayer, R. E. "The Teaching of Learning Strategies." In J. Segal, S. Chipman, and R. Glaser (eds.), *Relating Instruction to Research*. Hillsdale, N.J.: Erlbaum, 1985.

Weinstein, C. E., and Mayer, R. E. "The Teaching of Learning Strategies." In M. C. Wittrock (ed.), *Handbook of Research on Teaching*. (3rd ed.) New York: Macmillan, 1986.

Wergin, J. F. "Basic Issues and Principles in Classroom Assessment." In J. H. McMillan (ed.), *Assessing Students' Learning*. New Directions for Teaching and Learning, no. 34. San Francisco: Jossey-Bass, 1988.

White, S. L. *Managing Health and Human Services Programs*. New York: Free Press, 1981.

Wigdor, A., and Garner, W. *Ability Testing: Uses, Consequences, and Controversies*. Washington, D.C.: National Academy Press, 1982.

Winograd, P., and Hare, V. C. "Direct Instruction of Reading Comprehension Strategies: The Nature of Teacher Explanation." In C. E. Weinstein, E. T. Goetz, and P. A. Alexander (eds.), *Learning and Study Strategies: Issues in Assessment, Instruction, and Evaluation*. San Diego, Calif.: Academic Press, 1988.

Wittrock, M. C. "Students' Thought Processes." In M. C. Wittrock (ed.), *Handbook of Research and Teaching*. (3rd ed.). New York: Macmillan, 1986.

Wyatt, M. "The Past, Present, and Future Need for College Reading Courses in the U.S." *Journal of Reading*, 1992, 36(1), 10–20.

Yanok, J., and Broderick, B. "Program Models for Serving Learning Disabled College Students." *Review of Research in Developmental Education*, 1988, 6(2), 1–4.

Index